Felix Körner

Revisionist Koran Hern
Contemporary Turkish University Theology

MISK

MITTEILUNGEN ZUR SOZIAL- UND KULTURGESCHICHTE DER ISLAMISCHEN WELT

herausgegeben
von
Rahul Peter Das, Werner Ende, Erika Glassen,
Angelika Hartmann, Jens Peter Laut, Stefan Leder,
Ulrich Rebstock, Rotraud Wielandt

BAND 15

Revisionist Koran Hermeneutics in Contemporary Turkish University Theology

ERGON VERLAG

Felix Körner

Revisionist Koran Hermeneutics in Contemporary Turkish University Theology

Rethinking Islam

ERGON VERLAG

Bibliografische Information der Deutschen Bibliothek

Die Deutsche Bibliothek verzeichnet diese Publikation in der Deutschen Nationalbibliografie; detaillierte bibliografische Daten sind im Internet über http://dnb.ddb.de abrufbar.

Gedruckt auf alterungsbeständigem Papier.
Umschlaggestaltung: Jan von Hugo
Satz: Daniel Groß, Ergon Verlag

www.ergon-verlag.de

Printed in Germany

ISBN 3-89913-373-0

ISSN 1436-8080

PARENTIBUS

MISK heißt die Reihe, in der diese Arbeit erscheint. Auf Arabisch und Türkisch bedeutet das Moschus. Wer jemandem beim Arbeiten über die Schultern schaut, bekommt den Geruch des andern mit. Hier habe ich türkischen Theologen über die Schultern geschaut bei ihren Versuchen, einen grundlegend neuen Ansatz für das Koranverständnis zu entwickeln. Wer uns lesend dabei zuschaut, wie wir miteinander arbeiten, manchmal auch ringen, wird zuerst Arbeitsschweiß riechen – mag dann aber auch den Duft solcher Nähe mitbekommen.

Diese Arbeit wurde im Mai 2003 an der Otto-Friedrich-Universität Bamberg als Promotionsarbeit im Fach Islamkunde angenommen. Frau Prof. Dr. Rotraud Wielandt hat mich durch mein islamkundliches Studium mit menschlichem und oft übermenschlichem Einsatz begleitet. In Bamberg wurde ich optimal gefordert und gefördert. Sie hat den Löwenanteil dazu beigetragen. Der Doktormutter sei von Herzen Dank gesagt.

Ich danke auch Herrn Prof. Dr. Georg Kraus, der freundlicherweise das Koreferat übernommen und einen spannenden systematisch-theologischen Rigorosumsteil gestaltet hat.

Herr Prof. Dr. Jens Peter Laut und Herr Prof. Dr. Ulrich Rebstock haben wie Frau Prof. Dr. Rotraud Wielandt den vorliegenden Text gründlich gelesen, mir zahlreiche hilfreiche Korrekturvorschläge gemacht und erfreulicherweise beschlossen, ihn in die Reihe MISK aufzunehmen. Auch dafür danke ich herzlich.

Beim Promovieren haben mir eine Reihe von lieben Mitmenschen geholfen. Sie haben sachkundig Rat gegeben, Literatur besorgt, gute Fragen gestellt, einen tröstlichen Lebensrahmen gebildet und mich so ermutigt: Meine Geschwister Tilman und Julia und ihre Familien; Elisabeth Halter und viele andere Schwestern vom Serafischen Liebeswerk Solothurn; Pfarrer Markus Bolowich und zuvor Pfarrer Hans Hübner mit Frau Maria Stappenbacher; Pfarrerin Berthild Sachs und Stefan Brandenburger; Peter Dippolt, Karin Hartbecke, Marcus Hüttner, Christoph Körner, Guido Müller mit seinen Lieben, Thomas Würtz – und eine ganze Reihe Bamberger Familien (Dietzel, Dörfler, Einwich, Geimer, Hofmann, Holderberg, Mantz, Meyer, Müller, Ruß, Strauch), P. Georg Braulik OSB sowie meine Mitbrüder in der Gesellschaft Jesu, insbesondere Jean-Marc Balhan, Patrice Jullien de Pommerol, Jack A. Lucal, Alexander Eck, Dan Madigan, Friedo Ricken, Christian Rutishauser, Felix Schaich, Johannes Maria Steinke, Christian Troll, Sebastian Watzek und Ansgar Wucherpfennig.

Ich widme diese Arbeit meinem Vater und dem Andenken unserer verstorbenen Mutter.

Felix Körner

Outline

NB: A detailed table of contents can be found on pp. 9–13.

A Note on Typography

This system of typographical marks has been used to distinguish between diffent languages:

French words are set within French-type single quotation marks (‹…›).

German words are set within German-type single quotation marks (‚…’).

Latin words are set in SMALL CAPITALS.

Words in Arabic, other Semitic languages, and pre-1928 Turkish are written in the ‚Deutsche Morgenländische Gesellschaft’ transcription and set in *italics.* In quotations (including titles), other scholarly transcription systems have been retained.

Post-1928 Turkish words are written in the new Turkish alphabet and also set in *italics.*

(..(..))	As in mathematics, parentheses can be used also within parentheses.
“..“..””	Likewise, quotations, even within quotations, are marked with *double* quotation marks.
[…]	Brackets are used only in quotations to mark additions by the present author.
‘…’	Phrases which are not quotations and which are still to be singled out—e.g., when an opinion is epitomised, an hypothetical objection is proffered or the level of speech changes from metalanguage to object language—appear in English-type single inverted commas.
°.. (..)	If it is not clear to which words exactly an explanation in parantheses refers, the sign “°” is set at the beginning of the words which will be explained in the parentheses.
x:y	Numbers stated in this form: ‘2:257’, indicate Koran Suras and verses.

Contents

Introduction

Rethinking the Title

Why 'Koran', why 'hermeneutics', why 'revisionist', why 'university theology', why 'Turkey'? These questions will be answered in due course.[1] But why 'Rethinking Islam'? Rethinking Islam is a multilevel process.

Firstly, 'rethinking' captures a typical move of theological reflection. Every new experience challenges the mind to *return* to the received tradition in order to understand both present and past experience anew and to *transform* the course of reflection, practice and tradition in this light. The prefix 're-' captures the return as well as the transformation.

Secondly, 'rethinking Islam' expresses what the authors to be presented here are committed to, in a twofold sense. 'Islam' can be understood as the *object* of 'rethinking'. Thus, the subtitle means that Islam is being rethought. But 'Islam' can also be taken as the grammatical *subject* of 'rethinking Islam', i.e., Islam which is rethinking itself. This is a welcome ambiguity in English because it allows for the implication that the revisionists want to do their rethinking as members of Islam, thus demonstrating Islam's ability to reform itself.[2]

But thirdly, 'rethinking Islam' might be heard as the claim that the present author himself is rethinking Islam. If a Muslim writes a book 'Rethinking Islam', that is not problematic.[3] But can a non-Muslim use such a title and thus imply, 'I am taking part in the rethinking'?

---

1 On 'Koran' cf. below, p. 19. On 'hermeneutics' cf. below, p. 22. On 'revisionism' cf. below, footnote 120 on p. 60. On 'university theology' cf. below, p. 57. On 'Turkey' cf. below, p. 47.

2 In morphologically more explicit languages these two senses of 'rethinking Islam' call for two different expressions. *'İslâm'ı yeniden düşünmek'*, ‚den Islam neu denken' over against *'yeniden düşünen İslâm'*, ‚neu denkender Islam'.

3 There is a French book by a Muslim which appeared under the title 'Rethinking Islam' in English translation. Mohammed Arkoun, *Ouvertures sur l'Islam,* Paris 1989: IDEM (translated by Robert D. Lee), *Rethinking Islam. Common Questions, Uncommon Answers,* Boulder (Colorado) and Oxford, 1994. The present study's title was not influenced by that book but rather by a Turkish publication: Adil Çifti, *Rethinking Islam with Fazlur Rahman* (below, footnote 246 on p. 109). Since in the case of Arkoun's book, 'Rethinking Islam' is only a translation's title, it should be seen as neither confusing nor plagiarising to use 'Rethinking Islam' as a subtitle.

A demarcation of religious studies (‚Religionswissenschaft') over against theology held by some scholars of religion is this:

> 'While religious studies are an empirical discipline which looks at the phenomena without asking for the reality of God and revelation,[4] theology presupposes the reality of God and revelation.[5] Therefore in religious studies one must refrain from discussing theological propositions, let alone making any.'

A proposition clearly to be excluded, as illigitimate theologising and dogmatic, from the precincts of religious studies according to that demarcation would be this:

> 'Muslims can apply historical criticism to the Koran without losing their faith.'[6]

This demarcation raises a number of questions. Firstly, there are theologians who try as theologians to establish—rather than presuppose—the truth of claims like 'God acts'.[7] Quite independent of the convincingness of

---

4 Joachim Wach, classically, conceives of religious studies as an empirical discipline which brackets truth questions. („Einklammerung der Gültigkeits-(Wahrheits)frage", Joachim Wach, *Religionswissenschaft. Prolegomena zu ihrer wissenschaftstheoretischen Grundlegung*, Leipzig 1924, p. 26, quoted after Dirk Kemper, "Religionswissenschaft", *Historisches Wörterbuch der Philosophie*, vol. 8, Basel 1992, cols. 771–4, col. 773.)

5 E.g., Matthias Gatzemeier, "Theologie", *Enzyklopädie Philosophie und Wissenschaftstheorie*, vol. 4, Stuttgart 1996, pp. 250–6, p. 250 says that theology „die Offenbarung und die kirchliche Lehre als unabdingbare inhaltliche Vorraussetzung annimmt", i.e., it presupposes revelation and church doctrine.

6 Rotraud Wielandt warned in her thematically and methodologically exemplary study *Offenbarung und Geschichte im Denken moderner Muslime*, Wiesbaden 1971, p. 158, n. 5, that Islamic studies should not decide what Muslims can or cannot say. According to her, possible propositions in Islamic studies concern "what °has been a valid rule of faith (‚als Glaubensnorm gegolten hat') for a certain group of Muslims. But one cannot principally deny them [scil. Muslims] the possibility to redefine (‚neu zu definieren') that rule". The point of Wielandt's caveat is that Islamicists cannot prescribe to Muslims what they should or should not say. This is an important point to be made. But while a scholar cannot as a scholar prescribe to anybody anything, the scholar can, and can only, *argue*. Wielandt's statement should not be misunderstood as a plea against argumentation. On the contrary, Wielandt is one of the few proponents of Islamic studies who study the views presented in a way that advances the state of the theological discussion (e.g., ibid., p. 170, with a call for intellectual uprightness). Many of her studies demonstrate that it is well possible for a scholar to discuss faith positions scholarly, that is, also, independently of one's own creed, cf., e.g., ibid., pp. 157–8, or below, p. 43, section 6. The esteem her studies find among Muslim theologians (cf., e.g., below, footnote 19 on p. 21) demonstrates that it is possible to argue in Islamic theology as a non-Muslim without being misunderstood as dogmatic.

7 Wolfhart Pannenberg argues against Friedrich Schleiermacher's view of theology as the scientific study of Christianity (‚Wissenschaft vom Christentum') that such a concept lead theology into the dilemma of historicism or subjectivism (Wolfhart

their arguments, the demarcation collides with this practice. Therefore, either those theologians have misunderstood theology—or the demarcation has. Secondly, if the demarcation is questionable concerning theology, perhaps it is doubtful when speaking about religious studies, too. Among the phenoma considered by religious studies are religious truth claims. Does the most rational way of taking religious truth claims seriously not include to take them seriously as truth claims? Why should one not be allowed to reason about religious, and theological, utterances quite independent of one's own religious stance? And why should one not call this practice 'religious studies'?[8] Thirdly, a reflection on the status of 'can' in

---

Pannenberg, *Wissenschaftstheorie und Theologie,* Frankfurt am Main 1973, pp. 299–302 (chapter 5.1): „Die Theologie wurde auf diesem Wege entweder zu einer historisch-antiquarischen Disziplin, oder sie verfing sich in den Aporien einer nur dezisionistisch anzueignenden Positivität, die mit ihrem Anspruch auf Wissenschaftlichkeit nicht vereinbar ist. Die Frage nach der Wahrheit des Christentums ist diskutierbar erst im Rahmen einer Wissenschaft, die nicht nur das Christentum, sondern die Wirklichkeit Gottes zu ihrem Thema hat, auf die sich der christliche Glaube beruft. [...] Der Gedanke Gottes als der seinem Begriff nach alles bestimmenden Wirklichkeit ist an der erfahrenen Wirklichkeit von Welt und Mensch zu bewähren. [...] Wollte Theologie als Wissenschaft von Gott prinzipiell *dogmatisch* verfahren, so bliebe sie in den Aporien der Positivität und damit auch des Glaubenssubjektivismus gefangen. Indem ihr aber „Gott" als Problem zum Thema wird, kann sie die Positivitätsproblematik durchbrechen und dann auch mit neuer Glaubwürdigkeit ihrerseits die Enge dezidiert untheologischer Wirklichkeitsauffassungen in Frage stellen." Theology's theme is the reality of God. Is God rightly considered to be the all-determining reality? This must be verified in light of our experience of reality. But, of course, since reality is, within history, not yet complete, the concept of God has so far to remain a hypothesis. (Ibid., p. 302) Cf. also IDEM, *Systematische Theologie,* vol. 1, Göttingen 1988, p. 60 (chapter 1.5): theology presupposes only the historical reality that Christianity *has claimed* the decisive truth of the Bible. „Doch nicht schon vorauszusetzen ist die göttliche Wahrheit, die die christliche Lehrüberlieferung beansprucht: Dieser Anspruch ist in der Theologie darzustellen, zu prüfen, wo möglich zu erhärten, muß aber eben darum als offen und nicht schon vorweg entschieden behandelt werden. Es macht geradezu das Interesse an der Theologie aus, daß im Gang ihres Denkens und ihrer Argumente das Recht dieses Anspruchs auf dem Spiele steht." The point of theology is that religious truth claims are at stake. Cf. also Siegfried Wiedenhofer, "Theologie und Religionswissenschaft", *Lexikon für Theologie und Kirche,* vol. 9, Freiburg [3]2000, cols. 1443–4, col. 1443: „Im 20. Jh. gibt es (v. a. unter dem Titel einer "komparativischen Th[eologie]" od[er] einer "globalen Th[eologie]") sowohl v[on] seiten der Theologie als auch v[on] seiten der Religions-Wiss[enschaft] bzw. Religions-Philos[ophie] eine ganze Reihe v[on] programmat[ischen] Versuchen, fragwürdige Dichotomien (wie subjektiv – objektiv, dogmatisch – wissenschaftlich, Innensicht – Außensicht, Bekenntnis – Erkenntnis) zu überwinden u[nd] v[on] neuem in eine wechselseitige Verarbeitung u[nd] Kritik einzutreten (u. a. N. Söderblom, R. Otto, G. van der Leeuw, F. Heiler, Pannenberg, Panikkar, Hick, Tracy; M. Eliade, Smith, Schaeffler)."

8 That in common English usage 'studying' is not confined to documentation but includes analysis and examination can be checked in the dictionaries. Cf., e.g.,

the proposition 'Muslims can apply historical criticism to the Koran without losing their faith' is in place. This may (i) be the conclusion drawn from a logical reasoning which discusses the coherence of a position, and therefore its designation as dogmatic may be inadequate. What decides the truth of the proposition is then the validity of the arguments proffered. Or (ii) it may be an empirical observation of the type 'there are Muslims who …'. What then decides its truth is whether it rests on correct observations. Finally (iii) it may be a magisterial decision with a claim at authority without arguments. Then it is an attempt at suspending the question of truth.[9]

The discussion of the above demarcation has brought to light a possible authoritarianism, or possible misunderstanding, of propositions in religious studies. Furthermore, it has produced this question: 'Why should one not be allowed to reason about religious utterances quite independent of one's own religious stance?' This is not only a rhetorical question. It should draw the attention of scholars of religion to three particular challenges to be faced in their discipline. Firstly, religious utterances are not necessarily propositional. They can then still be discussed and follow a certain logic. But other methods than only the exchange of arguments may be needed. Secondly, modern rationality usually accepts and validates only one type of consciousness as providing reality contact. The possible rationality of, e.g., a vision or contemplative absorption is typically underestimated.[10] And thirdly, it is true that one need not be a believer to question the coherences of a belief; but if one does not share the experience of a particular religion, even when professing another creed, one's arguments are in danger of missing the point. This is so because the partners in interreligious discussions are in particular danger of misunderstanding the words the other uses. This study has to take those challenges just like any other attempt in religious studies. It has to be aware of its inherent dangers and to face the fact that its success will be measured also in their light.

On the other hand, Western scholars of religion should not pretend that all the material they study is equally exotic and beyond the framework of their own rationality standards. The material studied here is Turkish university theology. Modern theology was founded in Turkey precisely to

Webster's New Collegiate Dictionary, Springfield (Massachusetts) 1979, s.v. "study […] *n[oun]*": 2d(1).

9 What Wielandt, rightly, rejects in her *Offenbarung und Geschichte*, p. 158, n. 5 (cf. above, footnote 6) is a dogmatic in the sense of non-argumentative ruling 'Muslims can …' from the precincts of religious studies.

10 Cf. Dieter Henrich, "Rahmenbedingungen der Rationalität. Überlegungen zum Verhältnis von Kulturform und Kunstform" (1982), IDEM, *Fixpunkte. Abhandlungen und Essays zur Theorie der Kunst*, Frankfurt am Main 2003, pp. 221–32, p. 225.

be on one level with Western theology.[11] If we are not only presenting thoughts but also discussing them, this should be seen as taking seriously that founding idea. And if the discussion becomes passionate, this should be seen as proving that what Turkish theologians produce can actually be taken seriously; and that in fact they throw out exciting challenges.

This study is therefore working with the following presupposition: in principle, we are operating with the same vocabulary and we are talking about the same realities. Any frictions that may be felt *can* be caused by that presupposition; they do however not disprove the success of the presupposed common language. Quite on the contrary.

Returning to the Koran

Calls "AD FONTES"[12] tend to be uttered in a spirit of reform or indeed reformation. Certainly the Koran had never lost its leading role for the Muslim communities. But once it had been declared as merely one, if the primary, source of jurisprudence among others and was therefore being read through the optic of the Hadith corpus, its refreshing force weakened. Furthermore, the *immediate* contact with the text sometimes became an otherworldly and/or aesthetic experience—recitation, not reading—with little interest in contents.[13] It has been observed by scholars of different points of view that this type of traditionalising has limited the wealth of Koranic theology.[14] Consequently, returning to the wells of the Koran itself seems promising on three grounds. There are plenty of undiscovered elements in

11 Cf. below, at note 98 on p. 55.

12 Cf. Hans-Georg Gadamer, *Hermeneutik,* vol. 2, *Wahrheit und Methode. Ergänzungen, Register,* Tübingen 1993, pp. 383–4. It seems that the oft-quoted meaning of *'šarīʿa'* 'the place where the animals drink' (cf., e.g., Norman Calder, "sharīʿa", *EI²,* vol. 9, Leiden 1997, pp. 321–6, p. 326) has never been seen in the light of Humanism's concept of FONS ('spring, well, source').

13 Cf. Alford T. Welch, "The Ḳurʾān in Muslim Life and Thought", *EI²,* vol. 5, Leiden 1986, pp. 425–9. Welch stresses the Koran's orality, pp. 425–6.

14 Fazlur Rahman, *Islam & Modernity. Transformation of an Intellectual Tradition,* Chicago 1982, p. 3. Josef van Ess, *Zwischen Ḥadīṯ und Theologie. Studien zum Entstehen prädestinatianischer Überlieferung,* Berlin 1975, pp. 56–7: authors rejecting divine predestination (who were later called Qadarites) argue on a solely Koranic basis, while their adversaries adduce (often forged) *Ḥadīṯ*s in order to prove that every human act is predestined; a point which became a part of standard theology through Ašʿarism. It was already William Montgomery Watt, in his (now partly obsolete) *Free Will and Predestination in Early Islam,* London 1948, p. 19, who considered the turn towards predestinationism in Muslim theology to be the breaking through of a pre-Islamic, Bedouin sense of living, from which Koranic theology had parted.

it,[15] the findings can be more suitable to the modern mind than what traditionalists say is Islamic,[16] and the findings are likely to get resonance among Muslims today—after all, it is their own origin which is seen in a new light.[17]

The History of Rethinking: The State of Research

In focussing on the Koran, one is faced with two fundamental options.[18] One may either study how the Koran *should* be handled today, or how it *is being* handled today. The latter option has been chosen in this study. This choice may surprise systematic philosophers and theologians because they might see it as avoiding the more relevant question of how the Koran *should* be handled. They should however consider these points: (a.) If one answers the question 'how the Koran should be handled today' without considering what Muslims are actually doing, the answer may be original; but one can then because of the answer's independence from the Muslim discussion not *see its originality.* (b.) On the other hand, studying what Muslims are actually doing may prove worthwhile because one will probably be reporting about things so far *unrecorded in the non-Muslim world.* (c.) One may find *inspiring insights,* even in methodological theory, and even for one's own 'how to handle'-problems from people thinking in, or coming from, traditions different from one's own. (d.) Reversely, if one finds Muslims drawing from one's own tradition, their application may shed *new light on one's own tradition.* (e.) If one is reporting about a linguistic or geo-

15 E.g., where in Islamic theology has a thrilling verse like 2:257 been taken as the starting point for a Koranic anthropology? "God is the friend of those who are believers. He brings them out, from darkness to light. The unbelievers' friends are the idols, who bring them out from light into darkness." Belief starts from darkness, unbelief from light. This does not mean that people have either the dark or the light disposition. After all, darkness/light position is being inversed through contact with "the friend". Does it not rather imply a general description of the human situation as including darkness *and* light? And does the verse not imply a description of the path of believing as beginning in darkness? Of course however a methodologically sound Koranic anthropology must not pick individual verses only.

16 Cf., e.g., Fazlur Rahman, *Major Themes of the Qur'an,* Minneapolis ^{2}1989, p. 15: "with regard to man's actions and his destiny vis-à-vis God, God and man are not rivals therein—as the later Mu'atazilite and Ash'arite theologians thought".

17 Cf. also Fazlur Rahman's arguments for grounding his theology on the Koran, below, p. 110.

18 The following paragraphs are not intended to suggest that the present author has surveyed the whole globe before settling on the subject stated in the title. Rather, they are meant to *justify* the choice of the theme, which he was encouraged to study by Prof. Wielandt. (Cf. below, p. 43, section a.)

graphical area unfamiliar also to other Muslims, the discoveries may as well be interesting and inspiring *for the Muslim world.* (f.) A Muslim voice suggesting an answer to the question of 'how the Koran should be handled today' would normally be heard as a valid participant in the debate of today; non-Muslim students of Islam intending to discuss questions Koranic however will only be understood as *participants in the same discussion* if they first express and explain the state of the discussion.

Before setting out on the expedition, a look at the extant maps is worthwhile. Which spot seems of particular interest on the maps of modern Muslim Koran interpretation that have been drawn by Western scholarship? What attracts our curiosity are unmapped areas. Turkey is, as will be seen, a great blank on the Western maps of Muslim exegesis. The expedition will be directed there to look for new approaches to Koranic studies. But what has been gained if any should be found? If such approaches prove viable, a precious key has been found and the expedition will prove to be a successful treasure hunt. What is the key needed for? It opens the gate between two lands. The lands are 'Muslim identity' and 'today'. And the key may also fit in the gate between 'religious traditions in general' and 'modern minds'.

The state of research has to be presented on two levels of reflection at the same time. A report on the state of research will have to be a history of Muslim Koran interpretation *and* of its Western analysis. Muslim Koran exegesis and its Western analyses can only be presented overlapping because (a.) a wealth of Muslim contributions comes in languages not easily accessible to Western scholars, which makes it nearly impossible for a Western individual to provide a comprehensive study of the primary sources; one has to rely—if critically—on what the colleagues have prepared; (b.) there is a cross fertilisation between Muslim thinkers and Islamicists;[19] (c.) Muslim thinkers themselves provide surveys of the history of research from their points of view.[20]

If we want to find the fitting key, we need not only the maps but also an amateur manual in locksmithing. It has to clarify what exactly we are looking for. So, before presenting the state of research of Muslim exegesis, a glimpse at the state of today's discussion on interpretative methodology should be ventured.

---

19 Cf., e.g., the great interest studies like Paret's receive among Muslim theologians: below, p. 135. Furthermore, the present author heard Muslim theologians express that works by Josef van Ess or Rotraud Wielandt should be translated into Turkish.

20 E.g., Fazlur Rahman, *Islam,* Chicago ^{2}1979, pp. 193–234.

1 Reviewing Hermeneutics

The word 'hermeneutics' has been used in this study's title. It will be used in its body, too. Both the present author and the authors studied will fondly speak of 'hermeneutics'. It is not an unambiguous word, though.[21] A reflection on the word and on the history of hermeneutic practice and theory is therefore appropriate. Reflecting on hermeneutics may however prove valuable not only because it clarifies a concept frequently used in this study. It may also help us to clarify the goals, chances and dangers of such a study. After all, this study certainly presupposes an *understanding* of the texts it deals with.[22]

1.1 Why Interpret in the First Place?

Interpretation can be defined as the process of transposing something other into one's own understanding.[23] If this definition is correct, interpre-

---

21 And it is not one of the most commonly understood words either. Glenn W. Most, then Princeton, said in 1981 that many people especially in America think that hermeneutics is a German philosopher whose first name is Hermann and whose last name they didn't quite get. (Odo Marquard, "Das Fiktive als ENS REALISSIMUM", Dieter Henrich and Wolfgang Iser (eds.), *Funktionen des Fiktiven,* München 1983, pp. 489–95, pp. 491–2, quoting Glenn W. Most's Dubvrovnik talk "Rhetorik und Hermeneutik – Zur Konstitution der Neuzeitlichkeit".)

22 Gerhard Ebeling gives another reason for studying the *history* of hermeneutics. a. He starts from the observation that the task of hermeneutics has changed in the course of people's dealing with texts. b. Understanding, he adds, is something that happens within and according to the historical situation of all human existence. c. The more one is aware of this, Ebeling continues, the wider becomes the task of hermeneutics. (One may here add this justification for (c.): because more aspects of the author's and interpreters' situations come into sight as relevant for understanding.) d. From this he concludes that if one wants to understand what hermeneutics is, one has also to study its history. (Gerhard Ebeling, "Hermeneutik", *Die Religion in Geschichte und Gegenwart,* vol. 3, Tübingen ^{3}1959, cols. 242–62, col. 244.) But Ebeling's point can easily be taken as a truism (studying history helps) or a plea for relativism (interpreting *is* understanding).

23 Cf., e.g., Georg Wieland, "Hermeneutik. Begriff", *Lexikon für Theologie und Kirche,* vol. 5, Freiburg ^{3}1996, cols. 1–3. According to him, the task of hermeneutics is „den Sinngehalt des Fremden und Anderen in das eigene Verständnis zu übertragen. Wo diese Übertragung gelingt, spricht man v[on] Verstehen. Den Vorgang selbst kann man als Deutung od[er] *Interpretation* bezeichnen": Interpretation is taken to be the process of the transposition of contents from the strange and other into one's own understanding. (Ibid., col.1.) Georg Wieland says that the object to be understood encounters my own familiar world „mit dem Anspruch auf Verständnis—with the claim to be understood". (Ibid.) But the urge to be understood need not be in the object. It is true that understanding has to subject itself to the

tation presupposes a distance between the interpreter and what he or she interprets: an otherness. If one says one interprets the Koran, one is already accepting the Koran's otherness, i.e., that it is not within one's direct grasp. Or, the other way round, if one says one can apply the Koran immediately, without having to interpret it, one is rejecting its otherness (or the definition of 'interpretation'). "The theory and art of interpretation"[24] is commonly termed 'hermeneutics'. So, if one is doing Koran hermeneutics, and already if one says one has a Koran hermeneutics, one is aware of the gap between oneself and the Koran.

1.2 Levels of Hermeneutics

Of course, one cannot prevent people from using words the way they want to. Scholarship should not regulate but clarify. So besides offering definitions, we are to observe word usage. And 'hermeneutics' is used in different ways. 'X's hermeneutics' is often used simply to mean 'what X does with the text'. This should be termed the *neutrally descriptive* usage of 'hermeneutics'. Here, it is helpful to distinguish between 'X's explicit' and 'X's implicit hermeneutics', i.e., what X *says* X does with the text—and what X *actually* does with the text.[25] Then, there are people who call their own dealing with texts 'hermeneutical'. They seem to indicate that they transport a text's meaning into their own contexts while being aware of the problems involved in understanding. This might be called the *normative* usage of 'hermeneutics', because this usage allows for statements like 'X's procedure is fundamentalist rather than hermeneutical'. And finally, there is a philosophical tradition named 'hermeneutical' and associated with authors like Martin Heidegger and Hans-Georg Gadamer. Often, interpreters using the words 'hermeneutics/hermeneutical' seem to claim that they have understood and observed the points of that philosophical tradition. In this third case, 'hermeneutics' is a *name.* It may often be impossible to decide exactly which usage is involved when the authors to be presented here use 'hermeneutics'. The present study starts with a neutrally descrip-

---

object. But it is in fact all objects IN TOTO 'under' which understanding 'stands', i.e., it is a totality which is being understood.

24 Ibid.: „die Lehre und Kunst der Interpretation". On the 'art' aspect cf. Hans-Georg Gadamer, "Klassische und philosophische Hermeneutik" (1968), IDEM, *Wahrheit und Methode,* vol. 2, pp. 92–117, p. 93: "ARS, i.e., an art-theory like the art of rhetoric or of writing or of calculating—a practical skill (‚Fertigkeit') rather than 'science' (‚Wissenschaft')".

25 Cf. Felix Körner, *Muḥammad Šaḥrūrs Koranhermeneutik in al-Kitāb wa-l-qur'ān,* Bamberg 2000 (unpublished M.A. thesis), p. 7.

tive usage of 'hermeneutics' when surveying how modern Muslims actually deal with the Koran. But the normative usage will prevail in the main part of the study. In that, it is following the studied authors' own diction. And, as will be pointed out below (e.g., p. 74), some of them venture an explicite ‹reception› of Hans-Georg Gadamer's philosophy and consequently use 'hermeneutics/hermeneutical' also as a name.

1.3 Gadamer's History

A short review of the history of hermeneutics must serve as a backdrop for the detailed hermeneutical discussions to follow. Since Gadamer's view of hermeneutics plays such an important role for the Turkish theologians to be presented here, we will give him the word also for the historical survey.[26]

Although 'hermeneutics' was first used in 1654 to designate the art of interpretation and its theoretical justification, one can already find methodological awareness in the Biblical exegesis of the Fathers of the Church.[27] Reformation theologians, striving for the Bible's literal meaning, disputed the patristic "fourfold sense of Scripture". Still, their efforts, like Humanism's hermeneutics, were directed towards regaining "the normative". They were looking for a new understanding of the original meaning (‚Ur-Sinn') of an existing tradition. They were not concerned about diffi-

---

26 The arcticle mentioned above in footnote 24 on p. 23 will serve as a basis. It is the 1968 original of what was cut down to the (however prestigious) dictionary contribution: Hans-Georg Gadamer, "Hermeneutik", *Historisches Wörterbuch der Philosophie,* vol. 3, Basel 1974, cols. 1061–73.

27 Gadamer, "Klassische und philosophische Hermeneutik", p. 93, with reference to Augustin's *DE DOCTRINA CHRISTIANA.* Claus von Bormann, "Hermeneutik. Philosophisch-theologisch", *Theologische Realenzyklopädie,* pp. 108–37, p. 113 mentions that hermeneutics becomes vital when a vital tradition is shaken, and he names pre-Christian hermeneutics. But in fact he only records interpretative methodology, not hermeneutical awareness: „Hermeneutik ist immer entwickelt und gepflegt worden, wenn eine Tradition, die lebenstragend war, brüchig wurde und nun eine Korrektur oder ein Neuanfang gesucht wurden. Sie wurde weniger methodisch und mehr erfinderisch betrieben, wo es ausreichte, die Tradition für die Bedürfnisse der Zeit umzudeuten, um sie als Ganzes zu erhalten, so in der *Homerauslegung* der Stoa mit Hilfe der Allegorese (während die Alexandrinische Schule philologische Kritik im einzelnen leistete) oder im jüdischen Midrasch („Auslegung"), dem es darum ging, durch einzelne Regeln die Heilige Schrift als sinnvolle lehrhafte Einheit zu bewahren, was schließlich auch nur durch Allegorese gelang (Philo). Sie wurde methodisch unter Benutzung der Regeln der Rhetorik gebraucht, aber im Ganzen in starker Abhängigkeit von dogmatischen und ethischen Voraussetzungen, wo das Ziel war, einen überkommen Kanon (das Alte Testament) festzuhalten, aber mit der kirchlichen Lehrmeinung überall auszugleichen, wie dies Augustin [...] vorbildlich für das ganze Mittelalter vorführte."

culties in understanding a tradition. (That was to become Schleiermacher's motive later.) The hermeneutics of theology, classics and jurisprudence was contents centred and not particularly interested in philosophical questions. CLAVIS, key, is a common book title in that type of practical literature. But besides that, formal hermeneutics now turned up for the first time: under the heading of logic, developing more and more into general semantics. It was a theologian, Johann J. Rambach, who, influenced by the rhetoric of antiquity and guided his own homiletic interests, set up (in 1723) the triad of SUBTILITAS (subtlety) INTELLEGENDI, EXPLICANDI and APPLICANDI. 'Subtlety' may be seen to imply "that the 'methodology' of interpretation—like any application of rules whatsoever—requires a judgement which cannot again be secured by rules".[28]

Schleiermacher's hermeneutics takes a new approach. He tries to shed in his reading any dogmatic constraints. He does that not only with the intention of establishing theology's "scientific" status;[29] his approach is also in line with the Romantic presupposition that *the dialogue* (‚das Gespräch') is a source of truth irreplaceable by dogmatics. Rather than trying to be a normative text's intermediary, Schleiermacher wants to communicate with the dark (‚umdunkelt'), far-away traces of another human mind: the way to historicism (‚Historismus')—i.e., non-normative interest in the past—is open. Documents are now being interpreted especially from a psychological point of view.

Heidegger says that human existence itself is identical with understanding or, earlier, with historicality[30] (‚Geschichtlichkeit'). Historicality is for him not a limitation of knowledge but its positive condition. He uses the traditional image of the circle for the process of understanding. For him however it is not a vicious circle but an open and productive one. One starts from one's own particular situation, meets the new information from this perspective, and has one's own situation reshaped by this encounter. The late Heidegger sees truth as the event which opens the space of both discovering (‚Entbergen') *and covering* (‚Verbergung'). According to

---

28 Gadamer, "Klassische und philosophische Hermeneutik", p. 97, with reference to the introduction to the second edition of Kant's *Critique of Judgement.*

29 This attempt at making theology scientific has the opposite effect of a surrender of theology's scientific status if it stops inquiring about truth: cf. above, footnote 7 on p. 16.

30 In many translations, both ‚Geschichtlichkeit' and ‚Historizität' are rendered by 'historicity'. Following the suggestion of Elmar Waibl and Philip Herdina, *Wörterbuch philosophischer Fachbegriffe/Dictionary of Philosophical Terms,* vols. 1–2, Munich 2001, s.v., the—admittedly unusual—word 'historicality' is used for 'Geschichtlichkeit' here to avoid confusion. The difference plays a role in the authors studied below.

Gadamer, it was this view which made a re-evaluation of all discovering, including understanding, possible.

Gadamer was able to criticise the traditional view that understanding is only a reproduction—duplication[31]—of the production of author's mind.[32] Legal hermeneutics had always been seen as creative rather than merely reproductive, but also as therefore not objective and scholarly. As one can observe however when a dramatist attempts to "interpret" a text "appropriately", fidelity to the original and creativity are not mutually exclusive but equally necessary.

With these observations in mind, Gadamer now transcends the text-centered scope of hermeneutics. Hermeneutics is about interpration. And historical events, too, must be interpreted. Understanding an historical event is not identical with—or easier when—"experiencing" (‚erleben', Dilthey) or "re-enacting" it (Collingwood). That, says Gadamer, would be a subjectivistic reduction of the problem. He is harking back to Hegel, who wanted to see RATIO (‚Vernunft') at work in history. In other words: rather than trying to slip into other people's minds, Gadamer wants to look at reality himself—seeing the world not *as* others but *with* others. Is Biblical interpretion more on the 'as others' or the 'with others' side? Gadamer discovers that it has long been following the model 'as others' and he states: the traditional hermeneutical model of 'congeniality of author and interpreter' only lead to the "horrific image of inspiration theory".[33] More modern minded scholars offered historical exegesis as an alternative. But historical exegesis does not provide a more satisfying solution when it looks for the New Testament authors' self-understanding, says Gadamer (with an obvious allusion to Bultmann). Because, one could add, what comes into view thus is only other people's minds, not 'the world out there, which we want to understand'.

Rudolf Bultmann's programme of demythologisation can be seen as mediating between the romantic individualist approach (introspection),

---

31 Gadamer is inconsistent in his wording here, because he calls both duplicating retrieval and creative new actualisation 'reproduction': "Klassische und philosophische Hermeneutik", p. 104.

32 It is, in Gadamer's presentation, not quite clear why the discovery of truth's 'covering' (‚Verbergen') feature should lead to the insight that understanding is more than duplicating the author's mind. The missing link seems to be the point that Heidegger called our attention to what is beneath the propositional surface of language. Possibly, his almost pejorative, nostalgic terming of revealing as ‚Entbergen' is meant to lead to the association that language has a function of ‚Bergen' i.e., sheltering, harbouring, nesting people—and otherwise invisible mysteries.

33 Ibid., p. 105. Gadamer seems to allude to models which declare the Biblical author and the Christian interpreter as co-enlightened by the Spirit.

and the normative approach (explaining belief). Gadamer however says that Scripture's °salvific meaning (‚Heilssinn') must be more than the authors' self-understandings. He clearly advocates a stronger outreach to the outside world. The reader must bring his understanding to new reality contact. In Gadamer's words: The salvific meaning of the text is actualised only when the interpretation includes application. This revisionist hermeneutics required a new theoretical basis, which Gadamer provided in the two concepts of 'pre-understanding' (‚Vorverständnis') and 'history of effect' (‚Wirkungsgeschichte').[34]

According to his analysis, efficacious interpretation has always, though often unconsciously, played a role in lawyers' and theologians' interpretations. Their contribution to the hermeneutic reflection should be taken seriously, Gadamer demands. But the strongest starting point for Gadamer's rethinking was the experience of art. Here, he says, scholarly theory is secondary to experience, but INTELLECTIO, EXPLICATIO and APPLICATIO are intertwined, none of them is secondary to an other.

Application is a constituent part of understanding, not a later step, because "rules are determined by or even abstracted from actions". (p. 108) A hermeneutic which stresses the reader's pre-understanding and need of application is not the legalisation of a reading which subordinates the text to the reader's preconceived intentions. Uncovering the inevitability of a pre-understanding and the application structure of understanding is, rather, explicating the conditions in which any understanding actually takes place. Gadamer is clear in saying that one must be ready to leave one's own presuppositions. But the distance (and one might even say, discrepancy, disagreement) between text and interpreter does not thwart understanding. On the contrary, it gives "life and suspense (‚Spannung')" to any understanding. (p. 109) The new questions and insights the interpreter has gained from elsewhere shed new light on the things the text is talking about and the reader now also tries to see. Their horizons fuse (to use Gadamer's classical formulation). By that, Gadamer designates the process

---

[34] Both words had already a tradition in philosophical theology.—Since the presentation followed here is now both by and about Gadamer at the same time and since self-interpretation, as Gadamer himself says, (ibid., p. 104) is "of questionable validity", a distanced explication of the two concepts is required. Gadamer observed that interpreting does not mean that one is simply entering into the author's mind. One cannot—and need not—leave one's own mind, knowledge, questions, one's own perspective. In Gadamer's words: One has to start from his own "pre-understanding", and one has to be aware of that. One's pre-understanding is however not totally independent of the text. Even before one reads the first word, the text has already influenced on one's pre-understanding. The pre-understanding is part of the text's "history of effect".

in which the interpreter takes what the text points to into his own, thus growing, range of knowledge. But how can the distance between text and interpreter be bridged? Language, Gadamer trusts, can do that.

Gadamer concludes his survey with the observation that his own understanding of hermeneutics means an extension of the traditional question of understanding on three levels: a. His hermeneutics is competent in all kinds of communications, not only in the special case of monological argumentation (as logic is)—therefore hermeneutics must not be subordinated to the much more restricted discipline of logic. b. Understanding something includes understanding the question it answered, i.e., to see not only its propositional content but also the history of its motivation. c. But this widening of the question of understanding must also be applied to the practice of the person who is trying to understand. Real understanding must include self-criticism. In laying open what restricts our grasp on the world, philosophical hermeneutics has an important criticical role to play. It has to remind any scientific and technical attempt at dominating nature and society of its limits.

1.4 Fusing Horizons with Gadamer

Gadamer's approach is undoubtably a groundbraking advance in the reflection on understanding. But if understanding should progress, one should also have an eye for the problems in other people's views. Gadamer's views do raise several points of discussion. And discussing rather than simply sharing the author's view is quite in line with Gadamer's own idea of understanding.

Firstly, one should mention that Gadamer's philosophy easily disappoints those who are looking for a text hermeneutics in Gadamer's work. His whole "Philosophical Hermeneutics" works on a different level. He observes what happens when someone understands a text and then applies his findings to all areas of human life. Gadamer expressly refuses to offer a method of interpreting texts. His philosophy may have effects on methodologies of interpretation, but Gadamer is extremely sceptical of method, and he does not draw the methodological conclusions himself. But since he stresses that the understanding of a text and its application are inextricably linked, applying his hermeneutics in trying to find interpretative methods seems to be a Gadamerian thing to do. At least one of the Turkish authors studied below has gone this way.[35]

---

35 Cf. below, p. 78.

Secondly, Gadamer has a problem with propositions.[36] On the final pages of his *Wahrheit und Methode* he distinguishes between „was man meint" and „der ‚reine' Sinn", i.e., that which one wants to say, and that which one says literally.[37] This is a relevant distinction. But if exaggerated, it can lead to discarding all possible propositional truth in favour of the "infinity of that which is unsaid".[38] Although Gadamer's philosophy is steering towards the possibility of object relations in other parts of *Wahrheit und Methode,*[39] he cannot, for all his "unsaid horizon of meaning", accept here that people can make propositions which have a validity that does not depend on the speaker's situation. One should consider:[40] (a.) Even though everything is said within a particular horizon, one can still *distinguish* between the speaker's subjectivity and the object spoken about. (b.) Any understanding of the unsaid horizon of meaning must also start from that which is being said, i.e., from propositions. (c.) The result of understanding, again, lives in propositions.—Sometimes, Gadamer's formulation seems to advocate a fragmentation of understanding. What he describes, the singular 'I see'-instance, is only a section of understanding. Does not understanding mean that I see all parts in their places and thus see their meaning? If understanding is nothing but seeing individual things, my horizon can easily become the horizon of someone else. That however must end in text tourism. We can visit other horizons without bringing them together into one whole. People's understandings however offer more than only points of view. The position I encounter when reading a text or in a face-to-face dialogue is at the same time an explication of how things belong together. Therefore, in our fusion of horizons, necessary as it is for understanding, we might encounter a—constructive—clash

---

36 Cf. already Wolfhart Pannenberg, "Hermeneutik und Universalgeschichte" (1963), IDEM, *Grundfragen systematischer Theologie,* vol. 1, Göttingen 1967, pp. 91–122, pp. 112–4.

37 Hans-Georg Gadamer, *Hermeneutik,* vol. 1, *Wahrheit und Methode. Grundzüge einer philosophischen Hermeneutik,* Tübingen ([1]1960:) [6]1990, p. 473 (part 3, 3.b). Gadamer uses the ambiguity of ‚Aussage' ('proposition' and 'testimony, deposition in a lawsuit') to illustrate his point that what people are made to *say* is often not what they *mean.*

38 Ibid.

39 A mere historical understanding does not allow the text to say *something true.* (Ibid., p. 308) Gadamer produced the concept 'fusion of horizons' precisely to procure "understandable truth" in texts. (Ibid., p. 309) And language refers to things in the world; it is therefore objective in the sense of object related: „Aus dem Weltverhältnis der Sprache folgt ihre eigentümliche *Sachlichkeit.*" (Ibid., p. 449; Gadamer's italics) Cf. also below, p. 120.

40 Wolfhart Pannenberg, "Hermeneutik und Universalgeschichte", p. 114, and IDEM, *Wissenschaftstheorie und Theologie,* p. 168.

of theories because my own horizon may provide other data which put my partner's explication into a new context, and vice versa.

Thirdly, in *Wahrheit und Methode* Gadamer has problems with the concept of universal history. We cannot, he says, understand the past or present in view of the totality of events, because the course of events is not yet finished and human experience is finite and therefore incapable of seeing the whole.[41] Gadamer is right in stressing that the course of events is unfinished and our experience is finite. But understanding still works in view of an anticipated whole, as Gadamer unconsciously admits when mentioning the "totality of that which is unsaid".[42] And although the content of these anticipations will change, they cannot be replaced by anything more limited. The horizons of past and present can only then fuse without either one appropriating the other completely, if this fusion takes place in the greater horizon to which both past and present horizons belong. According to Gadamer language suffices to bridge the different horizons. (cf. above, p. 28) But having a bridge is only one thing. The other is: something must come across. In a fusion of hozizons, what comes across is a claim of factuality. It is this claimed factuality which provides the material for understanding.

Finally, a comment is due on Gadamer's insight that understanding a text is to understand which question it answers.[43] But where do we get the question from? From our dialogue with the text itself? That is Gadamer's answer.[44] In this, he presupposes that every text is a successful answer to its questions. But can an author not fail to do his or her assignment? In this case, it will be difficult to read the question out of the text's content. This

---

41 *Wahrheit und Methode,* vol. 1, p. 361 (part 2.ii.3.b), in discussion with Hegel.

42 Pannenberg, "Hermeneutik und Universalgeschichte", p. 116. While Gadamer has not tackled Pannenberg's criticism concerning the propositional character of language (cf. the second point in this series of comments), he accepted Pannenberg's reminder of the conscious horizon of the whole of history, in which all understanding takes place. „Niemand kann bestreiten, daß Historie Zukünftigkeit voraussetzt. Eine universalgeschichtliche Konzeption ist insofern unvermeidlicherweise eine der Dimensionen gegenwärtiger historischer Bewußtheit 'in praktischer Absicht'". Hans-Georg Gadamer, "Rhetorik, Hermeneutik und Ideologiekritik. Metakritische Erörterungen zu 'Wahrheit und Methode'" (1967), IDEM, *Hermeneutik,* vol. 2, *Wahrheit und Methode. Ergänzungen,* pp. 232–50, p. 246.

43 Gadamer, *Wahrheit und Methode,* vol. 1, p. 375, with reference to Collingwood. On Collingwood cf. below, p. 160.

44 He, approvingly, reports Collingwood as saying that „man diese Frage [scil., auf die der Text eine Antwort ist] aber nur aus dem Text gewinnen kann—one can obtain that question [scil., to which the text is an answer] only from the text". *Wahrheit und Methode,* vol. 1, p. 375. Gadamer and Collingwood have not stated what exactly they mean by 'text' here. The above criticism presupposes that they thought of the content.

is a relevant distinction even if the question was not assigned to the author from outside: a text can, e.g., through its form, promise an answer it is unable to provide. Furthermore, it was Gadamer's own insight that our preliminary understanding is a creative factor in understanding. An exclusively intra-textual understanding seems neither desirable nor even possible. There must be extra-textual coordinates which enable us to say things like: 'A fundamental religious text must contain an explanation of the world.'

1.5 Key Results

This review of Western hermeneutical reflection[45] has provided three important insights for the study of religion.

Firstly, understanding is more than empathy. In reading texts from an historical (temporal, cultural, religious) distance, one can bring to light what could not be seen from other perspectives, including the author's own. This insight can encourage a study like the present one. And such a study can be a test of the insight's truth. We will not only present other people's opinions. We will try to understand them also by fusing horizons; in other words, by discussing their views.

Secondly, one cannot develop one's method before starting to work. This warning against a methodological obsession should keep us alert on two levels. On the one side, we will be dealing with authors discussing methods of Koranic interpretation. We should also consider what happens to their methodological reflections when they actually interpret the Koran. On the other side, we are trying to find an appropriate method for religious studies. The quality of any proposed method will only prove when set into action.[46]

---

45 A survey which leads interpretative methodology beyond Gadamer is Anthony C. Thiselton, *New Horizons in Hermeneutics,* London 1992. Cf. also Jean Grondin, *Introduction to Philosophical Hermeneutics (with a foreword by Hans-Georg Gadamer),* New Haven (German 1991:) 1994.

46 This is not a wholesale rejection of methodological reflections. The renowned New Testament scholar Geza Vermes, e.g., starts one of his books by proclaiming his disdain for methodology *(The Religion of Jesus the Jew,* Minneapolis 1993, p. 7): he advocates "muddling through". John P. Meier, *A Marginal Jew, Rethinking the Historical Jesus,* vol. 3, *Companions and Competitors,* New York 2001, p. 16, proves that Vermes's disdain led him into some embarrassing traps. But Meyer should not be taken to say that a scholarly work must have its methodology set and stated before it can start to work. His point is really that one should be conscious and explicit about what one is doing as a scholar at any moment. Although Meyer's own book starts with an elaborated methodology (criteria of historicity), which he uses throughout, one should not doubt that every method is shaped also in dialogue

Thirdly, meaning is the function a part has in a whole. The whole however is not yet completed. History is still going on. We therefore have to keep an eye on the question which role the course of events plays for those who try to find (new) meaning in the Koran?

Though the introduction of the word 'hermeneutics' in Muslim exegetical reflection is recent, first generation Muslims have of course already done exegesis.[47] Consequently, there has been 'implicit hermeneutics',[48] which can be explicated.[49] Moreover, Muslims have very soon started reflecting exegetical methodology.[50] So, there is also an old tradition of 'explicit hermeneutics' in Islam. But could one go further and claim that there has been Muslim Koran hermeneutics in the normative sense, i.e., has there been an historical awareness? Muslims have seen the context dependence of the Koran in so far as they have taken into account from early on that the proclamation of the Koran was being occasioned by certain events (cf. the discussions of the *asbāb an-nuzūl*[51] and of *nāsiḫ/mansūḫ*[52]), and that its interpretation requires knowledge of the general and particular history of its environment.[53] But if the points made in the above review of hermeneutics hold true, an historical consciousness relevant for understanding a text should include more than that. It requires (a.) an awareness

---

with the material. Two arguments can be adduced fort hat. Firstly, Meyer had already worked on New Testament texts before he developed his method. And secondly, his method does not (and cannot) contain a comprehensive meta-method which tells him each time how to apply which criterion.

47 Cf. Angelika Neuwirth, "Koran", Helmut Gätje (ed.), *Grundriß der arabischen Philologie,* vol. 2, *Literaturwissenschaft,* Wiesbaden 1987, pp. 96–135, p. 120: explication of the text started before the corpus of the Koran was completed.

48 Cf. above, at note 25.

49 Cf., e.g., Ignaz Goldziher, *Die Richtungen der islamischen Koranauslegung,* Leiden 1920, or Andrew Rippin (ed.), *Approaches to the History of the Interpretation of the Qur'ān,* Oxford 1988.

50 The literary genre and traditional academic discipline of *uṣūl al-fiqh* are what Norman Calder rightly calls a meta-discourse: "uṣūl al-fiḳh", *EI*², vol. 10, Leiden 2000, pp. 931–2, p. 932. He also refers to the study of the *qawāʿid fiqhīya* (legal maxims) and *maqāṣid aš-šarīʿa* (intentions of the law) as meta-discourses. (Ibid.) Cf. also the articles Andrew Rippin, "tafsīr", *EI*², vol. 10, Leiden 2000, pp. 83–7, and Ismail Kurban Husein Poonawala, "taʾwīl", Ibid., pp. 390–1.

51 The occasions of the sending down (of Koran passages)—cf. Alford T. Welch, "Ḳurʾān", *EI*², vol. 5, pp. 400–29, esp. section 5b: "Traditional Muslim Dating", pp. 415–6.

52 The rendering obsolete of an earlier Koran passage by one proclaimed later—cf. John Burton, "Naskh", *EI*², vol. 7, Leiden 1993, pp. 1009–12.

53 Cf. Angelika Neuwirth, "Koran", p. 122: the oldest commentaries are (what might be called:) context supplies, or, in Wansbrough's typology, "haggadic"; p. 123: the oldest extant documents of Muslim *philological* studies are by Ḫalīl ibn Aḥmad (d. 791) and Sībawayh (d. 796). A primary interest of the development of Arabic philology was to understand the Koran.

of the interpreter's pre-understanding, (b.) an awareness of the effects text and tradition have on the interpreter's pre-understanding, (c.) an awareness of the distance between text and interpreter, (d.) an awareness of the fact that text and interpreter are in principal confronted with the same reality and only see it from different perspectives, and (e.) an awareness of the therefore positive influence of this distance on the understanding. Can such awareness be found in Muslim Koran exegesis? In other words, how hermeneutical is Islam?

In our search for the key we had seen the necessity of an amateur manual of locksmithing. This has been presented above. We know now what the key we are looking for should look like. So we can have a look at the maps drawn until date.

2 *Western Analyses of Tafsīr*

Three authors have pioneered in the Western mapping of modern Muslim Koran interpretation.[54] Their studies, though some of them are more than thirty years old, must still be considered as standard works of great value.

2.1 Baljon: Urdu Voices

The study by the Dutch scholar J. M. S. Baljon on modern *Tafsīr* (Koran exegesis) makes special use of Urdu commentaries.[55] Baljon takes 'modern' "in the qualificative sense"; (p. 2) 'modern' is "where the impact of Western *Weltanschauung* and way of life is somehow recognizable". (p. 15) Three Urdu commentaries are in the focus of his attention. Abū l-Kalām Āzād's *Tarǧumān al-Qurʾān,* which appeared in 1930; the *Ḥadīṯ al-Qurʾān* (1951) by Muḥammad ʿInāyat Allāh Ḫān ("al-Mašriqī"), who is famed for his programmatic *Taḏkira* of 1924; and the four volume *Maʿārif al-Qurʾān* (1941–9) by Ġulām Aḥmad Parwīz. Baljon regrets not to have studied any Turkish authors. They might, he supposes, have been of great value for his inquiry.

54 'Koran interpretation' and 'Koran exegesis' will not be distinguished terminologically.

55 Johannes Marinus Simon Baljon, *Modern Muslim Koran Interpretation (1880–1960),* Leiden 1968, p. vii. He begins his study with the year 1880 because it was in that year that Aḥmad Ḫān's influential commentary appeared. Page numbers in the text above refer to Baljon's book. Baljon's sometimes unusual English has in quotations been reproduced literally. Being not a native writer of English himself, the present author is aware of the travails and risks involved in composing an English text as a foreigner.

Why bother to read what Muslims write in languages so unfamiliar to the Western critic when there is plenty of material published by Muslims in European languages? Baljon argues that Muslims are when writing in European languages "constantly jealous of the good name Islam must maintain. Consequently, the exposé's are a-priori of an apologetic nature in the much restricted sense of the word". (p. 120) Rather than prosopographically presenting each author's views as a whole, Baljon chose to arrange his material thematically. That type of presentation provides an impression of Muslims' *thoughts*. It offers the results, without indicating the ways on which the authors got there. It does not offer the *thinking*. Therefore, it does not allow for the analysis of schools, camps, strands, trends, discussions and developments, nor for the tracking of presuppositions all the way out to their ramifications or into conceptual systems. But the advantage of this type of presentation is that one can use Baljon's book as a compendium. It allows for synoptic comparison.

In the authors he studies, Baljon sees either a "consistent elimination of all that is supernatural" or a more moderate "attempt to minimize as much as possible miraculous elements". (p. 24) He mentions lexicological, scientific and psychological explanations which his authors adduce as "means of de-supranaturalizing the text". (p. 27) Baljon finds among his authors "demythologizing", "romanticizing", "rationalizing", "historicizing" and "moralizing" readings at work (pp. 29; 63). Baljon's characterises the types of commentaries with words in '-izing'.[56] This already implies that he sees the interpretations as distorting what he considers to be the true meaning of the Koran. Only in his conclusion will he be explicit about that. Comparing Christian and Muslim exegesis, he assesses that "both of them sometimes cut queer capers". (p. 88) To prove his point, he quotes a protestant economist's 1952 statement "that Jesus' PARAENESIS in Matth. 6:26 not to worry about the day of to-morrow does not preclude the possibility of keeping a savings-bank book". Baljon comments: "Such a treatment of Bible wording may hardly be qualified as an interpretation E MENTE AUCTORIS". (p. 88) It is helpful to counter-check observations made in other groups with those made in your own community. So, the glipse at Christian New Testament exegesis is worthwhile. Here however Baljon has analogised more than necessary. In comparison with this reading of Matthew, is "finding telegraph, telephone, tramway and microbes recorded in Koranic passages" really to be counted as "[a]nalogous elucidations of Muslim modernists" (p. 88)? Is it not formally different to say 'a certain

---

[56] Perhaps Baljon would have described his own method as the '-izing'-izing of modern Muslim Koran exegesis.

modern behaviour is not against the text' and 'a certain modern invention/discovery/idea is expressly mentioned in the text'? Baljon lists many instances of Muslim commentaries which triumphantly declare they have found yet another scientific theory to be already in the Koran. He says that when encountering "such fantastic interpretations one is induced to make the sarcastic comment: "But how will this end, if later on scholarly views change?"" (p. 97) His question is a relevant criticism of so-called Scientific Exegesis.

Baljon concludes his study with an apologia of apologetics. (pp. 121–6) He claims that apologetics is a necessary consequence of religion. From the way he justifies this claim, one sees that what he means by 'apologetics' is the rational justification of religious claims. He does not see a principal problem with apologetics. Thirty-five years after Baljon however such a problem has become visible: because apologetics only reacts to objections, it never gets to expressing belief other than in the adversary's terms. Baljon has not refuted the "general" (p. 121) objection to Muslim Koran interpretation as pure apologetics. But by seeing the essential role rational justification plays in religious thought, he has contributed an important insight. Baljon distinguishes between two types of apologetics: "apologetics pertaining to primarily intellectual problems and apologetics regarding existential needs and moral issues". (p. 122) While the first, according to Baljon, works with counter-arguments, the second works by demonstrating that the "message" to be defended fits with the situation we live in as human beings. (p. 123) So-called Scientific Exegesis, he says, comes under intellectual apologetics. And Baljon calls it "a certain attempt at logical reasoning". (p. 124) This seems to be meant as an encouragement for the Muslim exegete to continue on the path of modern scholarship. Baljon continues however: "when it comes to constructing correlations between the requirement of the hour with answers from the message through 'interpretation' of Koranic sayings which plainly clashes with their actual meaning, such apologetics is no longer admissible". (p. 125) Thus, Baljon admits in his final pages that he finds problematic much of what he presented.

In this early study, Baljon has provided some criteria for the assessment of modern Muslim theology. His criteria should be revisited today. With hermeneutical discussions having continued since Baljon, one can today see three problems in his criteria. Firstly, it is difficult to decree that an interpretation clashes with the actual meaning if one is not able to show what the actual meaning is. Secondly, the question is not what is admissible and what is inadmissible, but what will hold the test of time and argument. Baljon already mentions where he sees the problem and where he sees the first Muslim attempts to solve it: "the Koranic notions are adapted to the world-view of the first hearers". (p. 125) And some Muslim scholars (he mentions Amīn al-Ḫūlī) have already seen that the Koran "makes use of an antiquated *Weltanschauung* and of obsolete social norms". (p. 125) Finally, when dealing with "existential apologetics" (to stay with Baljon's terminology), he says that it is not in need of rational justification: "As a drowning person derives no benefit from swimming theories, the confused Muslim world at the moment is not served in the first place with clever essays on the background of Koranic ideas. Accordingly, present-day Muslim interpretation follows a pragmatic line." (pp. 125–6) This is an important hint because it reminds every scholar of the necessity to analyse Muslim (and everybody's) thoughts within the contexts of their origins. However, the plea for pragmatism over against theoretical criticism should not be exaggerated. There may be a pragmatic necessity for theory.

2.2 Jansen: Egyptian Voices

Johannes J. G. Jansen's thesis on Koran interpretation in modern Egypt is another pioneer achievement in Western Islamic studies. He lists more than 300 Arabic titles in his bibliography.[57] Jansen defines 'modern' exegesis as 20th century exegesis. He says he found very few original contributions. Most of the modern commentaries, he says, draw heavily on classical works, especially on the commentary by az-Zamaḫšarī (d. 1144) and the *Tafsīr al-Ǧalālayn* by al-Maḥallī (d. 1459) and as-Suyūṭī (d. 1505). (p. 17)

Twice in his book Jansen makes remarks which prove, if read today, to be most relevant in the hermeneutical discussion, although Jansen himself was not yet able to see that. Jansen reflects on the origin and nature of Koran interpretation. He states that "from the very beginning, the exegesis of the Koran seemed somewhat artificial". (p. 95) He justifies this surprising statement by comparing the origin of the Koranic text with the making of the Bible. Christians and Jews themselves decided in a gradual process, he says, about their canons; it was only when the canons were closed that "there was a large-scale need for an interpretation". (p. 95) Jansen portrays the Muslim community's situation as fundamentally different. For the Muslims after Muhammad's death the Koran was already there, and they were in "immediate need to explain and apply" it. Although one should not overlook the disputes in the history of the Koranic text, Jansen's claim that the Koran's canonisation was faster and less disputed than the Bible's

---

57 Johannes J. G. Jansen, *The Interpretation of the Koran in Modern Egypt,* Leiden 1974, pp. 100–7. Page numbers in the text above refer to this book.

is received opinion.[58] But what Jansen is in fact claiming is this: the less you have participated in a text's origin the more difficult and "artificial" is your interpretation of it. Jansen is steering towards a most relevant point, but he has not yet made it. His remark can be expanded thus: there are two structurally different types of relations between a text and its interpreters. One is that a community agrees on a text; what is expressed in the text may be called the common ground; the interpreter is a part of that community; the most important criterion of correct interpretation is whether it agrees with the common ground; the text is only a means of the common ground's manifestation.[59] The other type of relation can be found when the interpreters are not (or do not consider themselves to be) the text's authors; the interpreters find themselves opposite the text; the criterion of correct interpretation is whether it agrees with the text. Both situations are common to us. The first type, the 'common ground' situation, is that of democratic jurisprudence (laws are made to express justice and can be reformed accordingly), and of ecclesial New Testament reading (each document was written and canonised to express the meaning of Jesus, who is the actual point of reference). The second type, the 'opposite' situation, is that of the interpretation of historical documents, literature (including newspapers and letters), and of the Koran. Neither situation is "artificial". Therefore, Jansen's assessment can in today's reflection be seen as too strong. But it has drawn our attention to a relevant hermeneutic distinction, which will play a role later on.[60]

According to Jansen, the modern commentaries' form and contents "are often surprisingly traditional", (p. 96) the only qualification being that modern commentators normally address a secularly trained public rather than theological colleagues. Jansen finds 20th century Egyptian Koran exegetes to work under three "aspects" (p. viii): natural history, philology, and day-to-day affairs. (p. 95) These categories are in part similar to Baljon's, who categorised his findings more vaguely into scientific aspects, practical issues, political thought and social life.[61]

When Jansen calls the background of so-called *Scientific* Exegesis "natural history" (p. 96) rather than '(natural) science' he implicitly criticises the

58 Cf., e.g., Theodor Nöldeke and Friedrich Schwally, *Geschichte des Qorāns,* vol. 2, *Die Sammlung des Qorāns,* Leipzig 1919, pp. 119–21.

59 A similar type of relation exists when an author discusses his or her own writing. Often, phrases like 'what I want*ed* to say is …' will be heard, but what is in fact being stated is—typically—what the author sees *now.*

60 Cf. the confrontation of the Biblical and Koranic concepts of revelation, p. 121, below.

61 Baljon, *Interpretation,* p. v.

standard of scientific information of those exegetes. Jansen then collects philological[62] approaches.

Philological exegesis, he finds, is very much in line with the classical philologists. He mentions Ibn ʿAbbās (d. 686), Abū ʿUbayda (d. 824/5) and az-Zamaḫšarī (d. 1144). (pp. 55–64) In Amīn al-Ḫūlī's (d. 1967) attempts to study the Koran as a work of literature, Jansen finds the following principles at work: interpreting a Koranic passage in the light of its historical background, (p. 66) of other passages on the same subject, (p. 67) of the Koranic usage of word roots, (p. 67) and of its psychological effect on its readers. (p. 66) Al-Ḫūlī's pupil Bint aš-Šāṭiʾ applies her teacher's approach to a few Suras. But in her choice, Jansen sharply notes, she sets her own priorities: it is the "purely "religious"" (p. 69) rather than legal or historical Suras which she analyses. Jansen's interpretation of Bint aš-Šāṭiʾ's choice is: she wanted to avoid trouble with more conservative Muslim circles. (p. 69) Although Jansen's has good arguments (p. 70) for his suspicion that she writes less than she knows, one wonders if her choice does not reveal what she finds most relevant in a text considered holy. Jansen observes that Bint aš-Šāṭiʾ starts from the presupposition that in its context every word can have only one meaning. If a word have several meanings according to the classical dictionaries, then what decides the intended meaning is the Koranic parallels analysed "with common sense". (p. 72) She uses pre-Islamic poetry for her semantic studies but, it seems, in a rather credulous way. (p. 73) Another of her presuppositions is, as Jansen sees, that she does not believe in ‚Reimzwang' (prosodic compulsion) as a motive for Koranic wording. Jansen praises al-Ḫūlī's and Bint aš-Šāṭiʾ's studies as equal to, or better than, the classical commentaries.

According to Jansen's observation, the true subject of *practical*—"day-to-day affairs"—interpretation is often "the degree to which Western influence on the secular and religious aspects of life should be tolerated". (p. 97; cf. p. 94) In the Koranic reading oriented towards *fiqh* ("the Islamic doctrine of duties", p. 84) Jansen observes: (a.) the starting point is always a close study of the Koranic text; (b.) no attention is paid to "the limited importance of Islamic law in the law of Egypt"; (p. 85) (c.) *fiqh* commentaries have an apologetic overtone; (p. 86) (d.) the profession that the gate of

---

62 Jansen's definition of 'philology' ("scientific efforts at discovering the purport of written or printed texts from the past" (p. 54, footnote 3)) omits the *language* point of view as DIFFERENTIA SPECIFICA and therefore unintentionally includes all of Jansen's other "aspects", indeed all scholarly interpretation. The approaches Jansen subsequently lists focus on semantics, grammar and textual structure. 'Linguistics' might be an apt characterisation of Jansen's second "aspect".

iǧtihād (legal reinterpretation) is open is merely rhetoric, (p. 86); and (e.) there is no unanimity as to what *'iǧtihād'* means. (p. 89)

Jansen says—and this is his second unconsciously pertinent remark—that exegesis that intends to find out historical truths is unknown to (scil., modern) Muslims. His explication of "historical" exegesis is exclusively future oriented: "certain Jews and Christians were often of the opinion that the date of a hoped-for fall of an inimical empire could be derived from close scrutiny of the Scriptures". (p. 96) The relevance of Jansen's observation should not be restricted to interpretations foretelling the future. Rather, the point that history is not a prominent subject for Muslim theologians other than in reconstructing an original Koranic context is a vital contribution to the debate on interpretation.[63]

Jansen saw this rule at work among modern exegetes: the Koran must be understood as the first Muslims understood it. (p. 97) His standard principle, like Baljon's, is that correct interpretation is E MENTE AUCTORIS, i.e., finding out what the author intended. (pp. 66; 96)[64] Jansen's own study unwittingly provides material to challenge this principle. Above, two remarks of Jansen's were interpreted in a way he himself was still unable to see. If interpreting Jansen meant only repeating what Jansen meant, we would not have been allowed in our interpretation to develop, as we did, from his text the ideas of a typology of text-interpreter relations and of multi-dimensional historical reading.

2.3 Wielandt: Philology, Philosophy, and Theology

In 1971, Rotraud Wielandt published a survey of Muslim philosophy of history. She covers works written between the end of the 19th century and the 1960s.[65] Wielandt focussed on a theologically vital question, viz., on

---

63 Cf. below, p. 163.

64 Baljon, *Interpretation,* p. 88. The principle seems to originate in Spinoza: Hans-Georg Gadamer, *Hermeneutik,* vol. 1, *Wahrheit und Methode. Grundzüge einer philosophischen Hermeneutik,* Tübingen 1990, p. 184 (part 2.i.1.a.α). Gadamer's observation that a work of art leaves its author and becomes an entity in its own right which can be understood independently of one's knowledge of the author, is a valid criticism of that principle. (Ibid., pp. 116–7) Gadamer's exciting wording ‚Verwandlung ins Gebilde' got the dull English translation "transformation into structure", which misses the aspect 'independent formation, subsisting configuration' of ‚Gebilde' (IDEM (translated and revised by Joel Weinsheimer and Donald Marshall), *Truth and Method,* New York 1989, p. 110).

65 Rotraud Wielandt, *Offenbarung und Geschichte.* She takes 'modern' as a mere chronological marker, "not as a qualifier to mean 'progressive' or 'open-minded'" (p. 6, n. 3). Page numbers in the text above refer to that study.

the tension between the doctrine that the Koran is revealed, and historical thinking. As the first Western scholar in this field, she also takes modern Turkish texts into account. But for the era she covers she has to state yet: "In this area, Turkish thinkers have made hardly any advance worth mentioning." (p. 14) The historical cause she adduces for this is that in the wake of the secularism which Mustafa Kemal urged, the public discussion of pertinent religious questions waned. (p. 14) But she seems to imply that the interest in these questions did not disappear forever when she designates the waning as "for a certain time". (Ibid.) And when she surveys the seeds of historical thinking about to sprout among Muslim intellectuals, she explicitly mentions Ankara University's İlâhiyat Fakültesi as a promising place of historical-critical Koran exegesis. (pp. 169–70) She justifies her hope with the observation that at Ankara's Theological Faculty "not in Koran exegesis but in other academic subjects which also belong to the obligatory curriculum modern historical methods are being applied, which is not the case, e.g., at al-Azhar". (p. 169) The fruits of the seeds she saw shoot up are to be gathered in the present study.

The authors she analysed were mostly of Egyptian or Indo-Muslim origin: Muḥammad ʿAbduh, Muḥammad Rašīd Riḍā, ʿAlī ʿAbd ar-Rāziq, ʿAbbās Maḥmūd al-ʿAqqād, Malek Bennabi, Muḥammad Aḥmad Ḫalaf Allāh, Muhammad Daud Rahbar and Asaf A. A. Fyzee. After studying the works of these thinkers in depth, Wielandt assesses the development of Muslim Koran interpretation as stuck in a dilemma. Either the Koran is seen as a fully human product and thus at the mercy of historical critique; or it is totally from God, and historical analysis cannot provide any clues to its understanding. (pp. 157–8) When she wrote her study, Wielandt saw only one way out of the dilemma. Some theorists already indicated that way, and Fyzee, she says, had already gone it: only through Muhammad's active participation in the process called revelation is the product comprehensible. In other words, the way out of the dilemma of the human or divine nature of the Koran is to give up the doctrine of verbal inspiration. If that is accepted in Muslim theology, "then the belief in verbal inspiration could be replaced by the conception that the Koran is not simply truth itself revealed by God, but Muhammad's testimony to it". (p. 158)

Thirty years on, what does Wielandt's suggestion look like? The authors presented in the present study have all DE FACTO (not all discuss the question explicitly) gone this way and have thus opened, and passed through, the gates to historical criticism. However, the thesis that verbal inspiration and historical criticism are mutually exclusive tenets should also be reconsidered.[66] An interpretation of the Koran from the context of 7th century Arabia does not require the surrender of a belief in its verbal inspiration. God could have inspired it verbally and used, in order to make Himself understood, wording and imagery of Muhammad's time. Has any Muslim thinker seen the compatibility of verbal inspiration and historical interpretation? Thinkers taking their starting points for revisiting the Koran from literary theory are able to do justice to both. We will encounter such thinking shortly in the al-Ḫūlī school and in Naṣr Ḥāmid Abū Zayd; and Wielandt has kept track of these more recent exegetical developments, which she portrayed and analysed in several subsequent studies.[67]

Recently, Rotraud Wielandt has prepared an encyclopaedic overview of early modern and contemporary Koran exegesis.[68] She sees six major methodological trends.

1. Rationalistic interpretation. Sayyid Ahmad Khan[69] and Muḥammad ʿAbduh tried—independently but similarly—to establish the thesis that the Koranic revelation does not contradict Enlightenment rationality. Their main methodological device to justify this was to explain away anything miraculous as actually designating in its original context something natural.
2. Scientific Exegesis *(tafsīr ʿilmī).* It "starts from the assumption that all sorts of findings of modern natural sciences have been anticipated in the Qurʾān and that many clear references to them can be discovered in its verses". (p. 129) The tradition of Scientific Exegesis goes back as far as Faḫr ad-Dīn ar-Rāzī (d. 1209) and can be found in the aforementioned Muḥammad ʿAbduh as well as most notably in Šayḫ Ṭanṭāwī Ǧawharī, and in many other 20th century exegetical works. Wielandt criticises this method as "projecting into the text what normally nobody would see there" (p. 129) and later (pp. 130–1) lists five arguments proffered by Muslims against Scientific Exegesis: it is untenable because it neglects (1) the exact meanings of the words interpreted and (2) their literary context in the Koran, (3) the intellectual horizon of the Koran's

66 Already in 1971, Wielandt mentioned the possibility that Muslim theology could hold that a human, contingent, historical element might have entered the Koran through God Himself *(Offenbarung und Geschichte,* p. 167).

67 Cf. the following paragraph; and Wielandt's detailed study "Die Wurzeln der Schwierigkeiten" below, footnote 72.

68 Rotraud Wielandt, "Exegesis of the Qurʾān: Early Modern and Contemporary", Jane Dammen Mc Auliffe (ed.), *Encyclopaedia of the Qurʾān,* vol. 2, pp. 124–42, Leiden 2002.

69 Cf. Christian Wilhelm Troll, *Sayyid Ahmad Khan: A Reinterpretation of Muslim Theology,* New Delhi 1978.

first audience, (4) the provisional status of scientific theories and (5) the religious, rather than scientific, character of the Koran.

3. Literary studies. Starting from a suggestion by Ṭāhā Ḥusayn, literary critics have dealt with the Koran as a supreme work of literature. Among them are Amīn al-Ḫūlī and his pupils, especially ʿĀʾiša ʿAbd ar-Raḥmān ("Bint aš-Šāṭiʾ") and Muḥammad Aḥmad Ḫalaf Allāh. The meaning of a text, they say, can only be what the first recipients understood, and any text, revealed or otherwise, can be analysed according to its artistic qualities. The choice of words, the figures of speech, the structure of sentences and larger units and different literary genres can be studied. For them, art "is primarily a means of appealing to the public's emotions and to direct them according to one's aims". (p. 132)[70] Ḫalaf Allāh drew the conclusion from this theory that the Koranic narratives about earlier prophets are largely unhistorical. God used them as "psychological facts". A work not coming from this school but also applying literary criticism to the Koran, though less systematically, is Sayyid Quṭb's exegesis. He does not challenge the historicity of the Koranic narratives.
4. Historical exegesis. Wielandt terms more precisely "exegesis taking full account of the historicity of the Qurʾān". (p. 134) The first proponent of this trend is (Muhammad) Daud Rahbar, who said in 1958 that if one sees that God modified His word during Muhammad's life, one should be able to interpret God's word flexibly today, too. She then describes Fazlur Rahman's hermeneutics, whom she sees in basic agreement with an earlier Muslim voice, ʿAllāl al-Fāsī. According to Fazlur Rahman, the general ethical norm expressed in a Koranic stipulation must be distilled from the historical formulation. This model takes up a classical Islamic approach, viz., the analysis of *maqāṣid aš-šarīʿa,* the intentions behind the legislation. Wielandt then describes Naṣr Ḥāmid Abū Zayd's paradigm, which rests on a particular linguistic and literary text theory. "The information contained in a message can only be understood if the sender transmits it in a code (i.e., a system of signs) known to the recipient." (p. 136) The ancient code has to be distinguished from the message. Subsequently, every generation has to do its own re-encoding. Finally, Wielandt introduces Muhammad Arkoun, who sees the whole Muslim exegetical tradition as the process of appropriating the ‹fait coranique› (the Koran as proclaimed) by the different factions of the *umma.* Semiotic and socio-linguistic instruments

---

70 In *Offenbarung und Geschichte,* p. 139, Wielandt supposes that this approach may be influenced by al-Ǧurǧānī's (d. 1078) literary theory.

should help to sift traditional interpretations from the normative meaning of the Koran for today.

5. New immediacy. Interpreters Wielandt placed in this category, like Sayyid Quṭb and Abū l-Aʿlā Mawdūdī, argue along the following lines. Since the Koran is exclusively God's message, it is "always contemporary". (p. 138) The Koran need not be translated but put into practice in the "Islamic system". We must return to the belief of the first Muslims. Therefore, Hadith material is more relevant for this type of exegesis than the classical commentaries, allegedly contaminated by un-Islamic traditions.
6. Thematic interpretation. It starts from the interpreter's own questions about a particular theme and then consults the Koran, rather than starting from the text's arrangement and reacting to it. Under this heading, Wielandt also cites an author who claims to do thematic interpretation although he is everything but a typical proponent of this approach: Ḥasan Ḥanafī. He starts from the premise that "there is no true or false interpretation" and that "the validity of an interpretation lies in its power". (p. 139) She criticises Ḥanafī as abandoning the hermeneutical circle. For him, she says, interpretation has become a "one-way street whose only destination lies in influencing the audience according to the preconceived intentions of the interpreter". (p. 139) The text is being used for "enhancing the power of the interpreter's revolutionary arguments, which are not subject to critical review". (p. 139) But, as Wielandt emphasises, Ḥanafī's approach is not typical of thematic interpretation.

What Rotraud Wielandt offers here is a groundbreaking advance in *tafsīr* analysis. Her work provokes further reflection. As seen above (p. 21), the presentation of the state of research works on two different but inseperable levels: what should be said about Muslim Koran interpretation; and what about its Western presentation?

a. The field we are talking about here is neither easy to survey nor well worked through. Therefore, the easiest commentary to be made on the state of scholarship is to point out gaps in the coverage. Two such gaps can be mentioned concerning Wielandt's *Encyclopaedia* article. No Turkish authors feature in it. And an Arabic author presently oft-mentioned as an important revisionist is omitted: Muḥammad Šaḥrūr. Turkish theology clearly deserves attention, and Wielandt is well aware of that. It was she who suggested the subject of the present study; furthermore, she is presently preparing an in-depth study of contemporary Turkish theology. As for the Syrian interpreter Muḥammad Šaḥrūr, it was again Rotraud Wielandt who drew the present author's attention to him and supervised his study. However, that study's conclusion is that Šaḥrūr grounds his ‹relecture› on a confused mixture of *tafsīr ʿilmī* and cabbalistic systematisations;[71] if this assessment is correct, Šaḥrūr gets undue attention.

b. Another comment may be in place concerning Wielandt's division of the scene into six trends. The division itself is helpful. And because it is the first typology which offers categories for all contemporary Muslim approaches, it is a milestone of scholarship. These questions may be posed for a further refinement: (a.) Is Naṣr Ḥāmid Abū Zayd's model to be placed under the same category as Fazlur Rahman's and Daud Rahbar's, or (b.) is the category rightly named "… taking full account of the historicity of the Qurʾān"? Concerning this latter question (b.), one has to compare early and classical Koran commentators' contextualisations with what the modern authors under this heading actually do. Is there so much more consciousness of "historicity"? As for (a.), Abū Zayd imagines God encoding His message for Muhammad, while Fazlur Rahman sees Muhammad as responsible for the Koran's wording. The latter position is closer to common views of "historicity", whereas Abū Zayd enables us to hold both the Koran's verbal inspiration and the necessity of its contextual reading without bothering about theological questions like the following: can it be God's style as transcendent and creator to encode and send messages to some of us and thus impose His will? Abū Zayd seems, rather, to belong in the third category, "Literary studies", whose actors all seem to bother little about questions theological.

c. This leads us to another comment on the presentation, which is in fact a comment on the content presented. Do the theories described not deserve some questioning? Wielandt's article has been written for an encyclopaedia and therefore, naturally, provides information rather than discussion. But the original and irreplaceable investigations behind the production of the encyclopaedia article should also be made accessible to the scholarly world. These questions might be contemplated. (i.) The problems raised by the al-Ḫūlī school are symptomatic of an exclusively literary approach. If the truth of the Koran is to be found in God's artistic ability to cause certain reactions, this amounts to a surrender of any direct truth claim made by the Koran's words; and what would be different, in this model, if one simply left God aside? (ii.) Abū Zayd should be asked: what was God's message like before He encoded it for Muhammad? Can there be code-free messages? Or, if

71 Körner, *Šaḥrūrs Koranhermeneutik* (cf. above, note 25).

the message existed in the *divine* code, what does God need His private code for? If it is the task of exegesis to distinguish code from message, is there a method to control this distinction? And if the message can be subtracted, does it then float code-free in the air, before being re-encoded? In this point, Abū Zayd is very close to Fazlur Rahman. (iii.) Both should be asked whether their approaches are not implicitly reducing the Koran to a deontic ('thou shalt') message. (iv.) The "new immediacy" trend seems completely unaware of any hermeneutical problem. The bridging of the historical distance between text and today cannot start with a reforming of the present world situation into a Koranic ideal, because first we have to find out what the Koranic ideal is. Either it is claimed to be expressed unambiguously in the text—then we hear the Koran with today's ears, which will distort its original meaning because the meaning of words changes. Or we accept that our way of understanding traditional words today is sometimes misguided and that we have to try to find out what the words really mean—then we are in the middle of historical studies, and have lost the immediacy, which is thus discovered to be naïve and misleading. This reasoning explicates the immediacists' underlying assumption that language—at least in the case of the Koran—is not changing. (v.) Ḥasan Ḥanafī should be asked first, whether he seriously means what he says, and if so, why he bothers at all to explain his view? If the criterion of correct interpretation is whether it mobilises the masses, he has abandoned propositional truth. Therefore, he need not argumentatively present it to a critical audience. He should, rather, test his theory on the masses. If they are mobilised, it must be correct. One wonders however who will be mobilised by it. People want to believe that what they believe is true, and not only an effective means for their mobilisation.

d. Even with the limited amount of space in an encyclopaedia, Wielandt gives insightful comments on the views portrayed. She can welcome an approach (e.g., Sayyid Quṭb's is not simply disqualified as an Islamist but said to "grasp the original meaning and spirit of the respective Qur'ānic passage more adequately than other exegetes had done for a long time" (p. 22)) and reject another (cf. her criticism of Ḥanafī, above § 6, p. 43). She can sharply contrast an approach with its inner-Islamic criticism (as in the case of so-called Scientific Exegesis, above, § 2, p. 41). She also sees Koranic exegesis in its socio-political contexts. Thus, she touches upon the collision of Koranic scholarship and politics, including the condemnation of thinkers like Ḫalaf Allāh and Naṣr Ḥāmid Abū Zayd in Egypt in 1947 and 1990 respectively. She mentions the petrifying monopoly of the traditional religious scholars,

(p. 25) and the cliché accusations of orientalism and colonialism, which block a ‹reception› of Western methods into Muslim Koran exegesis.[72]

3 Conclusion: Desiderata

Our survey of the state of research on modern Muslim Koran interpretation should now be combined with what we saw when reviewing hermeneutics. This should lead us to a listing of what the state of research leaves for other researchers to investigate. In other words, where on the maps are the blanks? 'Blanks' in the triple sense of *areas* unmapped, *aspects* unmapped even in mapped areas, and *objects* proved *inexistent* in the areas so far mapped.

a. Areas not yet mapped. The maps so far drawn prove to depict only a small area of Koran interpretation. We have not seen research on modern Muslim Koran exegesis other than in Arabic, Urdu, English and French. We have not found any study on exegesis in Persian or Indonesian, from Black Africa[73] or the former Soviet Union, nor by Turkish authors. All of these are certainly promising areas of research. Are there criteria for preferring one or the other area for an expedition's destination? The answer should be given only after searching the map for the other two types of blanks.
b. Aspects not yet mapped. Unrecorded aspects of *tafsīr* include, largely, a study on the applied methods' *origins*. Wielandt lists several interesting findings on sources of the approaches she studied. She traced Naṣr Ḥāmid Abū Zayd's methodology back to Claude Elwood Shannon's information theory, and the earlier modernist approaches to European Enlightenment sources.[74] Another remark on origins is in Jansen's study; he finds most of modern Egyptian exegesis to be in the vein of

72 Cf. her more detailed study on the context of methodological receptions: Rotraud Wielandt, "Wurzeln der Schwierigkeiten innerislamischen Gesprächs über neue hermeneutische Zugänge zum Korantext", Stefan Wild (ed.), *The Qur'an as Text,* Leiden 1996, pp. 257–82, where she also mentions the factors that more and more influential people, notably in Egypt, side with fundamentalists, that the integrity of a text (the Koran) is identified with the integrity of a status (religious scholars), and that the consequences of disagreement are being feared. (p. 278)—The article refers to Arab countries only.

73 Christian Wilhelm Troll, "Islamische Stimmen zum gesellschaftlichen Pluralismus", IDEM (ed.), *Der europäische Islam. Eine reale Perspektive?,* Berlin 2001, pp. 55–94, p. 76 presents a *South* African voice (however without discussing the approach): Farid Esack, whose Islamic hermeneutics of liberation claims that the Koran can only be understood by people committed to "liberative" practice.

74 "Wurzeln der Schwierigkeiten", p. 260, n. 10.

the classical commentaries.[75] In other presentations, we hardly ever learn from where the Muslim authors got their ideas. Furthermore, the authors' methodology is hardly being *discussed.* Here, the only exceptions can be found in Wielandt's works (cf. above, p. 45, §d and above p. 41, § 2).[76] Yet another badly mapped aspect is, ironically, *blanks.* Authors covering modern Koran interpretation rarely state which aspects of interpretation have not but could be covered by Muslim authors. The exception is Wielandt's study on revelation and history, which concludes that Muslims might rethink what revelation is.[77] If one does not dogmatically restrict Islamic Studies to recording what is there, one might even admit that it is precisely from an exterior point of view that one is likely to discover blind spots in Islamic theology. Stating desiderata is not putting something down, but challenging and thus promoting it. So, a major desideratum in Islamic Studies on Muslim Koran exegesis is the naming of desiderata.

It is precisely this desideratum which makes it difficult to judge from the state of research to which area an expedition should be sent first. So, how to judge? Another criterion would be to look for places which offer (a.) good conditions for a reception of new philosophical approaches, perhaps from Western traditions of thought, into Muslims' theology, (b.) a fertile ground for new ideas to grow, and (c.) a climate conducive to a comparably open scholarly discourse. When scanning the map with this gauge, *Turkey* proves to be the primary destination of our expedition. This will be demonstrated in the following section.

c. Missing objects. The extant maps cover the aspect of *historical awareness* in Muslim Koran interpretation. It is precisely because of this coverage that we can say with relative certainty that what has been produced in the mapped areas does not meet all challenges of contemporary hermeneutic reflection yet. Although we could find an awareness of the distance between text and interpreter with some authors (notably in ʿAllāl al-Fāsī, Fazlur Rahman and Naṣr Ḥāmid Abū Zayd), the positive role that distance can play has not been taken into account by them. Furthermore, an analysis of the Koran interpreters' pre-understandings could not be found; nor did these authors see that the point of understanding is not to try to slip into the author's mind.

We will have to keep these desiderata in mind when looking at Turkish Koran hermeneutics.

---

75 Jansen, *Interpretation,* p. 96.

76 Wielandt, "Exegesis", p. 11.

77 Wielandt, *Offenbarung und Geschichte,* p. 158.

4 Contextualising Rethinking (i): The History of University Theology in Turkey[78]

In the second edition of the—notoriously Arabocentric—*Encyclopaedia of Islam,* Louis Gardet writes that "in the universities of Muslim countries the faculties of religious sciences are called *kulliyyāt al-sharīʿa,* a term generally rendered by "Faculties of theology"; *fiḳh* [jurisprudence] is there taught as much as, if not more than, *kalām* [theology]."[79] He finishes his article with these hopeful questions: "Will anything take the place of *ʿilm al-kalām* [systematic theology] with a more widespread perspective and serving a practical, rather than a speculative, attitude? [...] Will there take place a synthesis of the different tendencies of *ʿilm al-kalām* operating through a revised set of philosophical equipment? The study of the text of the *Ḳurʾān* and a more fully developed anthropology seem here to be called for, not to replace the "questions concerning God" *(ilāhiyyāt),* but to open wider perspectives for their discussion. [...] It may be hoped that a new *kalām,* perhaps quite different from the old in its methods, arguments and approach, will one day arise to play its part in animating a cultural recovery in the religious sciences of Islam."[80] Had Gardet been able to take into account what has been going on in Turkey in the last decades, he would have seen many of his hopes on the way to fulfilment, some of his questions already answered affirmatively, and his generalising judgements on "Muslim countries" proven to be too general.

4.1 A Faculty Founded

The origin of Turkey's higher religious education of today is paradoxical in many ways. It is traditional and it is a novelty, it continues Ottoman lines and takes up Western structures, it follows a Kemalist programme and it may prove to be of worldwide relevance for Islam.

78 Gotthard Jäschke, "Der Islam in der neuen Türkei. Eine rechtsgeschichtliche Untersuchung", *Die Welt des Islams,* N.S. vol. 1 (1951), pp. 1–174; corrections and additions: ibid., vol. 2 (1953 (SIC)), pp. 278–87. Münir Koştaş, "Ankara Üniversitesi İlâhiyat Fakültesi (Dünü Bugünü)", *Ankara Üniverisitesi İlâhiyat Fakültesi Dergisi,* vol. 40 (1998), pp. 141–84. Mehmet Paçacı and Yasin Aktay, "75 Years of Higher Religious Education in Modern Turkey", *The Muslim World,* vol. 89 (1999), pp. 398–413.

79 Louis Gardet, "ʿilm al-kalām", *EI²,* vol. 3, Leiden and London 1979, pp. 1141–50, p. 1147.

80 Ibid., p. 1150.

The Ottoman Ministry of Education, established in 1847, inaugurated a European type of educational system which was meant to replace the traditional Muslim *medrese*.[81] In 1900, a Theological Faculty *(ʿulūm-i ʿāliye-i dīnīye šuʿbesi)* was created at the University *(dār ül-fünūn)*, in Istanbul. A decree of February 26, 1910 established a twelve-year pre-university course of theology which included in fact only traditional subjects and text books. One exception can be found in its seventh year, when "modern physics *(ḥikmet-i ğedīde)*" was to be studied. The university Faculty was by decree of October 1, 1914 replaced with a specialists' school at the Süleymānīye Mosque. A law of April 2, 1917 added a fourth department to this school, viz., literature, to the traditional three: *Tefsīr* and *Ḥadīs̱; Fiqh; Kelām* and *Ḥikmet.* Among the new professorial chairs introduced by an October 4, 1917 decree were three for Ḥanafī law and one for each of the other three great legal schools, plus one for occidental literature. The *medreses* were to teach more and more secular subjects but they could not be subjected to the control of the Ministry of Education, although Żiyāʾ (Gökalp) suggested it. Only Muṣṭafā Kemāl's programme "We will turn ourselves into the most modern nation" (p. 33) made it possible to stipulate the subordination of all *medreses* to the Ministry of Education. The result was: they were closed down. The day the Great National Assembly in Ankara decreed the abolition of the caliphate, it also issued a law (No. 430, of March 3, 1924) which instituted °*imām ḫaṭīb mektebleri* (schools for prayer leaders and Friday preachers) and of a Theological *(ilāhīyāt)* Faculty at the University (of Istanbul). Twenty-nine *imām ḫaṭīb* schools were established in Turkey. The Istanbul school's director had an "enthusiastic belief in the possibilities of reforming Islam to become a vital and inspiring force in the life of new Turkey". (Reported by Henry Elisha Allen; p. 122) But with a continuous decline in attendance, by 1932 all *imām ḫaṭīb* schools were closed. The only surviving, indeed thriving, type of junior theological education was that of the school for Koran recitation, *dār ül-qurrāʾ*. The *ilāhīyāt* Faculty was structured according to "modern scientific principles" (p. 121) and published a scholarly journal from 1926 onwards. But its students' numbers were decreasing rapidly, together with those of the *imām ḫaṭīb* schools. A decree of the Ministry of Education (dated August 29, 1929) abolished Arabic and Persian classes from the high school curriculum. Subsequently, knowledge of these languages was no longer a prerequisite for admission to the Theological Faculty. In 1933 and 1934, laws regulated a reform of the University. The Theological Faculty was turned into the °Institute of Islam

[81] The following section is based on Gotthard Jäschke's documentation "Der Islam in der neuen Türkei". Page numbers refer to this article.

Researches *(Islâm Tedkikleri Enstitüsü)* and considered as a department of the Literature Faculty's Oriental Institute.

In 1947, Turkey became a multi-party democracy. The call for a better training of the °religious staff *(din adamları)* was voiced. °Private seminaries *(özel din seminerler)* were opened, but students had to graduate from a secular school before being admitted to them. Less than a year later however parliamentarians demanded a re-opening of state-run preachers schools. Two 1948 newspaper statements will illustrate the atmosphere: (1.) "Not to the least shall we verge from the principle of laicism.[82] Religion however is not only the bond between the individual and God. It is also a social fact, a matter of the community. In the countryside, there are often no more *hocas* (religious staff) to bury the dead. If we do not educate religious staff, superstition will prevail. Already, we hear about heavenly letters passing from hand to hand. Religious fanaticism is bad. But fanatic irreligion does not match with our tolerant society, either. It was not in order to ban Islam from Turkey that we accepted the principle of laicism. Against the Soviet advance, we have to utilise the force of the Islamic Belt, stretching from Java to the Atlantic Ocean." (Cihat Baban; pp. 124–5) (2.) "We have to save from extinction, or rather, to train anew, a generation of religious staff, both knowledgeable *(bilgili)* and patriotic *(vatansever)*." (M. Tuncer; p. 125)

In 1948, the reinstitution of *İmam Hatip* schools was decided upon—however, not under the Directorate for Religious Affairs but under the Ministry of Education. The intention was to avoid a return to the dualism of religious and secular education, of *medreseli/mektebli* mentality "still existent in oriental countries" (Tahsin Banguoğlu;[83] p. 125). On January 15, 1949, both in Ankara and Istanbul, ten-month courses were established to train prayer leaders and Friday preachers. Soon after, this was done in eight further cities. The courses starting in 1950 were decreed to last for two years.

The People's Party decided in February 1948 to establish an Islamic Theological Faculty in Ankara. On June 4, 1949, the Great National Assembly issued a law concerning the Faculty's institution. Again, Banguoğlu demanded that the Faculty should counter reactionary movements: "It is a

---

[82] Though normally rendered as '(state) secularism', the word *'layiklik'* will be translated here by 'laicism' to keep the association with ‹laïcité› alive, which was intended by the Turkish coinage.

[83] The philologist Hasan Tahsin Banguoğlu (1904–89), one of the last pupils of the Turkologist Willy Bang-Kaup in Berlin, was M.P. between 1943 and 1950 and Minister of Education from 1948–50. (At the same time, and again from 1963–6, he was president of the Turkish Language Association).

torch which the fabulists flee like bats." (p. 127) He suggested that on top of the classical canon, the Faculty should offer courses in psychology, sociology, general and comparative religious studies; in addition to Arabic and Persian, European languages should be taught; and alongside teachers from the former Istanbul Faculty, some teachers from other Islamic countries should be employed, e.g., from Pakistan. Perhaps, he said, it was due to the revolutionary atmosphere that the old Faculty had been unable to find a sufficient number of students; with more than one hundred young men following the *İmam Hatip* courses in 1949, things seemed to have changed. When Ankara Üniversitesi's president Hikmet Birand welcomed the new Faculty to the 1949/50 winter term, he said: "°The religious spirit *(dinî ruh)* can be a great power °for Enlightenment *(aydınlatıcı)*[84]. [...] Religious reforms accomplished in past centuries by individuals are today being effected by life itself, by society *(cemiyet)*. To observe and record these events and, if necessary, take °the leading role *(rehberlik vazifesi)* is the task of an alert *(uyanık)* institute of religion." (p. 128)

4.2 A Faculty's Framework

This survey can serve as a backdrop. Now some spotlights should be switched on to give us a live impression of the scene.

4.2.1 Last Minute

In his review of the first volume (1952) of the Ankara Faculty's first academic journal, *İlâhiyat Fakültesi Dergisi,* Franz Taeschner judges that the founding of the Faculty was "a last minute effort because there are still some aged professors alive with the fully fledged *medrese* training". But he also sees that "besides the training of religious staff, the new Faculty considers as its task—which considerably surpasses the old *medreses*' scope—to confront the mental values of Islam with modern sciences, thus obtaining for Islamic theology a standing in modern intellectual life, as Christian theology has always had."[85]

---

84 Jäschke's "aufhellende Kraft" misses the implied historic moment.

85 Franz Taeschner, "Ilâhiyat [SIC] Fakültesi Dergisi", *Die Welt des Islams,* N.S. vol. 2 (1953), pp. 305–6; Taeschner is probably overestimating the continuous quality of Christian theology.

4.2.2 Lacking Students

Why could the Istanbul Theological Faculty not find enough students? "The graduates of *İmam Hatip* Schools, which [were] not given the status of Lycée at the time, could not register at the Faculty. Furthermore, graduates of the Faculty were simply deprived of many rights of graduates of other Faculties."[86]

4.2.3 Traditionalists, Secularists, and the New Faculty

Was the opening of the Ankara Faculty welcomed widely? There was resistance to it both from the traditionalist and the secularist/revolutionary wings of the (ruling) People's Party. The traditionalists "argued that secularism was misunderstood and misapplied in Turkey". Moreover, in their view, Islam had become inferior to the minority religions in Turkey, because, they said, it lacked an independent organisation. "Hence, they contended, the Presidency of Religious Affairs should be independent and equipped to educate the Turkish man for religious service."[87] On the other side, the secularists wanted to see religion confined to the private realm. They feared religion might be abused by the corrupt, they said. National

---

86 Ibid, p. 396.

87 Ibid., p. 397. In the very first period of the Ankara government, there was a Ministry of Religious Affairs and Pious Foundations, but already in 1924 a Presidency for Religious Affairs *(diyānet išleri reʾīsliġi)* was established, whose head was nominated by the Prime Minister. (Bernard Lewis, *The Emergence of Modern Turkey,* Oxford [2]1968, p. 413) The Presidency of Religious Affairs *(Diyanet İşleri Başkanlığı)* was decreed by the 1961 Constitution (article 154) and re-established by article 136 of the 1982 Constitution, with three further stipulations. It was committed to the principle of laicism, thus e.g., introduction of the Sharia was excluded; it was forbidden to interfere with the state; and it was commissioned to "strive for national solidarity and integration", which meant in fact, to create a uniform Turkish Islam. Its employees were to be civil servants. If laicism means that the state is neutral towards religion, the Presidency as it is must be seen as contradicting that principle. (Ursula Spuler-Stegemann, "Der Islam", *Südosteuropa-Handbuch,* vol. 4, *Türkei,* Göttingen 1985, pp. 591–612, pp. 595, 599.) Spuler-Stegemann says that an established Islam (‚Staatsislam') as practiced in Turkey cannot be justified by Islamic theology. (Ibid., n. 6.) Christian Rumpf, "Das Präsidium für Religionsangelegenheiten", *Zeitschrift für Türkeistudien,* vol. 2 (1989), pp. 21–33 makes a series of further relevant points. While, towards the end of the Ottoman era, the *šeyḫ ül-islām* and his staff had de facto gained the rank of a Ministry, the Presidency has never been elevated to such independence; it is only the Presidency of *Islamic* Affairs; this means discrimination against other religions in Turkey and contradicts the constitutional principle of religious equality (1982, art. 10); the Presidency has practically no influence on self-instituted sheikhs, on religious education in schools and on the religious foundations.

coherence was in their eyes provided by ethnical unity: "The ultimate power of a Turk is in his noble blood", was the Mustafa Kemal motto they used to support their view.[88]

4.2.4 Motivations

It may seem surprising that the founders of modern Turkey, inspired by Positivist views, cared for religious training and theological quality. Why did they? "Their arguments were founded on the premise that religious education was needed to uphold the moral requirements of Turkish society."[89] But there were also strict advocates of laicism who demanded that the State should not interfere with religion, and saw religion itself as a source of ignorance.[90]

The People's Party's suggestion to establish the Ankara Faculty should be seen also as a concession by a party whose reputation in matters religious was bad, to the very wide demand for religious freedom.[91]

4.2.5 Kemalism and Islam

What was the attitude of Turkey's founding fathers towards Islam? (a.) Anti-clericalism had for long been a reform factor in Ottoman history.[92] It certainly was part of their attitude. (b.) In spite of the supreme religious authorities' hostility to the nationalists, Muṣṭafā Kemāl tried to compromise by keeping the Caliphate, when the Sultanate had been abolished in 1922. (c.) His goal was civilisation, which for him meant Western culture. (d.) He seems to have been able to distinguish between Islam as a sclerotic blockage against modernisation, and Islam as a tradition able to evolve. (e.) Muṣṭafā Kemāl's position towards Islam should be seen as *pragmatic.*[93] He

---

88 Paçacı and Aktay, "Higher Religious Education", p. 397.

89 Paçacı and Aktay, "Higher Religious Education", p. 394, with reference to three 1924 passages, by Ethem Ruhi, Ahmet Cevdet and Hasan Hikmet respectively.

90 Ibid.

91 Ibid., p. 398.

92 Lewis, *Emergence*, p. 402.

93 Jens Peter Laut, "Zur Sicht des Islam in der Türkischen Republik bis zum Tode Atatürks", Wolfgang Schluchter (ed.), *Kolloquien des Max Weber Kollegs VI-XI (1999/2000),* Erfurt 2000, pp. 59–75, p. 66 considers the (few) genuine Atatürk 'hadith's in praise of Islam to be of "purely tactical nature". According to Laut, translations of the Koran were promoted under Atatürk in hope of the *"başka yok mu*-effect". Laut is referring to an episode reported by Albert von Le Coq from eastern Turkmenistan. von Le Coq was asked by the Turks there to translate the Koran's first sura, a prayer they recited daily, into their language. He did so and received the

considered Islam as a source of social, national coherence and ethical motivation. And one may presume he also saw that an assault on Islam as religion would have been the end of his own project of creating a modern national state. He disestablished Islam, restricted then prohibited religious education, introduced European legal codes, reduced then eliminated the power of religious scholars, prohibited religious brotherhoods and Westernised such Islam-connoting cultural symbols as dress, headgear, calendar and alphabet.[94] Bernhard Lewis sums up his evaluation by saying: "The basis of Kemalist religious policy was laicism, not irreligion; its purpose was not to destroy Islam but to disestablish it—to end the power of religion and its exponents in political, social, and cultural affairs, and limit it to matters of belief and worship. In thus reducing Islam to the role of religion in a modern, Western, nation-state, the Kemalists also made some attempt to give their religion a more modern and more national form."[95] This description of the Kemalists'[96] religious policy contains a tension: limiting the influence of religion, and modernising it. Modernisation can mean a new type of influence. Religion in a modern state can play an important role which does not rest on hierarchical privileges but on convincingness and people's personal involvement. Kemalist or not, the institution of theological faculties at state universities should be seen as giving religion a new scientific, social and thus political standing.

4.2.6 Naming the Project

Why did the founding fathers of the Faculty not give it a traditional name like *'kullīyat aš-šarīʿa'*? They clearly wanted a Western-style theology, i.e., one that would focus not on jurisprudence but on comprehensive theo-

surprisingly disappointed reaction *"başka yok mu*—oh, is that all it says?!" (Ibid., p. 67).

94 Lewis, *Emergence*, p. 404.

95 Ibid., p. 412.

96 Laut, "Sicht des Islams", rightly points out that the views of Atatürk and the early Kemalists were not necessarily identical. (p. 67) He quotes two "Kemalist Muslims" who, on the First and Second Turkish History Congresses, tried to rehabilitate Islam in the face of the new ideology, Mehmet Şemsettin Günaltay in 1932 and İsmail Hakkı İzmirli in 1937. Günaltay's strategy is to point out that Islam would never have risen to its glory without the Turks; (p. 70) İzmirli even claims that Muhammad was "most probably a Turk". (p. 72) This type of argument strongly recalls products of the Sun Language Theory. Geoffrey Lewis shows that one function of 'proving' the Turkish origin of words like *filosofi* was to justify their survival. *The Turkish Language Reform. A Catastrophic Success,* Oxford 1999, p. 64. Both the religious and the linguistic efforts might be understood as apologetic nostrification.

logical rethinking?[97] Was that their reason to use a different designation? The model of Western theology was explicitly quoted in a 1949 memorandum *(gerekçe)* by Ankara Üniversitesi's senate: *"garptaki örneklerine benzer bir İlâhiyat Fakülte[si]*—a Faculty of Divinity similar to its examples in the West".[98] And Ismayıl Hakkı Baltacıoğlu said: "The intention to establish a Divinity Faculty is not [tantamount to] resurrecting the *medrese*. For the difference between Faculty and *medrese* is quite fundamental. It is this: *medrese* studies are text-positivist *(nassî)* and a priori *(apriyori, kablettecrübî)*. Faculties, because they are °houses of science *(ilim evleri)*, strive for comparison *(mukayese)*, °empirical knowledge *(müşahede,* lit.: observation) and eventually, if possible, for explanation *(izah)."*[99] So, *'İlâhiyat'* may itself be the marker of a revisionist programme. But already the demand for academic theology voiced in 1924 by Ibrāhīm Efendī, the Isparta M.P., when Dār ül-Fünūn's courses were discussed was worded thus: "Add an *ilāhīyāt* Faculty!"[100] And it was understood.

'Ilāhīyāt' appears in many classical works of theology. But in Arabic it has never meant 'theology' as the whole academic discipline. It could be used in three ways. 1. synonymously with *'mā baᶜd aṭ-ṭabīᶜa'* and *'al-falsafa al-ūlā'* to mean 'metaphysics';[101] 2. to designate that discipline of classical philosophy which deals with questions concerning God as such (cf. ‚Gotteslehre' as a TRACTATUS of philosophy or theology)[102]; 3. in the conceptual pair *'samᶜīyāt'* and *'ilāhīyāt'*, to mean 'rational theology': *samᶜīyāt* are the *positive* chapters, not accessible by reasoning but grounded on accep-

97 When writing English, Turkish theological faculties name themselves "divinity", e.g., in the internet presentation: http://www.ankara.edu.tr/faculties/divinity/.

98 Koştaş, "İlâhiyat Fakültesi", p. 149.

99 Koştaş, "İlâhiyat Fakültesi", p. 149. Ismayıl Hakkı Baltacıoğlu (d. 1978), the "pedagogue, writer and calligrapher", (Mehmet Faruk Bayraktar, "Baltacıoğlu, Ismayıl Hakkı", *Türkiye Diyanet Vakfı İslâm Ansiklopedisi,* vol. 5, Istanbul 1992, pp. 36–7, p. 36) M.P. between 1942 and 1950, published several titles in the field of religion, too; most notably, an article "Towards Religion", in which he argues that religion is not only the source of social institutions but also lives within these institutions, and life is therefore as impossible without religion as it is without blood ("Dine Doğru", *Ankara Üniversitesi İlâhiyat Fakültesi Dergisi,* vol. 6 (1957), pp. 44–59.)

100 Koştaş, "İlâhiyat Fakültesi", p. 147.

101 Roger Arnaldez, "mā baᶜd al-ṭabīᶜa", *EI²,* vol. 5, Leiden 1986, pp. 841–4, p. 841. And Josef van Ess reminds us that "after all, *ilāhīyāt* goes back to τὰ θεολογικά/*tà theologiká", Theologie und Gesellschaft,* vol. 5, Berlin 1997, p. 359.

102 In the Christian context, the word 'θεολογία—THEOLOGIA' was still used in the 4th and 5th centuries in that restricted sense of theological theology (‚Gotteslehre'), as opposed to (the study of) God's revelation in the history of salvation. (Siegfried Wiedenhofer, "Theologie", *Lexikon für Theologie und Kirche,* vol. 9, Freiburg ³2000, cols. 1435–44, col. 1436.)

tance EX AUDITU, whereas *ilāhīyāt* are theology's rational *(ʿaqlīyāt)* chapters, based on arguments.[103]

4.2.7 A Different Institution

In the last decade, a non-university scholarly institution has gained the reputation of doing high quality Islamic studies in Turkey, viz., İSAM (İslâm Araştırmaları Merkezi, "Centre of Islamic Studies") in Istanbul. It was founded in 1993, is a branch of the Türk Diyanet Vakfı and seems to have unlimited financial resources. The Centre employs more than 100 renowned scholars, offers grants to doctoral students, runs a fine library, edits a research quarterly,[104] and is in charge of the publication of the completely new edition of the Turkish *Encyclopaedia of Islam.*[105] The Institute's scope includes all eras and areas of Islam. It betrays however a particular interest in Ottoman studies. One might understand the Institute itself as an hermeneutical project. Its aim seems to be to demonstrate the originality and present-day relevance of the Ottoman era's intellectual performance and cultural achievements.[106] The Institute's products, academic though they are, will not be discussed in what is to follow here.

4.2.8 Reforming Islam

A 1928 committee, chaired by Meḥmed Fuʾād (Köprülü), made the following four recommendations to the Ministry of Education concerning a reform of Islam. a. Form of worship: orderly mosques with pews and cloakrooms. b. Language of worship: all prayers, sermons, etc., in the national language. c. Character of worship: beautiful, inspiring and spiritual, with trained musicians and musical instruments. d. Intellectual quality of worship: real religious guidance by philosophically trained preachers.[107]

---

103 Louis Gardet, "ʿilm al-kalām", *EI²*, vol. 3, pp. 1141–50, p. 1147.

104 *İslâm Araştırmaları Dergisi*, 1997–.

105 *Türkiye Diyanet Vakfı İslâm Ansiklopedisi*, vol. 1–, Istanbul 1988–, 27 vols. by October 2004.

106 Members of the institute do participate in the present discourse on Koran hermeneutics. Cf., e.g., Tahsin Görgün, "İnşa–Haber (Performative–Constative) ve Kur'an'ın Anlaşılması. Sözeylem Teorisinin Tarihi Üzerine", Ömer Kara (ed.), *Yüzüncü Yıl Üniversitesi İlahiyat Fakültesi 17–18 Mayıs 2001 Kur'an ve Dil – Dilbilim ve Hermenötik – Sempozyumu*, Erzurum 2001, pp. 443–60.

107 Lewis, *Emergence*, p. 414.

One may ridicule these suggestions just as an *aḏān* (call to prayer) in Turkish: "*Tanrı büyüktür*" or "*Tanrı uludur*", etc., for "*Allāhu akbar*", etc.[108] Liturgical changes from above tend to clash with people's nostalgia because of liturgy's emotional appeal. But could the Theological Faculties not be places where such reforms are discussed and experimented with? Turkish theologians are, according to the present author's impression, very much involved in high standards of intellectual discourse. But they seem to be reticent, or uncreative, or uninterested, or shy, when it comes to rethinking a change of cultic practice.

4.2.9 Conclusion

Turkish *İlâhiyat* Faculties are explicitely oriented towards enlightened Islam, scientific dialogue and Western-style theology; they are embedded in universities; they therefore operate under the Ministry of Education rather than under a religious authority or private institutions: in that, they are a unique construction in the world of Islam. It is structurally one of the most promising grounds for a well-reflected renewed Islam to grow. So, if our expedition sets out anywhere—and does not get lost in the preparation—it should visit the Turkish Theological Faculties.

5 Contextualising Rethinking (ii): İlâhiyat in Action

5.1 Pedigree

For ten years, the Ankara *İlâhiyat* Faculty remained the only Muslim academic theologate in Turkey. In 1959, a Yüksek İslâm Enstitüsü ("Higher Islam Institute") was opened in Istanbul. Two reasons for its establishment were advanced. The number of *İmam Hatip* schools had increased, and the Faculty had acquired the reputation of training philosophers and sociologists rather than guides for people's religious practice.[109] Between 1959 and 1982, eight Higher Islam Institutes were established for the training of religious education teachers and employees of the Presidency of Religious Affairs.[110] In 1982, seven of the eight institutes were converted into *İlâhiyat*

---

[108] Jäschke, "Islam", pp. 74–7. The former was heard from the Fatih Mosque, Istanbul, from January 1932 on. The latter was the official version decreed by the Presidency of Religious Affairs in November 1932 and valid until Prime Minister Adnan Menderes had the muezzins return to the Arabic original in 1950.

[109] Paçacı and Aktay, "Higher Religious Education", p. 402.

[110] Spuler-Stegemann, "Der Islam", p. 598.

Faculties. Beginning in 1987, many more Theological Faculties were founded in Turkey. Their number now totals twenty-four.[111] Ankara has taken a leading role among the Turkish Theological Faculties, since "the staff and the deans of the new Faculties of *İlâhiyat* were mostly appointed from the Faculty of İlâhiyat in Ankara. In 1993, the deans of six of the nine Faculties were *İlâhiyat* graduates of the Faculty of Ankara. Only recently were deans from the original staff appointed after they were able to form their own Faculty."[112]

5.2 Recent Moves

Five recent developments in Turkish higher religious education deserve being mentioned: (a.) the 1988 introduction of a two-year programme on a level between *İmam Hatip* schools and the university faculties, for the professional training of religious staff, a school type called *İlâhiyat Meslek Yüksek Okulu;* (b.) the 1998 establishment of a two-year theological correspondence course, called *İlâhiyat Önlisans Programı* (Pre-licentiate Programme in Theology), which was developed co-operatively by Ankara University's *İlâhiyat* Faculty and the Open Education Faculty of Anadolu Üniversitesi, Eskişehir; (c.) the launching in 1998 of a four-year teacher training programme for primary education, named after the subject taught in schools "Religious Culture and Ethics" *(Din Kültürü ve Ahlak Bilgisi),* at ten Universities all over the country; (d.) the 1997 reform of the Ankara *İlâhiyat* curriculum, which was subsequently taken over by other Turkish faculties. The new curriculum was designed to be flexible and interdisciplinary. Its goal is "to train a type of *İlâhiyat* graduate who can depend on the Qur'an itself as the most basic source of the religion, rightly evaluate the cultural heritage, interpret the daily life as well as produce solutions to the problems that are faced;"[113] and (e.) the 1999 regulation which made university theology the standard training for Turkish imams: "In order to be able to be appointed as °prayer leader and preacher *(imam-hatip)* one must have °an academic education in religion *(dini yüksek öğrenim).* If however there are not enough university graduates among the applicants, [the appointee] must be an *İmam-Hatip* school graduate."[114] This regulation means that the theological faculties are, in principle, training all Turkish imams.

---

[111] The appendix (p. 211) provides a list of all Turkish *İlâhiyat* Faculties.

[112] Paçacı and Aktay, "Higher Religious Education", p. 405.

[113] Ibid., p. 407.

[114] Dated November 23, 1999 and published in *Resmi Gazete* 23885, 45 a). I am grateful to Dr. Nurullah Altaş for this reference. (The verb of the sentences, i.e., "must—*gerekir*" is found 36 lines down in the text of the regulation.)

5.3 Cadre, Curricula, Careers

The academic staff of Ankara Üniversitesi İlâhiyat Fakültesi counts presently (November 2003) 104 members in four sections and nineteen departments:[115] in the

Basic Islamic Sciences Section, Koran exegesis, Hadith, Law, Systematic Theology, History of Schools *(mezhepler),* Sufism, and Arabic; in the

Philosophy and Religious Studies Section, History of Philosophy, Islamic Philosophy, Philosophy of Religion, Logic, History of Religion, Sociology of Religion, and Psychology of Religion; and in the

History of Islam and Islamic Arts Section, History of Islam, History of Turkish Islamic Arts, Turkish Islamic Literature, and Turkish Religious Music; finally, there is a *Primary Education Section.*

The Faculty's range of subjects raises some questions. It seems that certain areas which belong to theology are deliberately left out.[116] Since some of these areas concern what a strictly laicist state might consider dangerous, the omissions may be partly due to state control. But one should remember that if such reflection is not allocated an official place in the academic scene, it will perhaps not be done academically; and if not academically, then probably less rationally.

Careers of graduates from the *İlâhiyat* faculties include employment by the Ministry of Education—especially as religious education or ethics teachers, by the Presidency of Religious Affairs, by the media and archival institutions.

---

115 http://www.ankara.edu.tr/faculties/divinity/sayfalar/index-9.htm. The Ankara Faculty's staff is outnumbered by the staff of Marmara University's Divinity Faculty in Istanbul. Its academic staff counts 121 members. (http://www.ilahiyat.marmara.edu.tr/elemanlar/listele.asp, November 2003.) It has the same number and structure of departments as Ankara Divinity, with the only exception that the Section/ Department "Primary Education" is *"Din Eğitimi"* (‚Religionspädagogik') at Marmara. Marmara Divinity started off in 1959 as the Higher Islam Institute (cf. above, p. 50) and was one of the institutes to be converted into university faculties in 1982.

116 This is not to say that everything offered under 'theology' in Christian institutions should also be taught in an *İlâhiyat* Faculty. But in the journal *İslâmiyât* (cf. below, note 121), e.g., Muslim theologians discuss questions belonging to Muslim fundamental theology and anthropology, Islamic social doctrine and political theology or Muslim spirituality. In the setup of Turkish *İlâhiyat* Faculties however there are no such departments yet.

Some of the younger academic staff constitute what they call "a tradition".[117] They see themselves as—creatively—continuing trains of thoughts of their own Ankara teachers such as Hüseyin Atay, who has recently gained fame outside of Turkey,[118] and especially Mehmed Said Hatiboğlu. Several academic teachers, now in their forties, have in the course of their studies spent some time at European or North American universities. These thinkers form a team, not homogenous but with an ambition to publish their ideas jointly. They are editing a series of books titled "Publications of the Ankara School",[119] thus presenting themselves as a movement of thought. The series contains translations of books—prominently by Fazlur Rahman–into Turkish and collections of articles as well as original contributions; and its publication policy betrays a particular interest in Christian theology. In English, members of the "school" characterise their own "tradition" as "Islamic modernism"[120].

They have also launched a scholarly quarterly, *İslâmiyât* ("Islamics"), [121] and at the same publishing house as the journal another series of books, *kitâbiyât.*[122] A free quarterly leaflet, *islâmiyât/kitâbiyât bülten* (Ankara 2001–),

---

117 Paçacı and Aktay, "Higher Religious Education", p. 412.

118 Rainer Hermann, "Den Koran lesen. Ein türkischer Gelehrter will den Islam gegen die Last von Tradition und Dogmatik erneuern", *Frankfurter Allgemeine Zeitung,* April 4, 2002, p. 12.

119 *Ankara Okulu Yayınları,* Ankara 1995–. 79 vols. by October 2004. Online information is available under: http://www.yenikitaplar.net/AOY.htm. One of the books to be discussed below (p. 65sqq.), Mehmet Paçacı, *Kur'an ve Ben Ne Kadar Tarihseliz?,* appeared in that series.

120 Paçacı and Aktay, "Higher Religious Education", p. 412. That self-designation together with the authors' effort to use insights so far not connected to Koran hermeneutics, (cf., e.g., below, p. 78) their own frequent thematising of method, (cf., e.g., below, p. 109) their willingness to experiment with new approaches (cf., e.g., below, fotenote 181 on p. 87), and their consciousness of doing something relevant to the whole of Islam, (cf., e.g., below, pp. 112, 166) seem to justify the word "revisionist" in this study's title. 'Revisionist' can be a derogatory designation in politics for someone deviating from a doctrine considered to be sacrosanct. The tenor of the present study should make it sufficiently clear that 'revisionism' is used here in the descripitive sense of 'new approach' rather than with an undertone of anathema. (Cf. Iring Fetscher, "Revisionismus", *Historisches Wörterbuch der Philosophie,* vol. 8, Basel 1992, cols. 951–3, col. 953.)

121 *İslâmiyât. Üç aylık araştırma dergisi,* 1998–. One of its founders, Professor Mehmet Paçacı, when asked about the journal's readership, told the present author that on a Faculty excursion the Ankara academics were surprised to hear in an Anatolian town that the manager of the local bank met regularly with his friends to discuss the most recent issue of *İslâmiyât.*

122 Ankara, 1999–. 30 vols. by October 2004. (The title of the book series is, morphologically, an allusion to the journal's title, and means "book matters, bibliography".)

with shorter articles and up-to-date information serves to advertise both the journal and the books and brings across the aura of a theological workshop. There are three other academic journals edited by members of the Ankara Theological Faculty: the official *Ankara Üniversitesi İlâhiyat Fakültesi Dergisi* ("Journal of Ankara University's Divinity Faculty", Ankara 1952–); *İslâmî Araştırmalar* ("Islamic Studies", Ankara 1986–), which lost many of its more inspiring contributors to *İslâmiyât;* and a specialised periodical on Islamic mysticism, called *Tasavvuf* ("Sufism", Ankara 1999–).

5.5 Ideology and Pure Research

The politicians' decision that Turkish universities should do Western-style theology has made for a climate especially conducive to the development of new Koran hermeneutical approaches. Indeed, the politicians did not only *allow for* modern hermeneutics to develop when instituting *İlâhiyat* faculties; they *wanted* to have it. This puts the scholars under °pressure to live up to felt expectations (‚Erwartungsdruck'). Can they deliver such a hermeneutics, can they thus prove Islam to be compatible with modernity—as understood, e.g., by a Kemalist doctrine? Is, on the other hand, the expected result not a distortion of hermeneutics and the Koran? The historic situation seems to decree that Islam can be modernised and one only needs to apply the correct hermeneutics. As we have seen (above, on p. 60) and will see in more detail, (below, at note 260) authors like Gadamer are sceptical of such mechanistic applications of method. So, do the circumstances already thwart the growth of a truly scholarly interpretation of Islam? But what is the alternative for someone who really wants to do precisely this: study Islam? One cannot easily change all the conditions under which one works. But one can take account of them. So, rather than claiming that pure research is only possible without any such pressure, one can ask whether there is an awareness of these particular conditions. Awareness of their own situation is widely expressed among Turkish theologians studied here.[123] Awareness of a certain pressure behind hermeneutical theology should make one particularly suspicious of easy answers, but it should not immediately put a result under the verdict of ideology.

The present author asked one of the few people who could rightly claim panoramic knowledge of the Turkish academic scene in Koranic studies,

---

İslâmiyât and *kitâbiyât* run a common homepage: http://www.islamiyatdergisi.com. One of the books to be discussed below (p. 109–133), Adil Çiftçi, *Fazlur Rahman ile İslam'ı Yeniden Düşünmek,* is a volume of that series.

[123] Cf. below, pp. 109, 166, and especially below, p. 84.

Murat Sülün of Marmara (!) İlâhiyat:[124] Where is the ALMA MATER of Koran hermeneutics in Turkey? Dr. Sülün unhesitatingly gave the honour to *the other place*—Ankara. Four authors from the Ankara "tradition"[125] will be analysed.

[124] He is a post doctoral student and co-edited the specialist bibliography: Murat Sülün and Ömer Çelik (eds.), *Türkiye Kur'an Makaleleri Bibliyografyası*, Istanbul 1999.
[125] Cf. above at note 117 on p. 60.

Analysis

Chapter 1
Mehmet Paçacı: The Koran is Universally Historical

Mehmet Paçacı was born in 1959 in Bolu (northwest of Ankara). He graduated from an *İmam Hatip* School in 1977 and subsequently took up studies at the Theological Faculty of Ankara Üniversitesi. He earned the Licentiate in 1982 and set out for doctoral studies in what was then the Faculty's *Tefsir-Hadis* Department. His doctoral research led him to Saudi Arabia in 1985 and to Manchester University in 1987, where he spent a year at the Department of Biblical Theology. His doctoral thesis, on Koranic and Biblical eschatology, was accepted in Ankara in 1989. Apart from his theological studies, Paçacı also followed a Master's programme in philosophy at Middle East Technical University, Ankara. He has been visiting lecturer in Kuala Lumpur, at European universities including the Gregorian University, Rome, and Otto-Friedrich-Universität, Bamberg, and is now Professor in the *Tefsir* Department of Ankara Üniversitesi İlâhiyat Fakültesi.

Mehmet Paçacı has a particular interest in hermeneutics, and in comparing and confronting the Koran with the Bible. He has published many articles, especially in the scholarly quarterly *İslâmiyât,*[126] co-founded by him, and also in English periodicals.[127] Six of his major articles in Turkish, mostly methodological, have been collected in a recent book.[128]

Paçacı: History Back and Forward

Paçacı develops his hermeneutical reflections out of a chord which sounds his view of history in three notes.

---

[126] Cf. above, footnote 121 on p. 60.

[127] E.g., "The Role of the Subject (mujtahid) in al-Shafi'i's Methodology: A Hermeneutic Approach", *The American Journal of Islamic Social Sciences,* vol. 14 (1997), pp. 3–15.

[128] Mehmet Paçacı, *Kur'an ve Ben Ne Kadar Tarihseliz?* (Ankara Okulu Yayinları 23), Ankara 2000. The book does not offer the most reliable version of Paçacı's articles. Their first publications, in scholarly journals, provide better texts. Upon the collection of the book, many printing mistakes have crept in. Not all are as pleasant as "Septugiant" (p. 160). Proof reading seems not to have taken place. Since however the articles have in some cases been altered deliberately by the author, the book provides the latest version of the articles. Therefore, the present study refers to the *book's* pagination.

a. A theology of history. There is one "revelation tradition" *(Vahiy Geleneği)* (p. 53),[129] in which one and the same message has been preached throughout the ages.[130] However, in the course of that tradition, the message was revealed in the form of different legislations, due to the different historical situations into which the one message was spoken.
b. A vision. Muslims will found °a new civilisation *(yeni bir medeniyet).*[131]
c. A quest for today's scholar. What in a religion is changeable?

Obviously, the centre tone, the vision (b.) functions as *motivation* for a theological harking back (a.) that is to provide the *material* from which the quest (c.) will *mould* its results. There may, among Paçacı's addressees, be scepticism towards historically investigating the history of Islam. This seems to be his reason for presenting what might be termed *a comparative history of religions' probing their own histories.* He cites (p. 54) Albert Schweitzer to say that Christianity had deserted the historical Jesus.[132] Once Church teaching had adopted Paul's transhistorical view of Jesus's being Messiah—and more—any historical investigation could according to Mehmet Paçacı only be threatening to Christian theology.[133] In 17th

129 References in parentheses refer, until further notice will be made, to Mehmet Paçacı's 1996 article "Kur'an ve Ben Ne Kadar Tarihseliz?", which has been reprinted (under a slightly varied titled: *"Ne Kadar"* has become *"Nekadar"),* IDEM, *Kur'an,* pp. 53–79.

130 Lest discussion of the views presented interfere with the coherence of presentation, and in order to allow for an uninterrupted reading, certain points presented will be taken up in a subsequent paragraph headed "Discussion". In that section they will be arranged thematically rather than in the sequence of their appearance in the present text. "Revelation tradition" will be reconsidered under *(G) Integrationist History of Revelation,* below, p. 73.

131 "New civilisation" will be taken up again under *(F) Islamic Civilisation,* below, p. 72.

132 Albert Schweitzer, *Geschichte der Leben-Jesu-Forschung,* Tübingen ²1913 (¹1906: *Von Reimarus zu Wrede. Eine Geschichte der Leben-Jesu-Forschung).* Paçacı used the book's English translation *(The Quest of the Historical Jesus. A Critical Study of its Progress from Reimarus to Wrede,* London ³1954), which says (p. 3): "Primitive Christianity was therefore [viz., because of Jesus's own eschatological orientation] right to live wholly in the future with the Christ who was to come, and to preserve of the historic Jesus only detached sayings, a few miracles, His death and resurrection. By abolishing both the world and the historical Jesus it escaped the inner division [viz., between the world's and Christ's reign] described above, and remained consistent in its point of view." The text makes a striking distinction between "to preserve of the *historic* Jesus only …" and "abolishing … the *historical* Jesus". But the German original has „historischen" in both places. (²1913, p. 2) Later in the present study, differences between various words starting in 'histor-' will play an important role. Here however, such distinctions are out of place.

133 This point will be taken up again under *(E) Christians and History,* below, p. 72.

century[134] Europe this consensus was challenged, and an historical-critical exegesis developed which countered "the dogma". (p. 55) Recent researches have, in Paçacı's eyes, demonstrated that Christianity's historical critique of its own sources was influenced by Muslims' historical treatment of the Koran. (p. 56)[135] Since for Muslims, it has never been a problem to consider their religion's founder as an historical, human being, handling his biography and also the holy text with methods of historical critique—textual criticism, source criticism, pointing out chronological and geographical errors—has never been problematic, either.[136]

"Orientalists"[137] applied the methods of modern historical research to the Koran: methods which—according to Paçacı's account—they had indirectly, via Christian theology, inherited from Muslims. He says that, coming from a Christian tradition, Orientalists feel history to challenge their own beliefs even when reading the Koran. Thus, William Montgomery Watt has to "defend his tradition" against the Koran by saying that the Koran presents—and rejects—what it calls Jewish and Christian positions, which have however, as Watt remarks, not actually been held by Jews or Christians. The stock example is Mary's membership in the Trinity. Paçacı criticises Watt for working with an ideal concept of these religions and for not treating the history of Judaism and Christianity as one whole. Paçacı calls to mind that there were groups on the Arabian Peninsula during the time of Muhammad which did believe what the Koran presents as Christian belief. (p. 59)[138]

But Paçacı sees that the clash of historical thinking and holy text has strong repercussions also in Islam itself. The clash can render that ancient text meaningless for today; but it can also create a fresh approach, asking how °the Koran has interfered *(Kur'an'ın müdahalesi)* with history throughout the ages? (p. 61) For Paçacı, Fazlur Rahman's hermeneutical project is that new approach. The precondition for understanding the Koran, says Fazlur Rahman, is to investigate the era of its "coming down". Revelation is complete, but it must be understood. And it can only be understood within the framework of the time when it was put into language. This approach, says Paçacı, is quite different from the Orientalists', who uncover a monotheist tendency in 7th century Arabia and see the Koran as a product

134 Paçacı has "16th century"—"In this subject, the first advance was made in the 16th century by Richard Simon, a French priest" *(Kur'an,* p. 54)—but it is obvious that he meant '17th', since Richard Simon's thesis appeared in 1686.

135 This point will be taken up again under *(B) Influences,* below, p. 70.

136 This point will be taken up again under *(C) Historical Critique,* below, p. 70.

137 A comment on "orientalists" will be made under *(A) Paradigms,* below, p. 69.

138 This point will be taken up again under *(D) Heretics,* below, p. 71.

of that tendency. Paçacı's account can be summarised thus: both Fazlur Rahman and the Orientalists explain the Koran historically; but whereas the Orientalists explain its coming into being, Fazlur Rahman explains its meaning.

Among Muslim Koran interpreters, Mehmet Paçacı discovers two opposed groups, which he calls universalists *(evrenselciler)* and historicalists *(tarihselciler)*.[139] (p. 62) Both groups consider the Koranic norms to be valid for all times. It is the method of interpretation that makes the difference. The historicalists' hermeneutics can be described as working in three steps:[140]

1. Contextualisation. Every formulation of the Koran is read within the historical context of the time for which it was originally formulated. Only this makes it possible to understand the text's meaning correctly.
2. Condensation. The Koran is taken to have a message for all times and peoples, in other words, a universal message. This message can, according to the historicalists, not be found directly in the ancient formulations. Rather, these historically relative formulations must be understood as expressing an intention which is not relative to an historical situation. This intention must be found and expressed ("distilled") in universal principles.
3. Re-contextualisation. Subsequently, those universal principles have to be converted into action in every era of human history.[141]

---

[139] These English renderings do not capture the Turkish coinages precisely ("people who consider (the Koran) to be universal" or "historical" respectively), and, of course, have plenty of unsuitable associations. These qualifications being made, the renderings will do their job better than bulky translations, or none.

[140] Fazlur Rahman calls his method "a double movement" (IDEM, *Islam & Modernity*, p. 5), the first being the movement of returning to the Koran, the second, the movement of application for today. This description however would serve to mask the fact that in asking backwards one does often not automatically find the principles to be applied today. The 'condensation' of the commands-read-in-context must be marked out as a separate effort. Fazlur Rahman has actually seen this. He expressed it by subsuming two "steps" under the first "movement": reading in context, and distilling the general norm. (Ibid., p. 6) It would have been more consistent however to designate the first movement's "two steps" as separate movements, because the direction of questioning is different in each. That can be demonstrated by using space metaphors. From today 'back' to the Koran (interrogation); from the Koranic commands 'up' to the general norm (interpretation); from the general norm 'down' to today's problems (intervention).—The triple headings (contextualisation, condensation, re-contextualisation and interrogation, interpretation, intervention) are not literally Fazlur Rahman's or Mehmet Paçacı's; but they are elaborating precisely Fazlur Rahman's imagery ("destilled", ibid., p. 5) and Paçacı's choice of words *("müdahale", Kur'an,* p. 61).

[141] The model will be discussed under *(H) Fazlur Rahman's Model,* below, p. 73.

"According to the historicalists, the view which rests on the principle that the individual, historical religious norms—the text—have become universal is in danger of missing the historicality (tarihsellik)[142] of the individuals and generations after the coming down of revelation." (p. 62) The relation between the commands of the Koran and history is "dynamic". (p. 77)

Discussion: Camps, History and Hermeneutics

(A) Paradigms

(Cf. above, at note 137 on p. 67.) The discussion of Mehmet Paçacı's method and view must set off with what seem to be quibbles. But minor observations sometimes give clues to major lines. Paçacı uses the word "orientalists" to treat Western Islamicists' attitude toward Islam alike as saying, "In no way has the Koran anything to say for today". (p. 60) Paçacı's observation is correct in so far as many Western Islamicists understand their own paradigm as historical. By this they mean that as Islamicists they do not *want* to say what it all means for today because they would see that as shifting the paradigm towards preaching. But many of them would accept it as not abusive, if the material they provide was used to answer other questions, including: what does it mean for today? If one is not trying to answer the question, one can hardly be held to claim that the Koran has nothing to say for today. Such a levelling artificially constructs camps.

---

142 "Tarihsellik" is one of several possible Turkish renderings of ‚Geschichtlichkeit', which goes back to Gadamer (Dilthey, Yorck, eventually Hegel). Its most unambiguous English translation is 'historicality' (Elmar Waibl and Philip Herdina, *Wörterbuch philosophischer Fachbegriffe/Dictionary of Philosophical Terms,* vols. 1–2, Munich 2001, s.v. ‚Geschichtlichkeit'.) The most recent (1989) English translation of Gadamer's *Wahrheit und Methode: Truth and Method,* by Joel Weinsheimer and Donald Marshall however, still translates "historicity", (e.g., p. 265) thus not being able to distinguish between ‚Geschichtlichkeit' and ‚Historizität'. 'Historicity' should be used, if 'has actually taken place' is meant, whereas 'historicality' (‚Geschichtlichkeit') has, in philosophy, acquired the terminological sense: the (contingency of knowledge due to the) temporality of existence (cf., e.g., *Enzyklopädie Philosophie und Wissenschaftstheorie,* vol. 1, Mannheim 1980, p. 752). Of course, the two words are not completely clear terms, either. Søren Kierkegaard's usage of the conceptual pair, e.g., is closer to the English 'historic'/'historical' distinction. Cf., e.g., Richard Schaeffler, "Geschichte, Geschichtsphilosophie", *Lexikon für Theologie und Kirche,* vol. 4, Freiburg ^{3}1995, cols. 553–7, col. 556.

(B) Influences

(Cf. above, at note 135 on p. 67.) But possibly the construction of camps is, in Paçacı, not intended to reinforce a blunt antagonism between Islam and the West of the world. His underlying motive seems to be the opposite. First, another seemingly unimportant point has to be considered. Paçacı quotes an article by Hava Lazarus-Yafeh as his only reference to support his claim that "recent studies have begun to bring to light the fact that today's critical investigations of the Bible have been brought on the way by material of the critical approach which was developed by Muslims in the Middle Ages". (p. 56) Lazarus-Yafeh however in her article states only carefully that Muslim authors "may have helped to foster early modern Biblical criticism".[143] A *suggestion* of Lazarus-Yafeh has, just by being quoted, become a "fact". Furthermore, in order to substantiate a claim that 'B was influenced by A' one needs to answer not only the question 'Do A and B have a similar theme?' but also 'Can B have known A?'.

(C) Historical Critique

(Cf. above, at note 136 on p. 67.) Paçacı is quick to call pre-modern Muslims' dealing with Muhammad's biography—and their dealing with the text of the Koran—indiscriminately historical, even historical-critical. One has to keep in mind that

a. historico-biographically interested material about Muhammad, i.e., *Sīra,* was in the first centuries taken far less seriously than material about Muhammad of ethico-legal interest, i.e., *Ḥadīṯ;*[144]
b. deciding the authenticity of traditions about Muhammad is notoriously difficult, and strictly critical views, although attenuated by more recent scholars,[145] hold that most of the material was simply made up by later generations;

143 Hava Lazarus-Yafeh, "Some Neglected Aspects of Medieval Muslim Polemics Against Christianity", *Harvard Theological Review,* vol. 89 (1996), pp. 61–84, p. 65.

144 Wim Raven, "Sīra", *EI²,* vol. 9, pp. 660–3, p. 661.

145 Harald Motzki, *The Origins of Islamic Jurisprudence. Meccan Fiqh before the Classical Schools,* Leiden 2002. Motzki introduces his new approach with a fifty page history of research. Gregor Schöler argues for and applies a similar approach in his *Charakter und Authentie der muslimischen Überlieferung über das Leben Mohammeds,* Berlin 1996.

c. as soon as the Koran is seen as pre-existent,[146] any interest in its history is in danger of being seen as heretically claiming that the Koran is historical.

Be that as it may, what Paçacı is doing here is a traditionalising of historical criticism: Muslims, don't be afraid of it, he says, our forbears did the same. So, instead of resurrecting ancient antagonisms, he declares the adversaries' camp—Western historical criticism—to be depending on 'us': apologetic nostrification.[147] This may be pedagogical. But since it comes along as a cluster of scholarly theories, it must also stand the tests of scholarship.

(D) Heretics

(Cf. above, at note 138 on p. 67.) Paçacı accuses W. M. Watt—and indirectly other Orientalists—of defending Christianity from an unhistorical dogmatic point of view against what seem to be for Paçacı unquestionable historical facts. Watt reacts to the Christian heresies quoted in the Koran by rejecting their being Christian. Paçacı wants him to admit there were Christians who believed these heresies. Two questions have to be kept apart.

a. Did a group exist which held a view like the one presented by the Koran? Investigating pre-Islamic Arab Christianity is notoriously difficult, and important.[148] But the Koran as sole basis for the claim that there were heretics of that sort is insufficient.
b. If a group claiming Mary to be a member of the Trinity existed: what decides whether they are Christians or not? Paçacı implicitely advocates the criterion of self-designation. Another possible, and equally scholarly, criterion would be the criterion of compatibility with the central creed. The application of this criterion need not be "dogmatic" in the sense of a non-argumentative magisterial claim.[149] Credal compatibility can be demonstrated.

---

[146] Josef van Ess, *Theologie und Gesellschaft im 2. und 3. Jahrhundert Hidschra. Eine Geschichte des religiösen Denkens im frühen Islam,* vol. 4, Berlin 1997, pp. 625–30.

[147] Cf. above, footnote 96 on p. 54.

[148] John Spencer Trimingham, *Christianity Among the Arabs in Pre-Islamic Times,* London 1979. René Aigrain, "Arabie", *Dictionnaire d'Histoire et de Géographie Ecclésiastiques,* vol. 3, Paris 1924, cols. 1158–1339.

[149] Cf. the discussion of claims in religious studies, above p. 17.

(E) Christians and History

(Cf. above, at note 133 on p. 66.) For an accurate judgement on how the early Church handled its own history the following points may be considered:

a. "Historical" cannot, when designating the early Church's ways of handling tradition, be understood as incorporating modern research methods. That would not be true of earlier Muslims' interest in the life of Muhammad and the chronology of the Koran, either. Nor did any other pre-modern movement deal with its tradition according to modern standards of historical research. In the present context, "historical" can meaningfully be used to designate 'reporting (in the contemporary mindset) what *happened'*—as opposed to 'what should be done', 'what it all means', 'what I saw in a vision' etc.
b. The New Testament canon itself gives a clue about how historical presentations were weighed over against other manners of speaking about Jesus. Gospels which claimed apostolic origin but, in the eyes of the Church, deviated illegitimately from what the Church considered to be the historical Jesus, were not accepted into the canon. And the sequence of those books which were eventually accepted into the canon speaks the same language. They are arranged according to the chronology of themes, first Jesus, then the apostles. And even New Testament books which are formally not accounts of events, e.g., Paul's letters, argue primarily on the basis of 'what happened'. New Testament Christologies can been seen as attempts to explicate the Jesus-*event.*
c. For some titles used for Jesus later, one can demonstrate with high probability that the historical Jesus never used them to designate himself. It was the Church which found it appropriate to give Jesus this or that title. But the claim such titles make need not be the counter-historical one that Jesus historically called himself thus. Rather, the titles claim that they are adequate means for a later era to express who Jesus was and has become in history.
d. Therefore many Christian theologians see information about the historical Jesus including information gained with modern critical methods not as threatening to Christian belief but as elucidating.

(F) Islamic Civilisation

(Cf. above, at note 131 on p. 66.) A short distinction is due concerning talk of a future Islamic civilisation. This can mean either

a. one unified humanity,

b. a unified and renewed Islam, with other civilisations neighbouring it, or
c. a movement which allows for other Islams[150] and other civilisations, even in the same location.

(G) Integrationist History of Revelation

(Cf. above, at note 130 on p. 66.) Let us now turn to Mehmet Paçacı's central theses. These include his view of history and his view on hermeneutics. Paçacı's outlook is based on the theory that there is one "revelation tradition". (p. 53) In that, he is following a train of thought which can also be found in the Koran and which might be termed *integrationist revelation history*. These questions should be posed:

a. Is this alleged revelation tradition one strand among the many claimants of divine authority, or do all religious ideas of humanity belong to it? As we will see, and discuss, later, (below, p. 102) Mehmet Paçacı favours the first, terming the tradition "Semitic". His criteria for exclusion and inclusion are linguistic. Criteria concerning the *content* of a message claiming to be from God should also be applied.
b. Is this integration of religions other than Islam not pressing them into a straight jacket which they themselves do not want to wear? Would not a fairer comparative history of religions try to understand each religion on its own terms?
c. Is this forced integration of others the only view of the history of religions the Koran offers? Later verses of the Koran seem to imply a greater distance between Islam and other religions than the earlier 'integrationist' visions.[151]

(H) Fazlur Rahman's Model

(Cf. above, at note 141 on p. 68.) As the last point of this discussion, Paçacı's hermeneutic solution is to be considered. It is the model of Fazlur Rahman. Honoured as it may be, it should still not be considered as undisputable. It deserves questioning, if only to be clarified. Apart from the question raised further below, (p. 111) the following should be contemplated:

---

[150] I.e., other interpretations of Islam; cf. below, footnote 252 on p. 112.

[151] Cf. Frants Buhl, "Faßte Muḥammed seine Verkündigung als eine universelle, auch für Nichtaraber bestimmte Religion auf?", *Islamica*, vol. 2 (1926), pp. 135–49. On the Koran's theology of history cf. also below, p. 163.

1. The universality of the Koran's message is, in that model, taken for granted. It may appear dangerous to a Muslim to challenge this universality, because its rejection seems to be the notorious "Orientalist" position. However, especially if believing in the Koran's universality is a precondition for being a Muslim, Muslim theologians should see it as part of their task to *argue* for this universal validity.
2. The conversion of Koranic formulations into abstract principles is of course the weak point of this model. One Koranic ruling can, even when seen in the context of the whole Koran and in its historical setting, be understood to be the expression of several, even contradictory principles. There will never be unanimity among Muslims as to what the correct formulation of such principles is. Secondly, there seems to be an optimistic view behind this model concerning the possible performance of abstractions, rules, laws. Rather than actually covering all individual cases, rules remain always secondary to real life.[152] Finally, rules always need further rules, regulating their application, AD INFINITUM. (Paçacı touches upon this problem himself p. 66 note 47.)[153] So, even if the umma were able to agree upon, let's say, the formulation of ten Koranic *principles,* the situation would not be much different from now, when we have the Koranic *formulations.* Because then we would have the same controversial discussion about the application of these principles, which are discovered to be divine. It seems that this model has only shifted the problem and is still, just as a Muslim completely fixated on Koranic formulations—if less obviously—legalistic.
3. The model implies the presupposition that the principles behind the Koranic commands are—as opposed to certain other texts—absolutely correct and that in the Koranic commands those principles are applied absolutely correctly. Here, the following problem arises. Can the command to kill unbelievers (2:191) be the absolutely correct application of an absolutely correct principle? If the answer to this is: well, not every Koranic command is the correct application of a correct principle, then a criterion is required to distinguish the absolute from non-absolute. Yet, the model does not contain such a criterion.

---

152 Cf. already Gadamer's observation mentioned above, p. 27; and Wolfhart Pannenberg, *Systematische Theologie,* vol. 3, Göttingen 1993, p. 111 (chapter 12.3.d): "Because of its general character, law cannot do justice to the individual case in its particularity." He also cites (ibid.) Aristotle's statement that law, due to its general character, is *biased* and in need of amendment and correction. (Eth. Nic. v.14: 1137b10.)

153 Cf. Gadamer's remark, above, on p. 25 at note 28.

°The basic intention *(temel amaç)* of the Koran, according to Mehmet Paçacı and Fazlur Rahman, is "to give human life a direction *(yön)*, and to change the world". (p. 65) The Koran wants to develop an ethical society. All other subjects touched upon in the Koran are subsidiary to this aim. To be ethical means to apply a universal ethical principle to a concrete, particular *(tikel)*, historical situation. This is also what the Koran does.[154] The individual °historical situations *(tarihsel durumlar)* are °*asbāb an-nuzūl* (the occasions of the coming down (scil., of the Koranic passages)). It is into these situations that the Koran pronounces its regulations. So, behind each historical regulation, there is a universal, general ethico-religious principle. "Equally, °it is possible to know *(bilebilmek mümkündür*, lit.: it is possible to be able to know) which particular command in the history of revelation abrogates which command, and to know the historical conditions into which the commands were sent down." (pp. 65–6)[155] Now the question which divides the parties must be asked: is the Koran historical or universal? Mehmet Paçacı differentiates. The Koran is historical in so far as it refers to individual historical situations. The Koran is universal in so far as, at the occasion of these situations, universal principles were manifested. It is God's address in human terms. (p. 65) This humanness *(beşerilik)* and historicality of the Koran made the institution of a transhistorical dogma and a super-human interpretative authority—as there is, in Paçacı's view, in Christianity—unnecessary. Rather, *iğtihād* took over, i.e. creative application. Its method has been to define the more general principles *(sabab, ḥikma*, "the RATIO LEGIS"), and, from there, the most general principles *(maṣlaḥa, ʿadāla*, "the common good, justice") behind the Koranic commands.[156]

God's commands are—in their own historical situations—absolutely correct, since stipulated by an omniscient Being. Compared with stipulations made by human beings they are only ontologically (as of divine nature) and epistemologically (as received via revelation) different; structurally, they are equal to human regulations, because otherwise they would be incomprehensible to us. (p. 66) These divine commands can now be transformed into general principles. "The singular, historical regulations in the Koran are the source for defining the general principles in them

---

[154] Cf. the discussion under *(E) Ethical Reductionism*, below, on p. 84.

[155] Cf. the discussion under *(H) The Background Situations*, below, on p. 87.

[156] Cf. the discussion under *(B) Authority*, below, on p. 80.

correctly." (p. 66)[157] When the principles are brewed,[158] so to speak, to be regulations today, these regulations are highly likely to be correct, too. Since their application has to rely on human abilities, there is however no absolute criterion to establish them as correct.

Paçacı now implements a new tool. He reconsiders Fazlur Rahman's three step process of understanding 'read in context—draw principle—apply' in the light of Hans-Georg Gadamer's hermeneutics. The result of Paçacı's implementation is his discovery that Fazlur Rahman's model misses the preconditions of understanding. Paçacı therefore places one aspect before it: the historical conditions of the "understanding element—the subject". (p. 67) This is the core point of Paçacı's approach as also reflected in the heading of his article, which became the book's title: "The Koran *and I*—how historical are we?" (not Paçacı's italics). It is, says Paçacı, extraordinarily difficult to deal with our own situation "because it is a problem on the existential level, or rather, because there is an existential gap *(boşluk)* we do not want to accept. A person who understands and applies the Koranic commands today falls into doubts.[159] Therefore, it has become more and more difficult to speak of an understanding. Because the process of understanding does not only include understanding the text but at the same time includes bringing in some way the text [...] to one's own situation." (p. 67) "To understand a text means to understand it anew in every moment, [means] to interpret it anew within the framework of new and different situations. Thus, just as the text is historical, so is the act of understanding. [...] From this point of view, Muslims live in an existential poverty caused by their inability to bring that Islam of which they count themselves members into the present." (p. 68)[160] Paçacı depicts the situation of Muslims in the 19th and 20th centuries in sombre tones. Life in all its ramifications is controlled by Western not by Muslim civilisation. Since Muslims are history's objects only, rather than its agents, they are "within history but at the same time outside of it". (p. 69) Perceiving this, their reaction is to emigrate mentally and declare those they consider agents of history to be Satan's slaves. The stereotype catchword normally uttered in reaction to this situation is that of the °apologetic demagogue *(savunmacı propagandist):* with Islam in power things would be different. The syllogism

---

157 Cf. the discussion under *(G) Exemplary Application,* below, on p. 86.

158 This is not Paçacı's metaphor. The image is developed from Fazlur Rahman's metaphor 'norms are to be distilled' (cf. below, at note 168 on p. 79). Now, upon application, the product of that distillation has to be 'dissolved' again, i.e., 'brewed'.

159 Lit., "The existence of a subject who understands the Koranic commands today and applies them is in a condition which heavily produces doubt."

160 Cf. the discussion under *(F) Gadamer's Hermeneutics,* below, on p. 85.

of self defence runs: it is the sinners who are to be blamed for this history's abhorrent condition—Islam, being °the most orderly order *(en düzenli düzen)*, is innocent—ergo Islam has no place in this history. Islam cannot solve the problems others have produced. Either there is Islam as one whole system, or there is no Islam. (p. 69) Paçacı's comment on this demagogic attitude is: the crooked consciousness of those unable to find their identity. He analyses this attitude. Its underlying principle is that Islam has something to say only in a situation very similar to that of the Koran's original context. Implicitly, Mehmet Paçacı confronts the Gadamerian postulate that interpreters of tradition should be aware of their own historicality, with the attitude of today's Muslims who decree that what they live in is not really history. One might sum up Paçacı's observation: Muslims decree their own un-historicality.[161] He sees a fatal dualism—'our time, which corresponds to our ideas and in which we can intervene' over against 'not our time'—behind this attitude: "[Genuine][162] Islam does not allow for such a dualism, which in the last analysis yields the field to secularism *(sekülarizm)* and splits time into two. Islam does not accept [the fact that there is something like] °Satanic historical situations and Godly historical situations *(Şeytan'a ait ve Allah'a ait tarihsellikler)*.[163] All time is Godly." (p. 78)[164] Paçacı appeals to the sensitivity of his Muslim readers by confronting them first with the terrors of poverty of our days and then with the question: how can this world be so unjust although Muslims live in it? (p. 71) Intervening in history today would however mean to adapt the Koranic commands to be applicable today, which appears to the universalists like changing the unchangeable. Paçacı therefore demands that one should distinguish the universal, unchangeable element from its historical "envelope" *(zarf/kap:* receptacle), which, apart from being "carrier" *(taşıyıcı)* of the general norm, has also the function of conveying the historical framework of the command. (p. 71) Of course, the historical conditions of the "understanding person" will also be at work in the process of understanding. He or she necessarily has a particular *(cüz'i)* perspective. Human beings cannot reach a universal *(külli)*, objective understanding. Rather, the interpreter's own historical situation will always colour his or her interpretation. This raises the Universalist's greatest fear: alteration *(değişme)*, distortion *(tahrif olma)* of religion, °private-taste legislation *(telezzüzle teşri)*. Ac-

[161] Cf. the discussion under *(C) Being Unhistorical*, below, on p. 83.

[162] For clarification, some words have been added, in brackets.

[163] In several passages of his article, Paçacı uses *'tarihsellik'* to mean 'particular historical situation' rather than 'historicality' in the sense of 'the general situation of historical beings'. Cf. above, footnote 142.

[164] Cf. the discussion under *(D) Godly Time*, below, on p. 84.

cording to Paçacı's analysis, this fear consists of two attitudes: a "passive, defensive *(savunmacı)*" one and an "active, conscious *(dirayetli)*" one. The first is the fear of losing one's point of reference and thus one's identity in the torrents of history. The second is the urge to give history one's own direction without losing one's point of reference. (p. 74) Fear is in place, if a tradition loses its point of reference. It is then bound to fall prey to another tradition. The best example, says Paçacı, for such a loss of identity through loss of reference point is what happened to Christianity after Jesus. "With Paul's additions, it lost the receptacles of the historical commands in which revelation's fundamental principles were kept." (p. 75) By freeing Christianity from the Law, Paul separated Christianity from revelation although Jesus, "a prophet of Israel," had come to confirm Moses' Law. "Christianity, by leaving its Semitic origin, its Semitic context, the Semitic concepts expressing its basic principles, left its substance. Through Paul—and other Christian theologians who hellenised Christianity—the essence was lost. Muslims, on the contrary, have always kept to Koran and *Ḥadīṯ*, even the philosophers among them." (p. 75) "Christianity, although it should originally have taken its place within the Semitic Tradition, lost its tradition, plunged into the Hellenic *(Helen)* tradition and got lost in it." (p. 75)[165] "Since °the historical situations *(tarihsellikler)*[166] constantly change, the interpreters' °manners of understanding and applying *(anlamlar, uygulamalar)* the basic concepts and universal principles which are in the Koran will all change." (p. 76) For this, a °commission for Koranic reinterpretation *(ictihad kurumu)* must be set up.

Evaluation: A New Synthesis

Can Gadamer's philosophy be reconciled with Fazlur Rahman's methodology? That was the challenge Mehmet Paçacı obviously wanted to take when writing this methodological article. From Gadamer's side he hears: 'When you read, don't think you have a lifeless book in your hands. Rather, you are sharing life with someone that has been part of your life a long time before you started noticing it. In fact, it is your mother. You have started talking with her. You do not want to—or will be able to—understand her through and through. But in talking, you yourself develop,

[165] Cf. the discussion under *(A) Hellenisation,* below, on p. 79.
[166] Cf. above, footnote 163.

and you develop your understanding of the world.'[167] From Fazlur Rahman's side Mehmet Paçacı received the instruction: 'Go to the Koran; distil its intention from the stale juice of its commands. The old water will evaporate. Then return to where you have started and bring the concentrate. Infuse in today's water and serve the fresh juice.'[168] A philosophical mind will be able to verify the truth in Gadamer's observation even empirically: understanding is a continuous process. A modern theologian, on the other side, will be aware of the importance of feeding something practicable out of tradition into present-day conditions. Paçacı must have seen himself in a pressing dilemma. Creatively applying Gadamer's point 'we are inextricably tied into history', he used it to urge Muslims not to emigrate from history. And in the sentence quoted above, "Since the historical situations constantly change, the interpreters' manners of understanding and applying the basic concepts and universal principles which are in the Koran will all change", Mehmet Paçacı has reached a remarkable level of synthesis. He has taken Gadamer's point of constant change as well as Fazlur Rahman's point of operational universal principles. The principles are there to be discovered. But each discovery will be a new one.

Discussion:
Pneumatology, Koranology, and the Gadamering of Fazlur Rahman

Again, a number of Paçacı's asides concerning Christianity deserve comments. They often are, compared with what Paçacı writes about Islam and philosophy, clichés. The reading of that type of remark suggested in the previous discussion section, p. 70, might help to understand Paçacı here, too.

(A) Hellenisation

(Cf. above at note 165 on p. 78.) When Paçacı writes that the substance of (Semitic) Christianity was lost in Hellenistic culture, one is reminded of von Harnack's dated theories.[169] Could it also be that Christianity found

---

167 This metaphorical scenario has not been drawn by Gadamer nor is it meant to reflect what according to this author Mehmet Paçacı understood Gadamer to say. Rather, it is presented here because it seems to capture Gadamer's core insight.

168 The distilling and diluting (brewing) imagery is elaborating Fazlur Rahman's own metaphor of distillation *(Islam & Modernity,* p. 6).

169 Adolf von Harnack, *Lehrbuch der Dogmengeschichte,* vol. 1, Tübingen (^{1}1886:) ^{5}1931, p. 546.

in Greek philosophy a unique means for expressing its universal significance?[170] (We shall deal with the idea of a "Semitic Tradition" further below, on p. 102.) Or is Paçacı not really making an historical comment about Christianity but a pedagogical one to his Muslim readers? It might be translated as: 'Let us not make the mistake of leaving our tradition. If we have an identity within an unbroken tradition, we have a point of reference and we can start the rethinking.' Whether or not that mistake was in fact made by Christianity seems to be irrelevant for him. Even a fairy-tale could have done the same job: illustrating a certain type of danger.

The claim that through Hellenisation Christianity lost its Semitic point of reference raises the question whether Christianity's point of reference is something linguistic. What is Christianity's point of reference? Revelation, as already expressed in Moses' Law, or Jesus Christ? This question should be tackled historically. Reducing Jesus to a prophet who confirmed Moses' Law does not square with the historical evidence. Historical scholarship is confronted with a Jesus who, rather than simply confirming the Torah, claims that in his appearance God's reign has begun, that the Law has to be interpreted in the light of that reign, and not vice versa, and that the attitude people take toward himself is decisive for their eschatological salvation.[171]

(B) Authority

(Cf. above at note 156 on p. 75.) Another aside deserves detailed discussion. Due to the Koran's "humanness and historicality", says Paçacı, Islam never needed a "transhistorical dogma" and an authoritarian Church. The *first* question to be asked here is the following. Is Christianity's situation really that different from Islam's—and is Christianity's solution that different? Have not both Christianity and Islam been placed into the same tension of canon and community, or, in other words, are not both obliged to tradition *and* times? Both religions had to face the twin challenge of a canonical text (which includes the optics of a canonical tradition, explicitly or otherwise), which they were both unwilling and unable to alter, on the

170 Cf., e.g., Wolfhart Pannenberg, "Die Aufnahme des philosophischen Gottesbegriffs als dogmatisches Problem der frühchristlichen Theologie" (1959), IDEM, *Grundfragen systematischer Theologie,* vol. 1, Göttingen 1967, pp. 296–346.

171 Cf., e.g., John P. Meier, *A Marginal Jew. Rethinking the Historical Jesus,* vol. 2, *Mentor, Message, and Miracles,* New York 1994, pp. 398–454, and especially Wolfhart Pannenberg, *Grundzüge der Christologie,* Gütersloh ^{2}1966, p. 53 (§ 3.I). (For compatibility with translations, reference is not only to pages). The book has been translated as *Jesus—God and Man* into English (Philadelphia and London 1968).

one side; and on the other side the changing community of believers. Structurally, the new questions, be they doctrinal or exclusively practical, have always been the same, namely: how can we live true to the tradition today? "Live" means: believe, speak, act. "We" means: people with a present-day mind set, and 'life set'. The Church's doctrinal development is a product of the dialogue between the Tradition (viz., the Biblical message) and certain situations in history[172] just like any *iğtihād* in Islam. So there is a structural parallel; however, there are basic differences as well, which will be considered in the second point, below. But if Paçacı points out that fundamental difference between (churchy) Christianity and Islam (liberated by a comprehensible text), and some pages down calls for an Islamic committee of legal reinterpretation, he may have come to see the problem himself.

Secondly, what does Mehmet Paçacı actually claim when saying the Koran is more human(e) and more historical than the Bible? He refers to the type of speech used in the two texts. Paçacı describes the Koran's way of speaking in this way: it tells you what to do in a certain situation. The element "in a certain situation" makes it historical in Paçacı's sense, i.e., contextualised, while the element "tells you what to do" makes it human, i.e., you are not confronted with high-flown concepts but with down-to-earth practice (‚Operationalisierbarkeit').—It is true that the Koran can be read as a collection of imperatives. To call the text "historical" because it must, according to many interpreters, be understood from within its original context is at least a surprising usage of 'historical'.[173] To call the text "human" because it tells you what to do (rather than, e.g., who God is and how He acts with humanity) implies an anthropology of obedience which not everybody would share.

Thirdly, according to Paçacı, the foundation of the Church as a "superhuman", unifying doctrinal authority was necessitated by the Bible's lacking humanness over against the Koran. An alternative view is suggested here. The fact that in Christianity a—more or less—unified doctrinal authority came into being, which has no exact Islamic parallel, is best explained not by a less human/humane Bible and a more human/humane Koran but by these factors:

---

172 Cf., e.g., Wolfhart Pannenberg, "Die Aufnahme des philosophischen Gottesbegriffs", p. 298.

173 Ömer Özsoy however uses 'historicity' precisely in this sense. Cf. below, p. 136.

a. Muhammad had not appointed a successor.[174] This was perhaps due to his double role as prophet and statesman. It is of course not up to a prophet to elect his successor. That is God's job. A charismatic leader turned statesman however might have started setting up a mechanism for his succession or publicly built up a successor. Muhammad did not do so. This may be why after his death the umma fell into an interim trance, from which the disputable solution of the Caliphate evolved. It could however never gain authority in the vital field of doctrinal unity, which includes interpretation of the Tradition. Instead, the text of the Koran assumed a monarchic role with no force authoritatively surveying its application other than *Ḥadīṯ*, which in fact became another text, raising similar questions.
b. In the early Church, the Apostles understood themselves as endowed with Jesus's ἐξουσία/*exousía* (authority). Jesus himself taught and acted with an authority which was scandalous to many. He claimed divine authority. The Easter events have been understood by the Church as God's justification of Jesus's claim. Jesus authoritatively chose in the course of his earthly ministry a certain number of his followers to be his representatives also as regards his ἐξουσία/*exousía.* One of the titles for this group of men was "the Apostles".[175] Thus, the Church had from the outset no principal problem with the idea of divine authority in human hands. Two qualifications are in place. (i) This authority must be understood soteriologically; that is to say, human beings can have God's authority only in order to serve His plan of salvation. And (ii) the bishops, heirs to the Apostles, were only one authority in the triad of Episcopacy, Canon and REGULA FIDEI, in other words: bishops, Bible and (the Church's DE FACTO) belief.[176]

---

[174] Cf. the chaotic situation after Muhammad's death (Muḥammad b. Isḥāq, (translated by Alfred Guillaume), *The Life of Muhammad,* Oxford 1955), which even led to the embarrassment that Muhammad, who died on a Monday (ibid., no. 1010), was only buried "in the middle of the Wednesday night" (ibid., no. 1020).

[175] Cf., e.g., John P. Meier, *A Marginal Jew,* vol. 3, p. 126, and *'rasul'* (prophet/apostle).

[176] Cf., e.g., Henry Chadwick, *The Early Church,* Harmondsworth 1967, pp. 41–4. Does the factor REGULA FIDEI not imply a view just as Platonist (in a popular sense of the word) as Fazlur Rahman's general norms behind the Koranic commands? If 'the faith' has its rule, could one not simply state the rule and thus possess the core point to be reformulated in each era? The problem is that one cannot state that rule in a way independent of the respective historical situation. The genitive 'FIDEI' in 'REGULA FIDEI' should not, or not exclusively, be understood as possessive (the rule which Faith has) but as explicative (= identificative): the rule which Faith *is.* Understood in this way, the factor REGULA FIDEI means: the Church's believing exerts a regulating power on the Church's practice (including its practice of reformulating the faith). It presses the Church to re-express its belief in reaction to each challenge.

c. The status of the Bible is different from that of the Koran. While the New Testament is the witness to Jesus Christ by the early Church (community building the canon), the Koran is understood to be God's word giving shape to the umma (canon building the community).[177] This makes it more natural for the Bible than for the Koran to be creatively reread, and for the witness to be re-expressed in each historical period. "More natural" however does not mean 'necessary, without alternative'—in either case.

(C) Being Unhistorical

(Cf. above at note 161 on p. 77.) The hermeneutics of resignation of those who say they can only act if the world is Islamic, is characterised by Paçacı with these words: "they decree their own un-historicality". Thus, he has deepened the oft-quoted insight that an Islamist position is lacking historical consciousness. In his view, historical thinking means in this context more than approaching the text with the instruments of historical critique. It means understanding oneself as an active member of the present historical situation capable of effecting changes. Paçacı cannot appeal to Gadamer's hermeneutics in this point. That however does not render his point invalid.

It has also to be pointed out that Paçacı is offering here an outline of some idea of what a present-day Muslim supposedly thinks. He is not quoting and analysing certain authors.

A thought similar to the grammatical analysis suggested here is expressed by Wolfgang Beinert, "Regula fidei", *Lexikon für Theologie und Kirche,* vol. 8, Freiburg ^{3}1999, cols. 976–7. He says that the REGULA FIDEI is "not a formal rule *for* Faith but the guideline given *by* Faith itself—nicht eine formelle Regel *für* den Glauben, sondern die *durch* den Glauben selbst gegebene Richtschnur" (col. 976; Beinert's italics). Cf. A. M. Ritter's observation that the Early Church did not see the need of putting its creedal unity into a unified creed: Adolf Martin Ritter, "Glaubensbekenntnis(se). Alte Kirche", *Theologische Realenzyklopädie,* vol. 13, Berlin 1984, pp. 399–412, p. 405: „wie im Urchristentum genügt der Kirche der ersten beiden Jahrhunderte noch immer eine substantielle Bekenntniseinheit ohne Bekenntnis*formel*" (Ritter's italics).

177 Cf. also Josef van Ess's statement "After all, Islam is the first among the revelation religions in which—PACE Wansbrough—Scripture is earlier than Tradition. [...] Therefore, Islamic theology was not in need of pneumatology. But just like Protestantism, which devalued Tradition together with the authority of the Church, Islamic Theology also fell into the danger of allowing Scripture a dynamic of its own." *Theologie und Gesellschaft,* vol. 4, p. 625.

(D) Godly Time

(Cf. above at note 164 on p. 77.) In the same context an excursus into systematic theology is due. Paçacı understandably reacts to the demonising of an historical situation and sees in it an excuse for resignation. "All time is Godly", says Paçacı. This triggers a whole cluster of questions like 'Is every historical situation intended by God just the way it turned out?, 'Does God want evil to exist?', 'In how far can an evil situation be called Godly?', or: 'Is the point that God makes good *from* evil?'. But, of course, one cannot expect all questions to be answered at the same time. And Paçacı has implicitly made a valid point in his usage of 'Godly situation'. For a religious person, considering a situation to be Godly means 'I have a task in it to fulfil'.

(E) Ethical Reductionism

(Cf. above at note 154 on p. 75.) Let us now turn to the hermeneutical discussion itself. We must start, like Paçacı, not with a cosmology or anthropology but with a Koranology, i.e., an answer to the question, what is the Koran? His answer is that it is a divine means to form an ethical society, and all other types of propositions in the Koran are tools to accomplish this main intention. This surprises, if one remembers that less than five percent of the Koranic verses are legislative.[178] Certainly, a text's intention cannot be deduced from word statistics alone. Investigating the earliest Koranic proclamations, one will be led to points like 'God is creator'; 'God's judgement is imminent'. Regulations are not prominent in that first preaching.[179] Fazlur Rahman, and with him Mehmet Paçacı, will have to subsume the whole of Koranic theology under the single intention of influencing people's behaviour. Consequently, they are what should be called *ethical reductionists.* Three questions arise:

a. What is the textual basis for this reduction?
b. Does this not reduce God Himself to the status of a means, subservient to the one aim: human action?
c. What is meant by "ethics"?

These questions are not lethal attacks on ethical reductionism. They can be tackled as follows:

---

[178] Some 200 verses out of some 6370. I am grateful to Prof. Dr. Ulrich Rebstock for this information.

[179] Cf., e.g., Rudi Paret, *Mohammed und der Koran. Geschichte und Verkündigung des arabischen Propheten,* Stuttgart ^{7}1991, pp. 76–9.

Conc. c. (What is meant by "ethics"?) "Ethics" can be understood in a broader sense to refer not only to (i.) what people do *to people*, but to *everything* people do, including (ii.) what they do to God (e.g., prayer), and including not only action but also (iii.) which attitude they take (e.g., trusting God). Furthermore, ethics need not consist merely of commands and prohibitions, i.e., of the *imperative material*, but can also include arguments for the commands, and views on consequences, i.e., a *motivation system*.

Conc. b. (Does this not reduce God Himself to the status of a means, subservient to the one aim: human action?) God is not the Koran. And the correct attitude towards God, e.g., giving Him absolute priority can be part of an ethics in the broader sense expounded in the preceding paragraph.

Conc. a. (What is the textual basis for this reduction?) The Koran describes itself as a *hudā* for human beings (2:2 & PASSIM), a Guidance. This may be understood as synonymous with "ethics" in the sense explained above.

These are valid answers to the questions posed. But still, an objection to ethical reductionism is due. Is the Koran, when its intention is seen only to be ethical, not domesticated illegitimately; are not thus whole dimensions of the Koran being lost? If Muslims understand the Koran to be revelation, do they not imply that it gives them information other than only instruction; that it aims at people's *knowing* something apart from *doing* something? An ethical reductionist could still reply: 'Knowledge without real-life consequences is futile.' That however is a presupposition which ethical reductionists should be aware of.

Much depends on which concept of revelation one holds. Revelation can be understood as God's communicating not only something but Himself; then, revelation can be seen as the process of God realizing Himself within creation. In the ethical context, this implies that God gives not only the order (and a motivating system) but also the power to fulfil it. In Islamic theology, the concept of *'tawfiq'* expresses this; it is God who "gives success" to human fulfilment of His will.

(F) Gadamer's Hermeneutics

(Cf. above at note 160 on p. 76.) Staying with hermeneutics, a central point must now be tackled. Paçacı rightly sees that Hans-Georg Gadamer's philosophy can shed new light on Fazlur Rahman's methodology. But Paçacı cannot claim that he has taken in 'Gadamer' by simply adding another point to Fazlur Rahman: the historicality of all understanding. Rather, 'Gadamer's hermeneutics' is too fundamental to be a methodological supplement to somebody else's methodology. Gadamer's *Wahrheit und Methode* is not a textbook of text hermeneutics; it is contorted and cryptic; it is full of cross references to other philosophers but it lacks examples that would clarify Gadamer's points; using the understanding of literature as a starting point for an ontological reinterpretation of life, its scope is far beyond a user's instruction for handling literature. It is therefore difficult to specify what Gadamer really says when it comes to hermeneutics in the sense of methodological understanding of texts. For the present context, Gadamer can be epitomised in this way:

a. You cannot develop a ‹passe-partout› methodology of understanding.
b. Tradition has had a greater influence on you than you can see.
c. It is the text which takes the role of asking—and shaping—the questions.
d. Developing an awareness of the text's influence on you clarifies your understanding.
e. In understanding, you do not leave your own perspective but bring new insights into your own vision.
f. Your particular, new look at the tradition does not distort but elucidate it.

In Mehmet Paçacı's thoughts one can rediscover some of Gadamer's points. Taking when encountering a text one's own historicality into account is just as Gadamerian as seeing the difficulty of understanding one's own situation within history. But if one tries to rethink Islam with the help of Gadamer, there is still material left for more revisionism. Would it not be exciting to observe how the Koran can reshape the questions we want it to answer; or how a modern mind's vision is enriched by newly taking in Koranic points of view? If tradition shapes our way of putting our questions and if the text should itself start re-shaping and asking the questions, then a phenomenon like modern Muslims' ethical reductionism may be only a preparatory phase to a new movement of rethinking Islam. What this may mean for the future of Muslim theology will have to be considered further below. (p. 107)

(G) Exemplary Application

(Cf. above at note 157 on p. 76.) Finally, two minor points have to be raised. The first concerns Fazlur Rahman's and Mehmet Paçacı's theory that there are general principles to be discovered beneath the individual Koranic stipulations. One wonders why God has left it to human beings to distil the general norms from commands, rather than stipulating the general norms straight away. Thus, one of the weak points in the process of application could have been avoided. A possible response to this would be: 'A norm is clearer when set out not in its general form but in an exemplary application.' This would be another silent presupposition of the model presented above.

(H) The Background Situations

(Cf. above at note 155 on p. 75.) Mehmet Paçacı is very optimistic about our historical knowledge when he says that we can know the historical situations into which the Koran was sent. It is slightly easier to get a general view of 7th century Arabia. But for a precise interpretation we must know the individual context of each verse. And it is a huge, and hardly begun, task to check each message about the alleged historical context of a verse with a detailed questionnaire including questions like: 'Can the alleged context have been reconstructed simply out of the verse's formulation?' Affirmative response does not automatically lead to rejection.

Paçacı: Method in Action

When considering an author's hermeneutics it is not enough to look at what he or she says about hermeneutics. Apart from *methodology*—'explicit hermeneutics'—one has to investigate *method,* i.e., what the author does when actually interpreting. Is the author true to his or her own principles? What is the author's 'implicit hermeneutics'?[180] Mehmet Paçacı is extensive in matters methodological—i.e., in thinking about Koran exegesis. In a 1998 article[181] he is actually *doing* exegesis of the Koran. Since the article ventures into areas not often touched by Muslim theologians, tackles several vexing problems of the discipline, offers some exciting solutions, and provides material for a case study in method, it is worth detailed presentation.

The article is formally an exegesis of Sura 112. But in fact it is an essay experimenting with a particular view of the history of revelation. It starts from the thesis that the Koran is "a book which came into being within Semitic Religious Tradition". (p. 156)[182] This can according to Mehmet

---

180 Cf. above, p. 23.

181 Mehmet Paçacı, ""De Ki: Allah Bir(אחד/أحد)'dir." Sami Dini Geleneği Perspektifinden İhlas Sûresi'nin Bir Tefsiri Denemesi", IDEM, *Kur'an,* pp. 155–84. Here, the—even typographically rather demanding—title (""Say: God is One—*aḥad/æḥād*—." An experimental exegesis of Sura 112 in the perspective of Semitic Religious Tradition") has been quoted from its original (and better) version in *İslâmiyât,* vol. 1/3 (1998), p. 49.

182 Point *(I) Semitic Religious Tradition* will discuss the concept in detail: below, p. 102. Cf. also p. 93.

Paçacı be demonstrated by the two facts that the Koran mentions the prophets which were members of that tradition, and that the Koran shares its theology, viz., monotheism, with that tradition. The Koran's belonging to the Semitic Religious Tradition, he says, has long been overlooked. Why? Because the Koran's criticism of the People of the Book was, according to Paçacı, falsely taken to be normative and transhistorical, and its self-referential passages, which ought to be understood in the polemical milieu of its origin, received undue attention. (p. 155) On the other hand, the Koran often merely alludes to, and therefore presupposes knowledge of, that tradition. From that, Paçacı deduces a fairly high level of routine familiarity with Biblical narrative among 7th century Ḥiǧāz Arabs.[183] That level however sank in later generations, a fact which gave, in Paçacı's account, rise to the usage of *Isrā'īlīyāt*[184] narratives in Muslim Koran exegesis. (p. 156) But no method was developed to handle the documents. The exegetes dealt with the material as if it were mere legend. But at least they dealt with it. Even that was criticised by the first generation Modernists (Muḥammad ʿAbduh, Muḥammad Rašīd Riḍā).[185] In their views, taking *Isrā'īlīyāt* into account was thwarting the Koranic objectives, which were, according to them, rationalistic. Mehmet Paçacı, on the contrary, holds that, because the Koran assumed its shape within Semitic Tradition, studying this tradition's pre-Koranic material ought to be a major exegetical method. (p. 156) With this postulate, Mehmet Paçacı sees himself in line both with the philological-historical tradition of Western understanding and with Fazlur Rahman's "first movement",[186] viz., back to the historical setting of the Koran. (p. 157)

Turning to the text of Sura 112, Paçacı first inquires about the occasion of revelation, i.e., into which immediate context were these words proclaimed? Tradition has two different answers to give. One is that the Meccan Qurayš, i.e., polytheists, the other that a Jew, i.e., a monotheist, asked Muhammad about the God he preached. Some traditions on *asbāb an-nuzūl* present a complete frame around Koranic texts, that is to say, not only an occasion for, but also a reaction to the revelation. In this case, one

---

[183] Point *(B) Biblical Ǧāhilīya* in the following discussion section will take this up: below, p. 95.

[184] *'Isrā'īlīyāt'* in Paçacı's, and other Muslims', usage is not identical with what Islamicists tend to mean when using the word. For Paçacı *Isrā'īlīyāt* is Biblical (plus para-Biblical) material and the exegetical occupation with it, whereas in Islamic Studies, *'Isrā'īlīyāt'* designates popular, edifying stories about personages of the Bible which are mentioned in the Koran. Gyula Vajda, "Isā'īliyyāt", *EI²*, vol. 4, Leiden 1978, pp. 211–2, p. 211.

[185] Cf. above, p. 40.

[186] Cf. above, p. 76.

tradition (which Paçacı found in the commentary by Ibn Abī Ḥātim (854/5–938)) has it that a Jew (ʿAbd Allāh b. Salām), upon hearing the Sura, professed the *šahāda.* (p. 158) There is a consensus among scholars about the *early Meccan* origin of Sura 112.

The first point of philological interest is the word *'aḥad'* in verse 1 ("Say: He is God, *One.")*. From a standard work of Old Testament scholarship,[187] Paçacı sets out to investigate the etymology of *'aḥad'*.[188] He then mentions that God's being one, singular, unique is a concept central to Deuteronomistic theology and has been "kept" in the course of the Old Testament's translation into Greek.[189] (p. 160)[190] He observes that Jesus, in the Synoptic Gospels, and Hellenistic Synagogal Prayers[191] perform the same profession of monotheist faith. (p. 161)

Paçacı now turns to the notorious CRUX INTERPRETUM of 112:2. The verse calls Gods God *"aṣ-ṣamad"*, which is a Koranic hapax legomenon. Paçacı quotes the groping efforts of Arab national lexicography reflected in Lane's presentation,[192] which claims the word family *ṣ-m-d* has something

---

[187] Ernst Jenni and Claus Westermann (eds.), *Theologisches Handwörterbuch zum Alten Testament,* vols. 1–2, Munich [4]1984 ([1]1971), which Paçacı used in its English translation.

[188] Point *(C) One* in the following discussion section will take this up: below, p. 96.

[189] PHILOLOGICA: (a.) A distinction between henotheism and monotheism is in place. Being one god and unique does not necessarily imply being God without anything else being God. A philosophical distinction of the meanings of "one" is helpful throughout. (Cf. below, footnote 239 on pp. 103–4.) (b.) *"Sadece"* is stated as one of the meanings of the Greek 'εἷς/*heîs*'. (Consistently, a graphical representation of the SPIRITUS ASPER is omitted, with 'εἷς/*heîs'* becoming "eis", which can easily be misunderstood to be a preposition (εἰς).) *"Sadece"* for 'εἷς/*heîs'* must be a misinterpretation of an English dictionary entry. The dictionary's 'only' (which, in its *adjectival* usage, is a correct rendering of 'εἷς/*heîs'* must have been misunderstood to be the *adverb* 'only'. Thus it was translated by the adverbial *"sadece"*. *'Tek'* would have been the word of choice. (c.) Paçacı mentions the fact that 'θεὸς εἷς/*theòs heîs'* appears in "Greek texts" (p. 160). He (rightly) relies on Walter Bauer's dictionary (he used a reprint of a dated English translation: Walter Bauer, *A Greek—English Lexicon of the New Testament and Other Early Christian Literature* (translated by William F. Arndt and F. Wilbur Gingrich), Cambridge (U.K.) and Chicago [4]1952). Bauer's remark however gravely weakens Paçacı's point. If "already Xenophanes, fgm. 23" (Bauer, *Lexicon,* s.v. "εἷς/*heîs*" § 2.b) used "θεὸς εἷς/*theòs heîs*" to mean "God is the only one", that makes a Greek 5th century B.C. occurrence of what one might well term monotheism: *Semitic* Religious Tradition?

[190] Point *(A) Cross-fertilisation* in the following discussion section will take this up: below, p. 95.

[191] Paçacı translates from James H. Charlesworth, *Old Testament Pseudepigrapha,* New York 1983.

[192] Edward William Lane, *An Arabic—English Lexicon,* vol. 4, London 1872, pp. 1726–7. When considering the form *"muṣmad"*, Lane, p. 1727, is here translated thus: "a person who has no need of entertaining anything in order to earn his living *(hayatını kazanmak için bir iş tutmaya ihtiyacı olmayan kişi)"*. That is not exactly what

to do with lordship, reliability, solidity and being elevated. Paçacı is especially interested in the meaning of *ṣamda:* rock. A collection of Old Testament verses containing the word "rock" (Hebrew: *ṣûr)* for God ensues. He shows that *ṣûr* is associated with God's reliability, His granting protection and refuge, that it occurs in contexts of warfare but also of guidance (Ps 31:3 etc.) and of God's incomparability *(karşılaştırılamazlık,* 1 Sam 2:2 etc.), and he finally quotes Dtn 32:18: "You are unmindful of the rock which has begotten you, you have forgotten God, who made you." One has to keep in mind that we are in the middle of an exegesis of Sura 112 ("no one is like Him"; "He has not, and is not, begotten") to see that we are steering towards exciting new shores here. Behind *ṣamad,* he says, is the Old Testament idea of God the rock. Mehmet Paçacı compares the Hebrew Bible passages containing "the rock" with their ancient translations. In the Septuagint, he finds that *ṣûr* is, when designating God, not translated literally but either as "God" or in words characterising God as helper, watchman, hard.[193] Why is the Hebrew word for "rock", *ṣûr,* not rendered by its most obvious equivalents 'πέτρα/*pétra*' or 'λίθος/*líthos*' in the Septuagint?[194] Paçacı's explanation is that "the word [πέτρα/*pétra]* was a symbol used in Hellenistic religions for the incarnation of gods" (p. 165).[195] He argues along these lines: In the Targums and the Pešiṭṭa the original's "rock" regularly appears as '*taqqīf*—strong one'.[196] The tendency of rendering 'the rock' more abstract is one current of a great cultural stream. The monotheist tradition was re-expressing its old tenets (God's oneness) in new terms ('the strong one') because it was aware of the confusion a stubborn reiteration of the old formula ('the rock') would have caused in the new context. "Rock" had become an incarnation symbol.[197]

The next verse (112:3) seems to be a direct contradiction of an Old Testament passage. Rather than being the "rock who has begotten you", (Dtn 32:18) the Koran says about God "He has not, nor is He, begotten". (112:3) For Paçacı, this does not refute the hypothesis of 'one continuous Semitic Tradition'. Rather, it is an example of changing surface expression

---

Lane says: "a people having no trade or occupation nor anything by means of which they may live." This is, however, irrelevant to Paçacı's argument.

193 ἀντίλημπτωρ/*antílēmptōr,* βοηθός/*boēthós,* φύλαξ/*phýlax,* στέρεος/*stéreos.*

194 Point *(H) Oral Literature* in the following discussion section will propose an answer: below, p. 101

195 Point *(D) An Incarnation Symbol* in the following discussion section will take this up: below, p. 96.

196 Point *(E) Dropping the Rock* in the following discussion section will elaborate this: below, p. 97.

197 Point *(J) Transition and Continuity* in the following discussion section will take this up: below, p. 106.

to what seems to be the opposite, in order to stay faithful to the tradition. (p. 166) Paçacı sees the reason for this in the fact that "begetting" was, once Christian theology became more prominent, no longer used to designate God's creating and protecting activities but God's having a Son, Jesus Christ. This, Paçacı considers to be a concept "foreign to Semitic Tradition". (p. 167)[198] Quoting (scil., Karl) Rahner, Paçacı calls it a great problem for today's Christianity to harmonise its monotheistic claim with "*İsa'nın tam bir tanrı oluşu*—Jesus's being one complete god." (p. 168)[199] So, while the Christian tradition steered towards reiterating God's begetting his only Son, the Semitic Tradition accentuated all the more clearly God's unbegottenness and His not begetting anyone. This clarity of accentuation culminates in the Koran. (p. 170)

In its last verse, Sura 112 states that "nothing is equal to" God. While Jesus heeded the Old Testament idea of God's incomparability, it was already Paul who tampered with it, calling Christ "in God's likeness". (Phil 2:6) (p. 172) Paçacı admits that there has been a development of the monotheistic concept within the Semitic Tradition. He holds however that the affirmation of God's oneness remained unaltered from Old Testament to Koranic thought. Yet, development took place, namely from a "racist" *(ırkçı)* to a universalistic view of God's salvation. (p. 173) Only after Jesus's preaching, deviations from monotheism occurred. Therefore, the Semitic Tradition, in order to make its core tenet clear in view of a new background, developed new formulae, among which we find "God is not a father". (p. 174) It was not the Bible which influenced the Koran, as Orientalists tend to claim, but the common Semitic Tradition which surfaced in both the Bible and the Koran, each time re-expressed according to the needs of the contemporary culture. (p. 175)[200] The process is explicable in this way: Jews were part of the society in which the Koran was revealed, and it used the cultural code[201] of that society to make itself understood. (p. 176)

Mehmet Paçacı pleas for Koranic scholars to see themselves as addressed by the pre-Koranic scriptures, too. Studying them together with the Koran, he says, opens new dimensions for scholarship.

---

198 Point *(F) Son of God* in the following discussion section will take this up: below, p. 99.

199 Point *(G) Monotheism Challenged* in the following discussion section will take this up: below, p. 99.

200 Point *(K) Changing Tradition* in the following discussion section will take this up: below, p. 106.

201 This is Abū Zayd's language. He received the "code" *(KWD)* idea from communication theory. Cf. above, pp. 42 and 46.

Evaluation: Isrāʾīlīyāt Revisited

The significance of Mehmet Paçacı's *Iḫlāṣ* article can hardly be overrated. It should be seen as an historic turning point in Muslim theology.

What strikes one at first sight is that Paçacı is consulting, reading and processing not only Turkish and Arabic texts but also works in English. What deserves special attention here is that he is not only, like some of his colleagues, taking Western Islamicists'—or methodological—works into account. He also ventures into Western *Biblical* scholarship, and *theology*. Furthermore, he is striving for first hand contact with the Old and New Testaments in their original languages. And on top of that, he even plunges into texts from what is conveniently called the Intertestamental period, including ancient Biblical versions, and into early Church documents, including apocryphal material. In all that, he shows great interest in matters of both language and theory. Many of the regions he explores are altogether new territory to Muslim theologians. Even the mistakes in the essay should not pedantically be listed for correction. They should, rather, be seen as reflecting the courage of a man leaving the well-protected domains of traditional *tafsīr*. Mehmet Paçacı is exemplary for his Muslim, and non-Muslim!, colleagues in not confining himself to secondary reports about what the others think, but looking freshly at the primary sources—including modern Christian theology—striving for philological backing, and doing his own thinking.

It is classical *tafsīr* practice to take the 'Biblical'[202] material—in that context termed *'Isrāʾīlīyāt'*—into account for an exposition of the Koranic narratives. The major intention of that practice was to fill the gaps which the Koran left open, with more or less imaginative information about actors and affairs mentioned. From the outset, a strict distinction between reference to another source and mere coinage has been hard to draw. *Isrāʾīlīyāt* were not treated as having influenced Muhammad or the Koran, but as *history alluded to.*[203] Mehmet Paçacı is again taking the documents of the Bible and its environment as means for explaining the Koran. So, what he is actually doing is re-opening the gates of *Isrāʾīlīyāt.* This is a precise description of what he is doing, because the scope of his reconsideration is as generous as classical *Isrāʾīlīyāt,* which did not restrict itself to the Biblical

202 Marilyn Waldman's caveat is to be heeded. Cf. footnote 243 below.

203 This is a pertinent, but apparently overlooked, point in the hermeneutics of classical Koran exegesis, because a *mufassir* taking into account *Isrāʾīlīyāt* implicitly admits (a.) that the Koran need not answer out of its own text all questions a reader might ask; (b.) that other sources of knowledge can shed light on the Koran.

canon either.[204] So MATERIALITER, Paçacı is in line with his classical predecessors. FORMALITER however he is in line with modern scholars (a.) in distinguishing textual evidence from mere guess,[205] (b.) in allowing for an influence from that material on the cultural repertory the Koran used, (c.) in—consequently—trying to see strands of historical transmission,[206] and (d.) in contextualising the Koranic passages within problems[207] of 7th century *Ḥiǧāz*.[208]

In short, Paçacı is re-opening the gates of *Isrāʾīlīyāt* as an historicist.

Paçacı's essay is of a vividly experimental character. The author makes his reader a witness to the results' slowly taking shape. Lengthy quotes of little demonstrative value convey a workshop atmosphere. Furthermore, the article seems to be an experiment conducted in order to test an hypothesis. At surface level it is the methodology that is the hypothesis: historically revisiting *Isrāʾīlīyāt* for Koran exegesis. The implicit hypothesis is that this methodology works, yields new insights, helps to understand the Koran. If the article was an experiment testing this hypothesis, the result is a positive one.

There is however another hypothesis for which the essay seems to function as a test. The article is trying out the particular view of history which Paçacı is taking without ever questioning it. He is operating with the concept of a "Semitic Religious Tradition"[209] The idea goes back to a tendency of 19th century scholarship, which liked to root characteristics of certain *religions* in characteristics of certain *languages.* The French semitist and novelist Ernest Renan (1823–1892) ascribed a monotheistic inclination to

---

204 Gyula Vajda (above, note 184 on p. 88) reports three levels of evidence falling under the category of *'Isrāʾīlīyāt'*: 1. Biblical texts strictly speaking; 2. narratives from the times of the Israelites; 3. folklore claiming Jewish origin.

205 He relies on critical editions of the texts, or modern translations.

206 Therefore, 'tradition' is an acceptable—indeed helpful, central—concept for him, whereas a classical outlook would claim independent acts of revelation to account for parallels.

207 In the case of Sura 112, *theological* problems.

208 That is what *asbāb an-nuzūl* studies have always tried to do. What makes this approach modern is that the context is reconstructed not (or: not only) through "messages" supported by *isnāds*, but through a presentation of the (e.g.) theological milieu as reflected in contemporary documents (which may include non-textual evidence).

209 Presently, at Ankara University's Theological Faculty, Mehmet Paçacı's academic home, among several younger scholars a veritable enthusiasm can be felt to study Semitic languages. "How is your Aramaic these days?" is a question which can actually be heard.—Cf. also the discussion below, p. 102.

nomadic Semites based on race, i.e., linguistic kinship.[210] Following on Renan, Conrad von Orelli tries in his *Allgemeine Religionsgeschichte* of 1899 to argue for a Semitic monotheist predisposition („Anlage') manifest in the Semites' "lack of imagination" (imagination might have added other gods), "lack of analytic and dialectic talent" (reflection might have discovered other than divine causation) and lack of colour in language (linguistic associations, in the case of the Aryans, helped produce mythologies)[211] and, positively, the Semites' concentration of life and commitment (which predisposes people to devoting all their activities to one aim).[212] This idea betrays on the one hand the racist background of such hypotheses and on the other that they are not verifiable through historical methods. They should therefore have no place in scholarly theology. How did the idea of a "Semitic Religious Tradition" get into Mehmet Paçacı's thinking? There is one clue in Fazlur Rahman. In a 1985 autobiographical note which was also published in Turkey (accompanied by a Turkish translation) he argues that God's revelation exceeds what we can find in Judaism, Christianity and Islam. He exhorts his Muslim brothers and sisters

> "to believe in the totality of divine guidance and in any book God may have revealed—not just the Qur'an and other Semitically revealed books."[213]

The context, dealing with Koran and the Bible on the one hand, and other revelations on the other, makes it clear that Fazlur Rahman considers Koran *and* Bible to be "Semitically revealed", i.e., revealed in Semitic languages. This remark may surprise a linguist, who is aware that the New Testament is in Greek and that Greek is a member of the Indo-European, not the Semitic, family of languages. It presupposes a particular Islamic view of revelation history, which implies that revelation is PER DEFINITIONEM a speech act: God inspired his revelation to ʿĪsā, who uttered it in either Hebrew or Aramaic, which are Semitic languages; in the process of the revela-

---

210 Later however Renan considered forms of life to be prime factors of shaping believes. In other words, desert monotony makes you a monotheist. Cf. Fritz Stolz, *Einführung in den biblischen Monotheismus,* Darmstadt 1996, p. 23 (3.1.1).

211 "eine gewisse kunstlose Einfachheit der Sprache, welche den Ursinn der Wörter viel getreuer erkennen läßt und im Gedächtnis bewahrt als bei den Ariern, deren schillernde, vieldeutige Sprache zur Entstehung der Mythen- und Götterwelt nicht wenig beigetragen haben", Conrad von Orelli, *Allgemeine Religionsgeschichte,* Bonn ^{2}1913, p. 284, quoted after Stolz, *Monotheismus,* p. 24. The idea of an ‚ursemitischer Monotheismus' did not remain unchallenged. The counter position, viz., Arabian paganism as the origin of Koranic theology, was famously held by Julius Wellhausen in his *Reste arabischen Heidentums,* 1887, ^{2}1897.

212 von Orelli, *Religionsgeschichte* (cf. above, note 211), p. 284.

213 Fazlur Rahman, "An Autobiographical Note—Kısa Otobiyografi" (translated by Bekir Demirkol), *İslâmî Araştırmalar* vol. 4 (1990), pp. 227–31, p. 228.

tion's translation into Greek it was heavily distorted so that one cannot say that the Greek text we have today is what God revealed ("Semitically") to ʿĪsā. But this singular occurrence of a similarly sounding word in Fazlur Rahman does not suffice to account for Paçacı's usage.

Discussion: Christology, Oral Literature, and Semitic Religious Tradition

Discussion will open with five additions to points raised in the article, *(A)*–*(E)*. Then, two christological issues will be focussed, *(F)*, *(G)*. After that, a new linguistic category—possibly an important solution—will be suggested, *(H)*. Finally in this section, the long announced analysis of the concept 'Semitic Religious Tradition' will ensue, first in a detailed investigation, *(I)*, then in two small remarks taking the results of *(I)* already into account: *(J)*, *(K)*.

(A) Cross-fertilisation

(Cf. above at note 190 on p. 89.) When the Old Testament—especially Deuteronomistic—concept of God's oneness appears in the Septuagint, it is dull to attest that it was "kept". Here, a concept re-appears in another linguistic tradition which actually had monotheistic tendencies itself.[214] Therefore in the Septuagint traditional Greek ideas of God's oneness get into a most exciting process of interference with the Jewish ones. This mutual transformation is underestimated if it is seen as a 'being kept'.

(B) Biblical Ǧāhilīya

(Cf. above at note 183 on p. 88.) When Paçacı accounts for the coming into being of *Isrāʾīlīyāt*, he adduces a sinking of the level of Biblical knowledge among the Arabs after the Koran's proclamation. But, one might ask, had that level been higher before? In this context, a hypothesis proffered by Angelika Neuwirth is relevant:[215] The Koranic text as we have it might only be one bit of Muhammad's preaching, which was in fact polymor-

---

214 E.g., Walter Burkert, "Gott. Antike", *Historisches Wörterbuch der Philosophie,* vol. 3, Basel 1974, cols. 721–5, col. 723. Cf. also remark (c.) of footnote 116, above on p. 59.

215 Angelika Neuwirth, "Vom Rezitationstext über die Liturgie zum Kanon: Zu Entstehung und Wiederauflösung der Surenkomposition im Verlauf der Entwicklung eines islamischen Kultus", Stefan Wild (ed.), *The Qurʾan as Text,* Leiden 1993, pp. 69–105.

phic. His preaching might have included more detailed narrative. If Neuwirth is right, then the Koran's mere alluding to narratives need not indicate a standard familiarity with Biblical narratives on the Arabian peninsula. Rather, the level of the Arabs' knowledge of the stories could then have been raised by Muhammad's own preaching.

(C) One

(Cf. above at note 188 on p. 89.) As the—almost irreproducible—title[216] of the article already suggested, the whole essay betrays intense philological ambition. Paçacı is quoting dictionary articles at length. Perhaps this should not only be seen as pedantic but also as a reflection of the laudable fact that he is using scholarly books hardly available in Turkey. But that does not make him completely safe from drowning in the riches of his material. So, he fails to mention two points of some relevance, after telling us what 'one' is in six Semitic languages.

a. To say that the word for 'one' is similar in many, perhaps all, languages of one linguistic family is not at the same time to say that the whole family shares the concept of monotheism, expressed by 'one' in some of them.
b. However, quite in line with Paçacı's train of thought, one might ask whether Sura 112's *aḥad,* unusual in Arabic, indeed *because* it is unusual, is in fact a direct—linguistically marked—intertextual reference to the Hebrew *æḥād* of Dtn 6:4. The title of the article already insinuated this punch line, and one is rather surprised not to be surprised by that insight somewhere in the article.[217]

(D) An Incarnation Symbol

(Cf. above at note 195 on p. 90.) Paçacı's exciting-sounding remark that 'rock' was, in Hellenism, an incarnation symbol, would have needed proof texts. The literature quoted by Paçacı does not deal with that remark. A

216 ""De Ki: Allah Bir'dir."[...]" Of course it was not reproduced correctly in the article's re-edition, Paçacı, *Kur'an,* p. 155.

217 The idea seems to have been uttered for the first time by Hirschfeld in 1902: Hartwig Hirschfeld, *New Researches into the Composition and Exegesis of the Qoran,* London 1902, p. 35. Quoted, though not accepted, by Ambros (cf. below, note 222). Arthur Jeffery, *The Foreign Vocabulary of the Qur'ān,* Baroda 1938 has no entry *'aḥad'.* In the final paragraphs of his article, upon discussing textual variants, Paçacı ‹en passant› comments upon the official text's *aḥad* as "keeping to the Semitic Tradition" (p. 182).

scholarly article, dated but not obsolete, deals with exactly this question and should be heard here. A. Wiegand wrote in 1890 that "in the Septuagint, and in general in the [scil., ancient] Greek translations, one can observe the intention to spiritualise the concept of God as much as possible, and therefore to weaken or remove all expressions which seem to confuse God and nature with each other". [218]

(E) Dropping the Rock

(Cf. above at note 196 on p. 90.) Paçacı's authority for the information that in Aramaic and Syriac translations, Biblical 'rock' is rendered 'strong one', is a 1961 notice by Raimund Köbert.[219] It *does* contain that information, but primarily it proposes a difficult hypothesis which Paçacı does not mention.[220] Since the article is not easily accessible in terms of libraries, language and lucidity, and because of the importance of the subject, it will be summarised here schematically.

1. Among the Koranic names of God, 'the rock' is missing.
2. This is striking, because
   a. 'the rock' is a particularly graphic name;
   b. 'the rock' must have been known as a name of God in the matrix of Islam.
3. In the Hebrew Old Testament, '*ṣûr*—rock' is prominent as a name of God.
4. In Rabbinic Judaism, like in the Greek translations of the Old Testament, it has been replaced by less graphic words.
5. Rabbinic Judaism, the background of Muhammad's Jewish informants, is one of the Koran's major matrices.
6. Therefore, it would be plausible for early Islam not to use 'the rock' for God, either.
7. *Aṣ-ṣamad* however can etymologically be shown to mean 'the rock'.
8. Its meaning was soon forgotten, because the tradition out of which 'the rock' as a name of God came had itself dropped the name 'the rock'.

---

[218] A. Wiegand, "Der Gottesname צור und seine Deutung in dem Sinne Bildner oder Schöpfer in der alten jüdischen Litteratur", *Zeitschrift für die alttestamentliche Wissenschaft*, vol. 10 (1890), pp. 85–96, p. 94.

[219] Raimund Köbert, "Das Gottesepitheton aṣ-ṣamad in Sure 112,2", *Orientalia*, N.S. vol. 30 (1961), pp. 204–5. Paçacı might have got the reference to this inconspicuous notice through Rudi Paret's commentary in loc., Rudi Paret, *Der Koran. Kommentar und Konkordanz*, Stuttgart [3]1986, p. 530. The information Paçacı quotes on Köbert's authority is however not in Paret's commentary.

[220] Nor does Paret ibid.

It seems that Köbert's point is the following. There was a *development* going on in Judaism in 7th century Arabia of which the Koran and early Islam are witnesses. While 'the rock' for God was a prominent element of Jewish religious language of an earlier stage, and thus got into the Koran, it was in these very decades falling out of the active Jewish vocabulary. Köbert's line of thought betrays a silent presupposition (made explicit above under (5.)) concerning the linguistic origin of the Koran, that not everybody would want to share: Jewish informants were influencing Koranic formulation. For those who accept this (or reinterpret it to be not an explanation of origin but a description of the linguistic atmosphere in which the Koran wanted to make itself understood) Köbert has an important point. Still, the hypothesis could be attacked from at least two sides:

1. If the Koran is here referring to the Old Testament rock imagery, why did it not use either a more common Arabic word meaning 'rock' *(ṣaḫr/ṣaḫra is* being used in 89:9//18:36, 31:16) or hold on to Hebrew and Aramaic words like *ṣûr,* etc., as it did in other cases, e.g., *kursī*[221]?
2. Within the strictly (possibly even: polemically) monotheist context of the Sura, 'rock' with its Old Testament connotations does not make much sense. After all, 'rock' contains ideas which counter the intention of Sura 112, e.g., "the rock who has begotten you" (Dtn 32:18).

These two attacks can be parried thus:

Conc. 1.: First of all, one might explain this through ‚Reimzwang' (prosodic compulsion: a rhyming word had to be found).[222] Secondly, and more plausibly, Schedl's idea (see next paragraph) might account for this.

Conc. 2.: There is a highly monotheistic-sounding rock passage in the Old Testament, which Köbert himself adduces: Ps 18:32//2Sam 22,32. The first half of the Islamic *šahāda* seems to be taken from the first half of this Old Testament verse, which in the Aramaic Targum and in Syriac reads *"lyt ʾlhʾ ʾlʾ Yy* (there is no god but YHWH)". The second half of that verse reads: "*Who* is a rock, if not our God?" So, "rock" does in fact have a field of connotation which might be heard as monotheistic.

221 *Kursī* (throne) should not only be seen as an example of the Koran's taking over imagery with its Hebrew or Aramaic word (Jeffery, *Foreign Vocabulary,* p. 249); it is also an instance of anthropomorphism kept.

222 This is in fact what, among others, Ambros contends in Arne A. Ambros, "Die Analyse von Sure 112. Kritiken, Synthesen, neue Ansätze", *Der Islam,* vol. 63 (1986), pp. 219–47, p. 243. But the explanation of a word through ‚Reimzwang' should not replace the explanation a word's meaning.

(F) Son of God

(Cf. above at note 198 on p. 91.) Paçacı considers the concept 'Son of God' as "foreign to Semitic Tradition".—In this context, the following fact may be considered. It was not in Hellenism that Jesus was first called, even exclusively, Son of God. Already Palestinian tradition allowed for such terminology and understood it in the following way: Jesus, endowed, anointed with Spirit becomes the Son of God. Hellenism did not introduce the formulation but a new understanding of it: Jesus is now seen as the epiphany (appearance) of the divine Son.[223] And even the formulation of the Son of God being begotten by God was formulated outside of Hellenism. It is the theology of Psalm 2, quoted in the Lucan account of Jesus's baptism (Lc 3,22), which designates Jesus's commissioning as his being begotten by God.[224] Being begotten by God need not imply being eternally begotten or being pre-existent. The idea of pre-existence did not come into Christology through the concept of being *begotten* by God but was deduced from Jesus's being *sent* by God. And even pre-existence does not imply being of one substance with the Father.[225] In short, the borderline of Hellenism is not where Paçacı wants it to be. Not all Christology is ipso facto un-Semitic, anti-monotheistic, incompatible with Old Testament thought.

Furthermore, an attempt to establish the interesting-sounding hypothesis that "begetting" language was dropped by Semitic Tradition because it came to be linked to Jesus's special relation with God would be welcome.

(G) Monotheism Challenged

(Cf. above at note 199 on p. 91.) It is a grave misunderstanding to see Christology as the claim that Jesus is one complete god. If that were the claim, Christianity would hardly be monotheistic. The claim is, in Rahner[226] just as in the Chalcedonian formula, that Jesus Christ is truly God[227]

---

223 Cf., e.g., Wolfhart Pannenberg, *Grundzüge der Christologie*, pp. 114–8, § 4.i.1.

224 p. 170, Paçacı himself states the fundamental role Ps 2:7 played in developing Christology. This however does not lead him to seeing an adoptionist Christology as a Semitic possibility.

225 Wolfhart Pannenberg, *Systematische Theologie*, vol. 1, Göttingen 1988, chapter 5.3.a.

226 In his 1972 Christology, Karl Rahner sums up Church teaching by quoting an earlier dictionary article of his own: "If thus, this one same Jesus is called Christ, then it is to be stated: *he* is true God—Wird somit dieser eine und selbe Jesus Christus genannt, so ist zu sagen: *dieser* ist wahrer Gott" (Rahner's italics). Karl Rahner, "Grundlinien einer systematischen Christologie", IDEM and Wilhelm Thüsing,

(and truly a human being). The article's wording does not meet Christian doctrinal claims:

a. not *"one* god" *(bir)* as if numbering separately in competition to God—rather, the wording of Jesus Christ's divinity goes back to his union with his "heavenly Father," in being obedient to Him, and in representing His eschatological salvation, thus excluding any kind of rival divinity;
b. not "complete" *(tam)* as if being seen independently—rather, Jesus Christ can only be seen in relation with his "heavenly Father", whom he trusts and represents;
c. not "god" *(tanrı),*[228] its lower case spelling implying countability, as if there were other gods beside the one God—rather, Christians say that Jesus is God because in Jesus, God wanted to communicate Himself fully (eschatologically) to creation; saying that Jesus is God says as much about God (who is then seen as the One communicating Himself in human history) as it does about Jesus Christ.

This is not to say that Paçacı has no point here. As Karl Rahner rightly sees, a formulation "Jesus Christ is truly God" challenges monotheism. But it does not turn monotheism into polytheism. Rather, it questions a dualist monotheism, which deals with God as with an object. If the formulation's proposition is true, our conceiving of God as only transcendent is insufficient.[229] The insufficiency of such a concept of God can also be seen outside of Christian theology. The truly infinite cannot have its limit at the finite.

Christologie – systematisch und exegetisch. Arbeitsgrundlagen für eine interdisziplinäre Vorlesung, Feiburg 1972, pp. 15–87, p. 73.

[227] Correctly capitalised also in Denzinger's edition of the definition, HENRICUS Denzinger and ADOLFUS Schönmetzer (eds.), *ENCHIRIDION SYMBOLORUM,* Freiburg [26]1976, NO. 301.

[228] Paçacı correctly capitalised it in another context two pages down, when translating the Nicene formula (p. 170). In the translation presented there, the words "seen and unseen" were taken as attributes of God *"görünebilen ve görünemeyen Allah'a inanırız*—we believe in the visible and invisible God". Actually, the two attributes can only refer to "all things" (genitive plural in the Greek original, Denzinger and Schönmetzer, *ENCHIRIDION,* NO. 125), of which "we believe" that God created them.

[229] Cf. the remarks by Wolfhart Pannenberg about the non-object personality of the Spirit in IDEM, *Grundzüge der Christologie,* § 4.iii.6. and his article "Nichtgegenständlichkeit Gottes," *Historisches Wörterbuch der Philosophie,* vol. 6, Basel 1984, cols. 803–5.

(Cf. above at note 194 on p. 90.) In the ongoing debate about the meaning of *aṣ-ṣamad* one important contribution, made more than twenty years ago, seems to be forgotten. As will be seen in due course, that contribution can serve to explain why such a difficult word was chosen, although a simple thing—rock—was meant, why many suggestions claiming to translate *'ṣamad'* were not simply conjectures from the context of the passage, and why its meaning can simultaneously be a clear Biblical allusion to 'the rock' and still, lexically, be a vague circumlocution meaning 'solid'. All this can be accounted for by a peculiar type of Jewish Diaspora intertextuality. The suggestion was made by Claus Schedl in 1981.[230] It can be systematised as follows:

1. Traditional explications of *ṣamad* include "to whom one flees" and "tough".
2. More likely than the existence of a (now lost) ancient Arabic translation of the Bible is the existence of an Arabic Targum, which was 'oral literature'; when in the Synagogal liturgy the Hebrew Bible was being recited, an oral vernacular translation was given for those who had problems in understanding the Hebrew text.
3. In this oral Targum, certain habitual renderings are likely to have established themselves as standard explanations of certain Hebrew words. For 'standard explanation' Schedl (p. 13) introduces the German term ‚Ersatzwort'.[231]
4. The Targumic tendency (as can be shown in the Aramaic, Syriac and Greek versions) is to render concrete metaphors concerning God through abstract words. Thus 'rock' became 'tough'.[232]

---

230 Claus Schedl, "Probleme der Koranexegese. Nochmals ṣamad in Sure 112,2", *Der Islam*, vol. 58 (1981), pp. 1–14. Other parts of that article contain what Schedl calls a "logotechnical" analysis, which will not be dealt with here. Schedl is mentioned as "taking his starting point [scil., concerning *ṣamad]* in Köbert" in the introduction to van Ess's account of early Muslim theologising on the *ṣamad* problem: Josef van Ess, *Theologie und Gesellschaft*, vol. 4, pp. 368–70, p. 368.

231 The word ‚Ersatzwort' is an established term in German linguistics. (Friedrich Kluge, *Etymologisches Wörterbuch der deutschen Sprache* (ed. by Elmar Seebold), Berlin [23]1999, p. xxii.) It designates a word which is deliberately introduced as a replacement for a foreign word. In Turkish, of course, examples of ‚Ersatzwörter' are legion, e.g., *'ulus/uluş'* for Ottoman *'millet'* (Geoffrey Lewis, *The Turkish Language Reform. A Catastrophic Success*, Oxford 1999, p. 55). In Old Testament scholarship and Jewish Studies, the word ‚Ersatzwort' is used to designate surrogate pronunciations of the sacrosanct tetragrammaton *'YHWH'*. Schedl's usage is a creative (possibly unconscious) and legitimate deviation from that terminology.

232 "Tough" is not exactly an abstract word. Still, the *tendency* is described well as "abstraction".

5. *Ṣamad* may be the Arabic standard explanation (NB, not claiming to be a literal translation), the ‚Ersatzwort', of *ṣûr.*

Schedl's theory has

a. great explicatory force. It explains why so many different explanations of *ṣamad* can be found. Many of them are neither mere guesses, nor are they strict definitions of the word; rather, they bring back to life the richness of the Old Testament 'rock' imagery, which is actually intended by the Targumic standard explanation;
b. great plausibility. A similar process of ‚Ersatzwort' establishing can be observed today when people recite texts difficult to understand, including the Koran. And a 7th century Synagogal liturgy in the Ḥiǧāz is conceivable as ‚Sitz im Leben' for a certain type of Arabic vocabulary;
c. great heuristic value. By introducing the category of ‚Ersatzwort', Schedl has in fact discovered a level of semantic relation between two words of different languages which is neither equivalence nor conjecture.

Paçacı's claim that it is the Old Testament *'ṣûr'* which is behind the Koranic *'ṣamad'* may sound rather far-fetched. But with a theoretical grounding like the one proposed by Claus Schedl the two words' nearness becomes understandable.[233]

(I) Semitic Religious Tradition

(Cf. above at note 182 on p. 87.) Mehmet Paçacı happily and frequently claims the existence of a "Semitic Religious Tradition". The term is problematic on more than one ground.

1. Its relation to Christianity is not clear. Paçacı is likely to say, Christianity is part of that tradition in so far as it is monotheist. In fact, he seems to use "Semitic" as a synonym for 'monotheistic'.

---

233 One might also adduce this argument: (a) The Koran *has* taken over the Hebrew word for 'rock', *ṣûr*. It appears in the form *'ṭūr'*. (Jeffery, *Foreign vocabulary,* pp. 206–7.) So, why should there have been the need for another word meaning 'rock', especially when a reference to Old Testament rock imagery is supposed to be implied? Is that not a strong point against the explication of *'ṣamad'* as 'rock'? (b) At all ten occurrences, the Koranic *'ṭūr'* has a specific meaning. It designates Mount Sinai. (c) With the most obvious word for 'rock' (at least in Old Testament contexts), *'ṭūr'*, already occupied for that particular signification, the Koranic vocabulary needed another word, if 'rock' was to be expressed. (d) Therefore, *'ṣamad'* was in fact a necessary complement of the Koran's linguistic inventory, because it was understood to mean 'rock' and to have a Biblical association but it was not understood to mean a particular geographical place.

2. Thus, the term is too general, since it is bound, by its own wording, to include religions which are clearly not monotheistic but expressed themselves in an indisputably Semitic language.[234]
3. On the other hand, it builds up a monotheistic camp which excludes monotheistic tendencies elsewhere. Non-Semitic 'monotheistic revolutions' like Akhenaton's[235] or Zoroaster's[236] find no place.
4. Likewise, it excludes anything Greek,[237] thus missing the important contributions of Greek philosophy to clarifying monotheist theology.
5. It implies a causal link between a family of languages (if not a race) and religious beliefs but does not bother to discuss the problems involved.[238]
6. It includes the a-historical claim that Israel has always been monotheistic. All steps of the history of Israel's belief before reaching what should properly be called monotheism are thus neglected. It does not distinguish between monotheism and other forms of worshipping one god only.[239]

---

[234] Cf., e.g., James B. Pritchard, *Ancient Near Eastern Texts Relating to the Old Testament,* Princeton [3]1974, and especially the 4000 page OPUS MAGNUM: Otto Kaiser (ed.), *Texte aus der Umwelt des Alten Testaments,* vols. 1–3, Gütersloh 1981–95, with a supplement *(Ergänzungslieferung),* Gütersloh 2001. Both works present clearly non-monotheistic texts, translated from Semitic languages like Sumerian or Acadian.

[235] Cf., e.g., Stolz, *Monotheismus,* p. 74 (3.4.1).

[236] Cf., e.g., Stolz, *Monotheismus,* p. 80 (3.4.3).

[237] This leads Paçacı to the claim that God's "property of unbegottenness is a characteristic of Semitic theology" (p. 167). The claim misses that the concept of originlessness is a classical Greek one, that it can be traced back to the earliest documents of Western philosophy (Parmenides frg. 8,27: being (τὸ ἔον */tò éon)* is ἄναρχον */ánarchon),* that God's "anarchy" (in the sense of originlessness) was stated by the Cappadocian Fathers, and that it found its way into scholastic theology in the form of the Latin term: divine ASEITAS (aseity, being caused by oneself, lit. 'through-Him-ness'). Cf. the philosophical dictionaries, e.g., "Aseität", *Historisches Wörterbuch der Philosophie,* vol. 1, Basel 1971, cols. 583–4.

[238] The origin of the concept and its possibly racist background are discussed in detail above, p. 93.

[239] On (the history of scholarship about) the development of Old Testament monotheism, cf., e.g., Rainer Albertz, *Religionsgeschichte Israels in alttestamentlicher Zeit,* vol. 1, *Von den Anfängen bis zum Ende der Königszeit,* Göttingen [2]1996, p. 98 (2.24): "Wohl kann ... von einem Monotheismus oder auch nur von einer Monolatrie im strengen Sinn zumindest in vorexilischer Zeit nicht gesprochen werden.—At least concerning the pre-exilic era one can certainly not speak of monotheism, not even of monolatria strictly speaking." But two distinctions have to be made. *Firstly* the contcepts involved have to be clear. To worship only one god is not necessarily to be a monotheist. Four terms should be kept apart, viz., henotheism, henolatria, monolatria and monotheism. Georg Braulik proposes this scheme:

7. On the other hand, by setting itself up to be a generic for several religions, at least for Judaism and Islam, it is conducive to a view which misses the differences and profiles of each religion.[240]
8. It suggests that monotheism is a matter of tradition rather than, e.g., insight.

Even if the term cannot be saved, is there a meaningful idea behind it? What Paçacı wants to prove is that monotheism, having to face all kinds of threats along the way, got more and more clarified. The *problem* with this view is that it illegitimately mixes historical and systematic considerations:

1. It pretends to know what monotheism is and therefore believes to have an easy job labelling everything as soiling and backsliding that does not fit its preconceived idea of monotheism.
2. At the same time, it *sociologises* monotheism, making it an exclusive strand. If you are, e.g., Aristotle, you are not a member of the monothe-

---

polytheism	*monotheism*	*worship of one single god*	*within one's own religious system*	*outside of one's own religious system*
henotheism		temporary	other gods	other gods
henolatria		constant	other gods	other gods
monolatria		constant	no other gods	other gods
	monotheism	constant	no other gods	no other gods

If this terminology is accepted, one must consider Israel's belief in YHWH until the Babylonian Exile to be a monolatria and thus polytheistic. Pre-exilic Israel had no relations with other gods besides YHWH but did not reject the existence of other gods in other religions, e.g., of neighbouring peoples. That is how "*YHWH æḥād*—YHWH is one" of Deuteronomy 6:4 must be understood. What caused the development from monolatria to monotheism? This leads us to the other distinction. *Secondly* to describe Israel's belief before the exile as standard monolatria is to miss its unique tendency. (Georg Braulik, "Das Deuteronomium und die Geburt des Monotheismus" 1985, IDEM, *Studien zur Theologie des Deuteronomiums,* Stuttgart 1988, pp. 257–300. IDEM, "Monotheismus. Biblisch-theologisch. Altes Testament", *Lexikon für Theologie und Kirche,* vol. 7, Freiburg ^{3}1998, cols. 424–6, col. 424:) From the start, Israel's experience is that YHWH claims exclusivity. And that means more than exclusive worship. It means radical delimitation from other populaces and their social hierarchies—social hierarchies, which reflect the hierarchies among the gods. Even when Israel speaks of heavenly assemblies and sons of God, other gods are portrayed as deprived of power, of individualities, names, and histories vis-à-vis YHWH. These gods will later be called "angels". When the egalitarian agricultural society called 'Israel' worshipped YHWH as their personal God, their monolatria was already leaning towards monotheism.—A similar picture should be drawn of Muhammad's earliest belief.

240 Behind this, the Koranic theology of religions seems to lurk, which sees all religions as equally furnished systems. A central concept of Old Testament theology is *election:* God chooses His people, Israel. (In fact, He chooses Israel over against other peoples, most of which must be called Semitic.) Through election, God is entering into a relation with human beings. In the history of this relation something *happens* to both sides. The Koranic outlook would not want to agree with that.

ist lineage. You must be a spiritual heir of Abraham. There is no other entrance to the club.

3. This is fatal because it deals with all challenges to 'our own private monotheism' as if they challenged monotheism itself, trying to polytheise it. Could it also be that those challenges actually ask serious, philosophically relevant questions? Could it be that they challenge whether 'our own private monotheism' is *monotheistic enough?*

The *strength* of this view is, that

1. it has inadvertently discovered a recurring pattern of monotheistic discourse. The accusation of Christian belief and theology as not, or not really, monotheistic, which may be found in Koranic passages like Sura 112, has in fact an ancient tradition.[241] Discussions in documents as early as the Gospel of John reflect the Jewish accusation of Christians as not keeping monotheism (John 10,33),[242] and the most likely historical reason that brought Jesus to death was his being accused of blasphemy. Even if the term "Semitic Religious Tradition" may be inadequate, it is important to see that the Koranic and Muslim accusations of Christianity conform to an ancient stereotype, and that there is a relation between Rabbinic Judaism of the first centuries C.E. and early Islam in that both contrast themselves as impeccably monotheistic over against Christianity;
2. it provides a motivation for comparing the Koran with other religious texts. Thus the Koran is taken out of its monolithic loneliness. Its textual relatives put it in perspective.

As was observed and discussed above (p. 78), Mehmet Paçacı agreed with Fazlur Rahman that the basic aim of the Koran is an ethical one. Surprisingly however, some of the most detailed Koranic studies by Paçacı, including his *Iḫlāṣ* article, do not even touch upon an ethical question. The article is historical, linguistic, exegetical in method, and its subject is theological theology, i.e., the doctrine of God. It is, so to speak, completely unethical. Is Paçacı silently admitting that he does not believe in ethical reductionism, or has he moved away from an earlier position, or does he simply write about something he would still claim as not belonging to the basic aim of the Koran, or do we have to re-define concepts?

241 "Has a tradition" is not to say that there is necessarily a causal link between the individual phenomena of the recurring pattern. It is simply to say, 'there were older instances of the same pattern'.

242 Ulrich Wilckens sees the central point of the Fourth Gospel in the question how God's uniqueness squares with Jesus's singularity as revealer: Ulrich Wilckens, *Das Evangelium nach Johannes*, Göttingen 1998, p. 333.

Let us call to mind a fundamental idea of Fazlur Rahman's hermeneutics. He thinks that one can distil from the Koranic commands a general normative system, which is ready to be re-applied throughout the ages. Under the text, one can discover an ever-valid subtext. Is that not the same way of thinking which produces the concept of a "Semitic Religious Tradition"? Beneath the texts we have an ever-valid position: monotheism, which re-expresses itself throughout the ages according to each time's respective challenges. One problem with this way of thinking is that it names the unnameable. It tries to define something—and definitions will always use words, which have histories and which are hampered by their own limited perspective—at one point in history and therefore cuts off its vital growth. If you operate with a once-for-all-time system of norms you will not be able to integrate new discoveries relevant for ethics. And if you operate with a once-for-all-time concept of monotheism you cannot take the challenges of new insights relevant to the doctrine of God.

(J) Transition and Continuity

(Cf. above at note 370 on p. 165.) In Paçacı's account, the monotheist tradition was re-expressing its old tenet (God's oneness) in new words *('aṣ-ṣamad')* because the traditional word 'the rock' had acquired a new connotation. The thesis contains two disputable elements:

a. 'Rock' was an incarnation symbol.
b. There has been a consistent monotheist tradition, which only chose new linguistic ways of expressing itself.

But the thesis is not depending on these two elements. Even if neither of them can be established, one could argue: the Koran came into being, linguistically speaking, at a point of transition from concrete metaphors to abstraction. And *aṣ-ṣamad* is an instance of this transition. And this may only be a sub-thesis to the main thesis that there is a continuity from Old Testament thought to the Koran.

(K) Changing Tradition

(Cf. above at note 200 on p. 91.) Neither Paçacı nor the article[243] he cites achieve the task of demonstrating that there was a tradition in the sense of

243 Marilyn R. Waldman, "New Approaches to "Biblical" Materials in the Qur'ān", *The Muslim World,* vol. 75 (1985), pp. 1–13. She makes the valid point that the Biblical narratives cannot count as *"ur-*stories" (p. 3) for the Koran, since both are mere flickers of a vast tradition.

a continuously held stance. Rather than conceiving a tradition as a stable root sending up young shoots here and there throughout the ages, one has to see that the tradition itself is changing.

Conclusion: Towards Muslim Fundamental Theology

Professor Paçacı's methodological reflections and suggestions are a major breakthrough. He makes the valid point that the historical situation of today's reader should consciously play a role in Koranic exegesis. And when he is not talking about exegesis but is actually doing it? Then, the readers' present situation comes to bear because Paçacı takes into account the views of today's "Orientalists" (very critically) and (happily) the discoveries of contemporary Biblical exegetes. This can be seen as expressing awareness of the present historical situation. But his awareness seems to be restricted to one-and-a-half strand of scholarship. If a modern theologian of such high philosophical qualification writes about God's oneness the reader is hoping to get new insights into questions like these: What does it mean for God to be one? What is it not to be a polytheist? Can oneness be reassessed terminologically? How could the Christian challenges be discussed with high philosophical standards? What are the life consequences of monotheism? What is the relation between monotheism and ethics? In other words, what does it mean to believe in one God only—anthropologically, existentially, even spiritually? Subjects like 'meaning of life', 'trust', 'love' seem equally involved as 'selfishness', 'liberation' and 'ecstasy'.[244]

These questions are listed here because it is from a thinker like Paçacı that one can expect more answers. In the present author's perception, Turkish theology is underexposed in modern *Kelâm.* This may be due partly to the structure of academic theology in Turkey.[245] Even though it has a strong focus on historical research, in systematic disciplines it still operates scholastically in a pejorative sense of the word: it obtains the questions to be asked from the traditional formulations themselves rather than from the conflicts and collisions of tradition and a modern mind. Mehmet Paçacı is admirably courageous—on the verge of being adventur-

---

244 Can the anthropologically central category of ecstasy be cross-fertilised with the concept *'islām'* in the sense of 'handing oneself over'? Cf. Wolfhart Pannenberg, *Systematische Theologie,* vol. 1, Göttingen 1988, pp. 125; 464–5, and IDEM, *Anthropologie in theologischer Perspektive. Religiöse Implikationen anthropologischer Theorie,* Göttingen 1983, p. 34, where he takes up Helmuth Plessner's concept of human being's "excentric position", which forms the basic orientation fulfilled in ecstasy.

245 Cf. above, p. 59.

ous—in taking up ideas of non-Muslim authors. He has thus substantially helped to open up the dialogue between modernity and Islam. His discovery of Gadamer's philosophy for Koran exegesis is crucial. But that type of cross-fertilisation has only just begun. Gadamer's observations can lead even further. If he draws our attention to the fact that tradition has shaped the interpreters and their ways of asking the text more than they themselves are aware of it, one might go on and ask: is the restriction of Koranic exegesis to ethical questions not itself an instance of a text's effective history? If one becomes aware of the effect, one can start handling it. Mehmet Paçacı has not yet ventured into having the dialogue of interpretation re-shape the questions to be asked and thus shape the theological re-expressions of the Muslim creed. But Paçacı should be seen as a man capable of this next step, in other words, of founding a Muslim fundamental theology.

Chapter 2
Adil Çiftçi: The Koran as Ethical Order

Adil Çiftçi was born in 1963 in Niksar (Province of Tokat, northeast of Ankara). He attended an *İmam Hatip* school and then studied at Ankara Üniversitesi's Theological Faculty, from which he graduated in 1985. In 1986, he took up further studies in the Sociology of Religion Department of the Theological Faculty at Dokuz Eylül Üniversitesi, İzmir. Between 1988 and 1990 he studied in London and, back to Turkey, was granted his doctorate in 1997. He is presently assistant lecturer in Sociology of Religion at Dokuz Eylül University.

Adil Çiftçi has worked extensively on, and translated several works by, Fazlur Rahman. In a recent study,[246] Çiftçi presents Fazlur Rahman's method of interpreting the Koran and by applying it himself develops a new Islamic perspective. As this will lead us also to a deeper understanding of Fazlur Rahman's hermeneutics, a detailed discussion of Çiftçi is now in place.

Adil Çiftçi's paradigm is Interpretative Sociology.[247] That is to say, he is trying to analyse Fazlur Rahman's life and work sociologically but with a special interest in "thought and mind" *(fikir ve zihin).* (p. 15) This leads Çiftçi to asking in his analysis not only "What does Fazlur Rahman say?", but also "What does he want to do, how and in which context?". (p. 18)[248] Çiftçi builds his presentation of Fazlur Rahman's hermeneutics basically on three of Fazlur Rahman's books.[249] Çiftçi betrays however, great familiarity with Fazlur Rahman's other writings, too. The starting point of Çiftçi's expositions is formed by Fazlur Rahman's view of present-day conditions. Today, Islam is in a crisis, Adil Çiftçi reports him to say, and the only salvation from it is "ethical thinking". (p. 19) Fazlur Rahman's method is intended as, and proves to be—in Çiftçi's eyes—a method of modernising Islam. (p. 117) Çiftçi, though not grouping them together in

---

[246] "Rethinking Islam with Fazlur Rahman": Adil Çiftçi, *Fazlur Rahman ile İslam'ı Yeniden Düşünmek,* Ankara (Kitâbiyât) 2000. Page numbers in the following section will refer to that book.

[247] Cf. Gibson Burrell, "Interpretative Sociology", IDEM and Gareth Morgan (eds.), *Sociological Paradigms and Organisational Analysis,* London 1979.

[248] Adil Çiftçi seems to miss the point that, without using the term, Fazlur Rahman reads the Koran himself with a kind of Interpretative Sociology.

[249] Fazlur Rahman, *Islam;* IDEM, *Islam & Modernity;* IDEM, *Major Themes of the Qur'an,* Minneapolis ^{2}1989.

this way, seems to see Fazlur Rahman's importance in what might be called his two methodological axioms.

On the one hand, Çiftçi rightly reports Fazlur Rahman's emphasis on "what the Text says", (p. 83) in other words his Koranic orientation. Fazlur Rahman's arguments for it are:

a. No other thing is considered as *divine* by Muslims as the Koran.
b. The Koran contains *all* revelations, it is the "comprehensive guide".
c. The Koran has always been regulating Muslims' *behaviour.*
d. The Koran is not only about metaphysics and individual ethics, it can also answer all *social* questions. (p. 96)

On the other hand, he characterises Fazlur Rahman as a "rationalist ethicist" *(rasyonalist ahlakçı),* (p. 18) by which Çiftçi means that Fazlur Rahman wanted to

a. draw from the Koran °a system of how to behave *(davranış sistemi);* (p. 18) and
b. stress the necessity of using reason for the solution of problems.

Fazlur Rahman's view was that revelation and reason never collide; traditional and rational thinking however do. (p. 18) Islamic ethics is defined by Fazlur Rahman as "a religious ethics grounded in the thought of God's universal reign" *(Allah'in evrene hakimiyeti fikrine dayanan dinî bir ahlak).* (p. 21)

Evaluation: Ethics in History

The first axiom brings the Muslim discussion about how to live Islam back to what is indisputably divine, Islamic, common ground. The second axiom however is a fresh approach to the old text. It presupposes the distinction between legal (i.e., containing concrete stipulations) and ethical (i.e., containing principles). And it amounts to rejecting the Muslim understanding of the Koran as *immediately legally* relevant. (p. 86) By seeing the Koran as an exemplary realisation of God's will for one situation in history, the legislative force of the text is reduced to the status of a model. What is to be realised during the generations is not that example of old, but the will, the intention, the ethics for which it was an example. This is how the Koran becomes ethically relevant.

So, according to Fazlur Rahman, the Koran is to be read not as a legal text to be obeyed slavishly but as an exemplary concretisation of a certain ethics. (pp. 86; 116) It would not suffice to state this bluntly. Two challenges could be raised against his view.

1. If the Koran is only an ethical, not also a legal book, why has no Muslim in the course of the tradition, nor the rightly guided *umma* throughout history dealt with the Koran in that way?
2. Why, if the Koran is an ethical book, does it come across as a legal one?

As if in response to the first challenge, Fazlur Rahman has tried to show that Muslims throughout the ages have in fact done exactly this: read the Koran as an ethical book.[250] Çiftçi does not explore that question in detail. But he offers an elaborate account of Fazlur Rahman's hermeneutics, based on his concept of revelation. This should be understood as a reaction to the second objection.

Çiftçi: Redefining Revelation

What is the metaphysical context of revelation?

a. God, on the one hand, is transcendent;
b. human beings, on the other hand, are deficient as regards ethical knowledge and practice.

In this situation, God helps, and He does so through revelation, i.e., via prophecy. For a rational mind, the concept of revelation is not without problems. Çiftçi's analysis of Fazlur Rahman's view of what revelation is, can be summed up in five points. (p. 64)

1. Revelation is a spiritual *(ruhi)* experience—as opposed to a physical one.
2. It involves an expansion of the recipient's self.
3. It entails no locomotion—e.g., in Muhammad's *miʿrāǧ* (ascension) experience.
4. Yet, the reality experienced in it is more-than-subjective *(öznel hislerini aşan).*[251]
5. The experience wraps itself in words.

Revelation is brought about by 'the Spirit' *(Ruh)*. But what precisely is that to say? Fazlur Rahman's concept of 'the Spirit' is the key to his view of revelation. Three different descriptions must be held together for a full understanding of Fazlur Rahman's concept of the Spirit:

---

250 In fact, this is what Fazlur Rahman calls *'iǧtihād':* to apply a rule to a new situation. That is at least how his slightly contorted five lines definition should probably be understood, IDEM, *Islam & Modernity*, p. 8: "the effort to understand the meaning of a relevant text or precendent in the past, containing a rule, and to alter that rule by extending or restrincting or otherwise modifiyining it in such a manner that a new situation can be subsumed under it by a new solution". Cf. also, IDEM, *Islamic Methodology in History*, Karachi 1965.

251 Lit.: going beyond his subjective feelings.

1. The Spirit is not a being outside of the prophet, not a third being coming between God and Muhammad. Considering the word 'angel' is helpful here. 'Revelation is mediated by an angel' is for Fazlur Rahman another way of saying: that which brings about revelation is neither separate from, nor plainly identical with God. (p. 65)
2. The Spirit is the content *(içerik, öz)* of revelation. (p. 67)
3. The Spirit is the Prophet's capacity to produce the appropriate verse in any situation. (p. 67)

Because of the ontological difference between prophets—human beings, i.e., creatures—and God, it is wrong to say that prophets are a part of God; they are the recipients of revelation, and God does not even speak with them directly. (p. 69) God's eternal word does not hit the prophet as if from outside. Thus, what people call 'inspiration' is in fact a fusion of horizons between God's Spirit and the prophet. (p. 72) Therefore, Fazlur Rahman was able to say—and it notoriously caused tumult in his home country—that the Koran as we have it is Muhammad's word. By this however Fazlur Rahman was not rejecting the Koran's divine status. The prophet is endowed with the ability to produce what is according to God's will. Put differently, the Koran is at the same time God's and Muhammad's word. (p. 72) Consequently, Fazlur Rahman rejects portraits of Muhammad's role as God's loudspeaker *(hoparlör).* (p. 75) It was the Spirit of revelation which gave Muhammad the unique mixture of idealism and realism that enabled him to withstand the massive resistance in his home milieu. (p. 78) This amounts to saying that the Spirit is Muhammad's ‚Sendungsbewußtsein' (conviction of his mission; prophetic self-understanding).

Reconsidering the crisis of Islam which Fazlur Rahman diagnosed, and the therapy he prescribed—ethical thinking—what he envisaged is now much clearer: if Islam is not to be irrelevant today, what can be done? 'Apply the Koran!', is the stock answer to that. It is, according to Fazlur Rahman, too simple, because it would mean that

a. we had to return to the Middle Ages,
b. we had to rely on an historical, contingent, accidental[252] Islam, rather than on the Koran and the *Ḥadīṯ,*

[252] The latter two words are neither Fazlur Rahman's nor Çiftçi's, but seem to capture the point both are trying to make. (On 'contingent' cf. below, footnote 370). Neither is the usage of 'Islam' with the indefinite article Fazlur Rahman's (he has "historical Islam" *(Islam & Modernity,* p. 147), and Çiftçi translates, of course, *"tarihî İslam"* (p. 94)). But this Turkish wording is open to the rendering "an … Islam", which breaks up the monolithic image of Islam implied in the easy answers. The problem with "an … Islam", on the other hand, is that it might suggest a splitting

c. nostalgically, an earlier Islam would have become "our God". (p. 94)

This implies an important caveat. 'Returning to the Koran' is ambiguous. It can mean

1. submitting to the Koranic commands; or
2. trying to understand the ethical system which expresses itself in those commands (and submitting to that system).

This ambiguity is due to two differing possible views of what the Koran, what revelation actually is. Is it the text as we have it, or is it God's will within that text? Fazlur Rahman, of course, holds the second position. Therefore, he finds himself cast into the middle of the questions of understanding, and he can write: approaching the Koran without method is to lose it. "It" is more precisely the Koran's ethical and metaphysical world view. (p. 95)[253]

Discussing Fazlur Rahman Discussing Gadamer Discussing Betti

Even when handling problems of understanding, understanding itself is a problem. The locus classicus of hermeneutical reflection in the work of Fazlur Rahman is his introduction to *Islam & Modernity*.[254] Çifçti quotes from that passage intensely. He misses however to point out the problems, caused by misunderstanding, in that passage. In order to avoid further misunderstandings, the perspective has for a moment to be shifted. The original texts have to be revisited and the discussion with Fazlur Rahman has to be taken up directly.

Fazlur Rahman's double movement/three steps approach[255] is a method for the normative application of a certain text to a certain situation. It therefore implies, and quite expressly so, that—together with the present situation and the intervening tradition—the meaning of a text "can be sufficiently objectively known". *(Islam & Modernity,* p. 8) Fazlur Rahman seems to feel the boldness of his claim, especially in the face of Hans-Georg Gadamer.[256] He considers Gadamer's view as "radically opposed",

of that unity of the religious community, which, if not understood as uniformity, actually allows for various *forms of living* (the one) Islam without hereticising otherness QUA otherness.

253 This point will be taken up as *(D) How Necessary Is Method?*, below, p. 129.

254 Esp. pp. 8–11.

255 Cf. above, footnote 140.

256 Fazlur Rahman has apparently studied Hans-Georg Gadamer's 1960 work, *Wahrheit und Methode,* in an English translation *(Truth and Method,* New York 1975). Unfortunately, he makes reference only to that translation's pagination, which makes it difficult to check citations. The authoritative—though not always the best (cf. below,

indeed destructive, to his own view, and agrees with a characterisation of Gadamer as "hopelessly subjective". *(Islam & Modernity,* p. 9) This accusation makes yet another shift of perspective necessary. An eye has to be cast on Gadamer's own writing. Gadamer himself develops his hermeneutical ideas by contrasting them over against the hermeneutics of Emilio Betti.[257] Since Fazlur Rahman uses much of Betti's language, and explicitly sides with him,[258] a brief schematisation of the latter's model can serve as our starting point here. For Betti, this is how understanding works:

1. Someone produces something, e.g., a text. This production can be described thus. An inner reality casts its shape onto the outer world. In Betti's (Hegelian) words: a mind creates forms of its objectivations (reifications); these forms of the mind's objectivations separate themselves from the mind.
2. Someone else understands this, e.g., reads the text. In Betti's words: a mind brings those forms back into such an inner whole which also created them and from which they separated themselves—back to a mind.
3. This mind (the interpreter) is not identical with the first mind (the creator). But since the two minds, being both human, are relatives, the reassembly of the forms works.
4. Creation and interpretation can be seen as movements: mind-to-objectivation; objectivation-to-mind. Interpretation is, consequently, the *inversion* of creation.

What has Fazlur Rahman made of this model? He thinks along Betti's lines, in that

a. his "first movement" of the interpretative process is backward (even the "movements" language is likely to be inspired by Betti's trains of thought);
b. he thinks of the creative mind which produced the text as the key to accurate understanding: getting into that mind—seeing its intentions—is vital.

But Fazlur Rahman has modified Betti's model in two aspects.

---

footnote 275)—edition of the text is: IDEM, *Wahrheit und Methode,* vols. 1–2, Tübingen 1990–93.

257 On p. 393 of his 1961 article "Hermeneutik und Historismus", IDEM, *Wahrheit und Methode,* vol. 2, pp. 387–424, which he appended to *Wahrheit und Methode* in 1965, Gadamer quotes from a German article by Emilio Betti of 1954: "Zur Grundlegung einer allgemeinen Auslegungslehre". Emilio Betti is an Italian historian of jurisprudence; his OPUS MAGNUM is *Teoria generale dell' Interpretazione,* vols. 1–2, Milano 1955.

258 Fazlur Rahman (seems to know and) quotes Betti only as quoted by Gadamer and refers precisely to the passage schematised in four points here.

a. He considers not the mind in isolation but the mind as confronted with a certain situation to be the producer of the relevant forms.
b. He adds to the description of interpretation his "second movement" as a constituent part of any hermeneutical process: returning to today's situation with an application.

Both modifications are valid points. But let us see what Hans-Georg Gadamer has to say against Betti. Gadamer criticises Betti's model as "strict psychologism of Romantic character".[259] This goes especially against what has been marked here as Betti's third point. In order to over-state Gadamer's problem:

1. Betti's objectivations—contrary to what their name implies—speak only within a subject, have no objective lives by themselves. They have not cut their umbilical cords, have not gained autarky. Therefore, Betti is stuck in reproductive interpretation and cannot see that a fresh view at an old object can very well produce a new *but faithful* interpretation of it.
2. The fact that the producing mind and the understanding mind are relatives is a weak basis for the interpretation to work. Being relatives does not mean having exactly the same structure. If understanding is seen as re-arranging the objectivations as they were in the producing mind, who guarantees that the two relatives are not different in precisely that point which would have been essential for the correct re-arrangement?

These are certainly serious criticisms. In the light of that, it does no longer seem fair to characterise Gadamer as "hopelessly subjective". Why does Fazlur Rahman still insist on that characterisation? This should become clear when we answer the question which alternative methodology of understanding Gadamer offers.

He offers—no method at all,[260] although the title of his book might imply he does.[261] Rather, he only describes—transcendentally, in the Kantian sense of exposing the conditions of the possibility of knowledge—how ‚Geisteswissenschaften' (the humanities) and thus human self-understanding actually operate. What are Gadamer's hermeneutical core points?

---

259 *Wahrheit und Methode,* vol. 2, p. 393.

260 E.g., *Wahrheit und Methode,* vol. 2, p. 394. But already in the corpus of the text, e.g., ibid., vol. 1, p. 300 (part 2, ii.1.b.β).

261 Gadamer said, the idea to title his book *"Wahrheit und Methode"* only came to his mind when the editor remarked he couldn't figure out what *"Grundzüge einer philosophischen Hermeneutik"* meant, which consequently was degraded to the book's subtitle. *(Wahrheit und Methode,* vol. 2, p. 493)

1. The starting point of understanding. Ontological hermeneutics sees that when setting out to read a text you are not a tabula rasa. You have already got ideas and questions. But they need not come in the way of your understanding. Rather, they are a part of the understanding process. Therefore, Gadamer, following Martin Heidegger, describes understanding as a circular process, which is however not a vicious circle, in which one would end up from where one started. One constantly re-develops the intention, attention, tentative comprehension (‚Vorhabe, Vorsicht und Vorgriff')[262] which one already had, in dialogue with the matter (‚Sache')[263]. Therefore, "understanding is to be considered, not so much as an act of the subjectivity, but as an entering into a process of tradition."[264]
2. The target of understanding. Gadamer sets a motto over the second part of his *Wahrheit und Methode,* upon which he never comments explicitly but which captures the point of his criticism against psychological hermeneutics. The motto is from the table talks of—Martin Luther: "QUI NON INTELLIGIT RES, NON POTEST EX VERBIS SENSUM ELICERE.—If you do not understand the matter, you cannot make sense of the words."[265] Rather than romantically considering a text merely as an expression of life, understanding means to take seriously the text's truth claim.[266]
3. The understandings of understanding. One can juxtapose the former two points plus Gadamer's alternatives, and his division of the history of hermeneutics into three epochs: the historical, the psychological, and the ontological. Historical hermeneutics has a problem with the starting point of understanding, psychological hermeneutics with its target. Of course, Gadamer considers himself, together with his teacher Martin Heidegger, to be the final phase's pioneer.

---

262 *Wahrheit und Methode,* vol. 1, p. 271 (part 2, ii.1.a.α). At the same time, ‚Vorhabe, Vorsicht und Vorgriff' can, on a more literal level, be heard as meaning: preliminary possession, preliminary view and preliminary grasp.

263 ‚Sache' includes both 'object' (the text) and 'subject' (reality; what the text is about).

264 Ibid., p. 295 (part 2, ii.1.b.β).

265 Lit.: "if you don't understand the matter, you cannot make sense of the words."

266 Ibid., p. 302.

Interpreting an ancient text *historically*[267] (‚historisch') means trying to remove out of one's sight everything that happened after the text was written. One wants to see the text in its 'then-setting'.[268] The aim is interpreting the text "out of itself".[269]—Gadamer's comment on this type of hermeneutics is the following: all that happened between the composition of the text and now has an influence on one's ways of understanding. If one does not notice that influence, it runs out of control.[270]

Romanticism, in the wake of the historical method, wanted to liberate the author's creative individual mind in its otherness from the grips of dogmatic interests in what is to be believed. It therefore wanted to interpret the text psychologically. This entails transposing oneself into the author's inner situation, and, from that divinised position, trying to create again the author's creation. The text is treated as a work of art. Whether or not it corresponds with reality is unimportant. Understanding a text is, then, understanding the author's (possibly unconscious) intention.—Gadamer's comment on this type of hermeneutics is the following: although it has the advantage of seeing the individual text undogmatically, in its strangeness, as an expression of an individual life, it has the drawback of putting the authority of texts over the authority of truth.[271]

Ontological hermeneutics does not offer another method that promises to lead one to unprejudiced understanding; only after understanding, one will be able to tell the helpful from the hindering prejudices.[272] Rather, it starts from the observation that understanding is a °typically human life factor (‚Existenzial'). Therefore, it must be seen within the interaction of the other typically human life factors, e.g., human beings' developing in history. Thus, the temporal distance between text and interpreter is discovered as hermeneutically productive.[273] Gadamer's call can be rendered thus: Don't try to transpose yourself—historically—into the text's 'then-situation', or—romantically—into the author's inner situation. Rather, bring the text's horizon into your horizon (everything you can see from

---

267 Here, "historically" renders ‚historisch', rather than ‚geschichtlich', which would mean the exact opposite. Paçacı's call for an "historical" understanding of the Koran, e.g., (above, p. 77) clearly means ‚geschichtlich', because he takes post-textual conditions productively into account. But there is no established terminology for this distinction in Turkish.

268 This is not Gadamer's formulation.

269 *Wahrheit und Methode,* vol. 1, p. 180 (part 2, i.1.a.α).

270 Ibid., p. 305 (part 2, ii.1.d).

271 Ibid., p. 201 (part 2, i.b).

272 Ibid., p. 301 (part 2, ii.1.d).

273 Ibid., p. 302 (part 2, ii.1.d), with reference to Martin Heidegger.

your own point of view), i.e., understand the text's discoveries from your 'now-situation'![274]

Has Fazlur Rahman understood Gadamer correctly?[275]

Fazlur Rahman had to rely on an English translation of *Wahrheit und Methode.* From there he got the translation "quality of being determined by effective-history" *(Islam & Modernity,* p. 9) for Gadamer's ‚wirkungsgeschichtliche Bestimmtheit'. 'Quality of being -ed' is a correct rendering of the suffix ‚-heit' added to a past participle. But the word ‚bestimmen', from which ‚Bestimmtheit' is formed, means 'characterise, orient, destine, determine'. Fazlur Rahman's talk of "preconditioning" *(Islam & Modernity,* p. 9) and "predetermination" (ibid.) betrays that what he understood Gadamer to say was this: history has not only a strong influence on the interpreter but decides the outcome of any interpretation with necessity. Against this view, which he thinks is Gadamer's, Fazlur Rahman has to adduce the fact "that there have been changes in history, sometimes radical". *(Islam & Modernity,* p. 10) That is an superfluous argument because it is not Gadamer's point to say that the power of tradition vitiates all historical changes. There is a certain conservative—tradition treasuring—inclination in Gadamer's philosophy.[276] But historical changes are well in his sight.[277]

---

[274] Ibid., p. 307–11 (part 2, ii.1.d). 'Now-situation' is not Gadamer's but the present author's choice of words.

[275] At first glimpse, there is a striking example of misunderstanding. Fazlur Rahman quotes Gadamer as saying "the contrast between historical and dogmatic method has no absolute validity" *(Islam & Modernity,* p. 10), where the text of Gadamer's collected works reads: „Der Gegensatz von historischer und dogmatischer Methode hat [...] eine schlechthinnige Geltung" (vol. 2, p. 443), which is the exact opposite. However, the problem is solved when checking the second edition of *Wahrheit und Methode* (Tübingen 1965). The passage in question is taken from its preface (p. xix). There, we find „hat [...] keine schlechthinnige Geltung", which means precisely "has no absolute validity". Which version is correct? The 1965 text has the LECTIO POTIOR, because one page down (p. 444) even the 1993 has „Denn erst im Scheitern des naiven Historismus des historischen Jahrhunderts wird sichtbar, daß der Gegensatz von unhistorisch-dogmatisch und historisch [...] kein schlechthinniger ist", which renders "the contrast [...] has no absolute validity". So, what appears to be an instance of Fazlur Rahman's misreading proves to be a misreading in the new German edition of Gadamer's collected works.

[276] E.g., in his plea for "authority and tradition" (part 2, ii.1.b.α) and for "the classical" (part 2, ii.1.b.β).

[277] (a.) When Gadamer writes a history of hermeneutics, it certainly contains massive changes, indeed a „Wesenswandel—changing essence" (part 2, i.1.a)—and he introduces his own suggestion as another essential change in that history (part 3: „Ontologische Wendung"). (b.) His observation that temporal distance is productive (p. 302: part 2, ii.1.c) implies that he sees tradition not as an unchangable heritage. (c.) Gadamer calls for an awareness of the effects of history. Rather than only making us see our fetters it can liberate our retrieval of tradition; cf. below, p. 119 on the punch line of effective-history.

What should be made of this flood of theories and counter-theories?

In claiming to propose *no method* because you see what works only when you have understood, Gadamer cannot be completely serious. On the one hand, that would deprive him of any criteria of correct understanding and thus of understanding altogether. On the other hand, his own philosophy does have methodological implications, and in fact most elucidatory ones. This will become obvious when we bring Hans-Georg Gadamer into a fresh dialogue with Fazlur Rahman:

The criticism Gadamer advances against *historical hermeneutics* is valid: the less you see what is influencing your sight, the more it influences you. Fazlur Rahman comes to the Koran with a preconceived question. How should we act? His whole hermeneutical reflection is a method of how to obtain an ethics—in fact, a new ethics—out of the Koran. This may look extremely modern, because ethics is an 'in' subject, which you can discuss with all sorts of people without a clash of world views, and because you get modern answers. Gadamer however points out that even your type of questioning may be influenced by the effects of your history and therefore—that is the not-so-conservative punch line of "effective-history"—that type of questioning need not be the only possible one. Only when you notice you are being controlled, can you start dealing with that control. Only when Fazlur Rahman notices how traditional it is to go to the Koran and ask 'How should we act?', and even how traditional it is to come back from the Koran and say 'I got a new answer from it', only then can he start wondering whether there are other types of questions one might ask. To illustrate this point in but one example, one might well go to the Koran and ask: 'What is it, in the light of God's future, to be a human being?'

The criticism Gadamer advances against *psychological hermeneutics* is also valid: if you think that understanding is only 'thinking yourself into' the other's otherness, you lose your interest in, and contact with, what you have already discovered to be true. Betti, who claims you have to return to the creative mind for understanding, is an exponent of this psychological approach. And so is Fazlur Rahman: the second step of his first movement is doing exactly this, viz., reconstructing the author's intention. In Fazlur Rahman's formula: distilling God's ethical norms. Now, Gadamer points out that the psychological interpreter misses the text's truth claim. Understanding does, then, not mean one agrees because one sees what is said there to be true, but one accepts it, be it as strange as it may, because that is what the author says. Thus, Gadamerian philosophy unmasks Fazlur Rahman as a 'revelation-positivist', whose final argument must be 'because

God wants it'. A rational support structure for this is neither necessary nor indeed possible.

Thirdly, the criticism Gadamer advanced against the possibility of ever understanding either a text or your own situation fully, and in that sense objectively, is valid, too. Our ability to know and understand things and ourselves grows. But that position does not make Gadamer "hopelessly subjective", *(Islam & Modernity,* p. 9) nor indeed does it follow that if Gadamer is right, the double movement theory has "no meaning at all" as Fazlur Rahman believes. *(Islam & Modernity,* p. 9) If you see that you will be able to see better in the future, that does not make you subjective. And it does not destroy a model which starts from the view you have so far. It only means that you must be prepared to correct your model again and again with the improvement of knowledge about the past and about the present and thus about history and values. If anything, it is that attitude which deserves the name 'objectivity'. Fazlur Rahman seems to miss the point of our constantly evolving state of information when he says "the objective ascertaining of the past (—which Gadamer does not allow) is possible in principle provided requisite evidence is available". (*Islam & Modernity,* p. 10)

Admittedly, the present study of Fazlur Rahman's hermeneutics has focused on a short "Introduction" to one of his books only. Adil Çiftçi has done the same. It would not be fair to say that this is all there is to say about Fazlur Rahman's methodology. It is only that he is nowhere else more explicit about hermeneutics. In all this, one should not forget that the "Introduction" is to a book which is not about the Koran, but about one particular challenge to Islam: *Islam & Modernity*. The limitations of Fazlur Rahman's model, as presented here, should be seen as partly due to Fazlur Rahman's deliberate restriction of hermeneutics to the particular subject of the book.

Why is Fazlur Rahman's reaction to Gadamer so allergic?

When describing the world(s) of contemporary Muslims, Fazlur Rahman likes to draw a scenario of radical transformations. In a world of fast changes, Fazlur Rahman grasps for something to hold on to. Gadamer seems to uproot the last hold on an 'objectively ascertained past', (cf. *Islam & Modernity,* p. 10) to which Fazlur Rahman wanted to fasten his method.

On the other hand, it may not only be Fazlur Rahman's own safety needs but also his way of advertising a new methodology to his Muslim brothers and sisters, that made him so obsessed with stability. If Fazlur Rahman thought many of his fellow Muslims would reject anything soft-sounding, he might have overstated the solidity of the ground even though he himself knew better.

Another, fundamental, factor seems to be at work here. Interestingly, it demonstrates how different hermeneutics depend on different theologies. What is revelation? Where does a (proposedly) revealed text point? Fazlur Rahman and Hans-Georg Gadamer are likely to give opposed answers to these questions. Fazlur Rahman implies that a revealed text points at God's otherwise hidden will-to-be-done. In listening to revelation, one learns about the kind of life God wants us to lead. That seems to be a Koranic concept of revelation.[278] And it is quite in line with Betti's view and with psychological hermeneutics. Hans-Georg Gadamer's view, on the other hand, squares so well with a Biblical—Christian, but also Jewish—concept of revelation that the Bible may in fact have been the starting point of his reflections. That concept considers the text to point at reality around us. It makes a truth-claim to be followed up in the world. Therefore the reader's own experience ("horizon") is fundamental. The text opens one's eyes to the things going on around oneself.[279] And it is the *events* which are in fact God's self-revelation. Now, this fundamental difference in the concept of revelation has a twofold consequence on the hermeneutical position one favours. Firstly, Fazlur Rahman's view is directed from the text to the proposed author (because that is where revelation takes place), whereas a Gadamerian, non-psychologist view is directed from the text to the world. Secondly, Fazlur Rahman's view tries to skip tradition and get a tradition-free sight on the revelatory intention 'back there' (which is impossible, cf. above, p. 115). For him, tradition is stain on my glasses. A Gadamerian, non-historicist view has a positive relation to tradition, during which human understanding has grown. Tradition is part of reality, and therefore—although Gadamer is nowhere theologically explicit—part of the locus of God's revelatory action.

278 How important is the Koranic view of revelation, viz., the theology of signs, *āyāt*? Do they serve only as props, proofs of the authority of the imperatives? Do they not reveal God's care? Is God's care for creation not a message in its own right? Of course, one can deduce also ethical insights from God's care. But should God's care for creation not be appreciated as a message that has more consequences than only ethical ones? On "signs" cf. also below, page 164 at note 366.

279 Cf. Wolfhart Pannenberg, "Dogmatische Thesen zur Lehre von der Offenbarung", IDEM (ed.), *Offenbarung als Geschichte*, Göttingen 1961, pp. 91–114, p. 91.

Çiftçi: Objective Understanding

We are now returning to Adil Çiftçi.[280] He observes, without adducing a reference, that several Turkish authors criticise Fazlur Rahman for having a Romantic hermeneutics. Fazlur Rahman's frequent formulation "understanding the Koran better" is taken as a proof for that. (p. 101) Çiftçi defends Fazlur Rahman with a counterquote: Fazlur Rahman himself considered the attempt of "understanding God better than He understood Himself—*Allah'ı, Allah'tan daha iyi anlama*" to be naïve. (p. 102) Through this quote, Adil Çiftçi believes, he has disproved the accusation of Fazlur Rahman's Romanticism.[281]

According to Çiftçi's Gadamer, the temporal distance between 'subject and subject' *(konu-özne)*, that is, between matter and reader makes objective understanding possible. (p. 102)[282] From that distance, the reader can enter into a real dialogical encounter with the text, °an I–thou relation *(ben–sen ilişkisi)*. The text's claim *(dedik)* can be heard. (p. 102) "In this dialogue, the interpreter encounters the text as having a different 'horizon' of understanding, as being a different 'world'. This encounter and conversation brings about a meeting of horizons: the text's horizon with the interpreter's horizon—that is objective understanding!" (p. 103)[283]

Çiftçi: Confronting Gadamer and Fazlur Rahman

Çiftçi accounts for Fazlur Rahman's claim that if "Gadamer is correct, then the double-movement theory I have put forward has no meaning at all" with two arguments. Both follow from what Çiftçi calls Gadamer's relativism. (p. 109) Gadamer cannot explain the Koran's superiority and divine status. And Gadamer vitiates the critical confrontation of tradition or of our thinking with the Koran. We would be stuck in the all-powerful tradition. A Koran disempowered by Gadamer could not pull us out. Çiftçi then refutes this "relativity" with Fazlur Rahman's argument. Tradition cannot be all that powerful since great minds have turned its course. (p. 110)[284] Adil Çiftçi then sums up his confrontation of Gadamer and Fazlur Rahman. The main point of dissent, and the source of all differ-

280 Page numbers in the text refer to his *Fazlur Rahman ile İslam'ı Yeniden Düşünmek* again.

281 Çiftçi's argument will be taken up under *(E) Being a Romantic*, below, p. 129.

282 "Objective understanding" will be taken up under *(B)*, below, p. 127.

283 This understanding of the meeting and fusing of horizons will be reconsidered under *(C) One World, Many Horizons*, below, p. 128.

284 This will be reconsidered under *(A) The Power of Tradition*, below, p. 126.

ences between the two authors is, for him, the fact that Gadamer considers the process of understanding-interpreting-applying to be one inseparable, indistinguishable action whereas Fazlur Rahman explicitly splits up the two actions of "objective ascertaining the past" and the response (the latter being influenced by values and the present situation). The objective, normative meanings *(anlamlar)* are being interpreted in, or according to, our own historicality *(tarihsellik)*. (p. 111)[285]

Adil Çiftçi declares that things will become clearer once we have understood what kind of a book the Koran really is according to Fazlur Rahman. "The Koran is not °a single 'book' *(tek bir 'kitap')*, because no one sat down and wrote it. It is [rather] the concretised state of revelation, which took up the problems and questions the Prophet encountered within more than twenty years." (p. 113) Two insights follow from that. Firstly, the Koran is "a living text connected with history". In its interpretation, the 'occasions of revelation' are to be taken into account even though they can, as Çiftçi admits, not be established in a verse-by-verse manner. (p. 114) Secondly, the Koran is not about God. It is not God's autobiography (p. 115) but "*hudan li-n-nās*, a guidance for human beings". (2:2)[286] Therefore, the Koran provides a consistent and comprehensive view of life and world, at least in the shape of a framework. (p. 116) Only because this is so, can the Koran be understood. Understanding is attributing the parts to the whole. The implicit link is clearly this: each individual Koranic command can be seen as having its place within the Koranic world view. Fazlur Rahman's Koranic world view is however not a fixed one. Here, just as is the case with individual norms, one has to find the intention behind the formulation and re-express it in accordance with today's state of human thinking.[287] Islam must be understood out of the Koran and brought into dialogue with the modern world. (p. 117) The danger of charging the Koran with un-Koranic contemporary thought can be evaded through the application of two control mechanisms. The first one is: one must always work with an °integral, complete *(bütüncül)* understanding of the Koranic message. The second is, using the correct method. (p. 117) The correct method however consists primarily in understanding the Koran as one whole. (p. 129) Fazlur Rahman criticises the traditional method of °analogical conclusion *(qiyās)* as inflexible, (p. 117) oriented towards individual verses rather than the inner whole of the Koran, (p. 118) and as drawing legal

---

[285] This remark will be discussed under *(F) Two Historicalities?*, below, p. 130

[286] This Koranic expression will be revisited under *(G) A Guidance*, below, p. 130.

[287] This will be discussed under *(H) Mental Reconstruction and the Applicability Dogma*, below, p. 131.

conclusions from non-legal verses. The alternative method offered by Fazlur Rahman is his double movement approach, whose first movement consists of the two steps: understanding a given Koranic statement's import in the light of its contemporary macro-situation; and distilling the statement's general objective out of it. Here, neither Fazlur Rahman nor Adil Çiftçi are particularly clear as to which role the Koran as a whole plays in this first movement. Fazlur Rahman writes (and Çiftçi simply translates it (p. 131)), "The first step of the first movement, then, consists of understanding the meaning of the Qur'ān as a whole as well as in terms of the specific tenets that constitute responses to specific situations."[288] This vague wording seems to conceal (and betray) the fact that Fazlur Rahman himself was not altogether clear about the role of the Koran as a whole. It is not obvious which role, according to his model, e.g., the doctrine of later revealed verses abrogating earlier ones should play. What is the Koran as a whole? Is it the Koran including the verses considered to be abrogated; or including the chronology and affirmation of abrogation? What to do with conflicting stipulations? Should one distil from them a common denominator, wide enough to encompass the differences (e.g., 'God's will to create justice'), or should one regulation be used to relativise another?

Adil Çiftçi describes Fazlur Rahman's method as a hermeneutic circle, although Fazlur Rahman, as Çiftçi notices, does not term his own method thus. (p. 133) For a correct understanding of the Koran, it is not enough to know Arabic well. What is needed is an historical approach. The Koran's intention must be understood as the answer to a question which was in the air when the Koran was proclaimed. Through that historical approach, the Koran can be authorised to interfere today. Using the circle which Çiftçi saw at work in Fazlur Rahman's method we could describe the process thus. The Koranic question-and-answer structure can itself be described as a circular process. People in the questioning situation require and get a response and are thus brought into a new situation, possibly needing new answers. This is the inner-Koranic circle. By reconstructing the questioning situation and discovering the similarity of present day situations, the circle is detached form its original situation. So, we can today mount the same circle and thus be brought to the response the Koran gives us. Çiftçi perceptibly remarks that the response is possibly a correction of the question. (p. 133) Explicitly dissociating himself from Gadamer's (and thus, implicitly, from Heidegger's) usage, Çiftçi introduces a concept "*ön anlama*—preliminary understanding", which should be seen as an exclusively passive

288 *Islam & Modernity*, p. 6.

habitus of the understanding mind: the, so to speak, shy state which humbly accepts correction or approval by the text. The value of this newly introduced concept is not obvious.

"On which criteria does he [viz., Fazlur Rahman] rely to be certain that, when drawing general ethical, religious and social ideas from the Koran, they have been drawn correctly?" (p. 134) Çiftçi answers his own question in a fourfold way, the four answers apparently being Çiftçi's own products. (p. 134)

1. What the Koran says about itself is contradiction-free.
2. In taking the Koran seriously, you achieve a contradiction-free world view.
3. The Koran speaks for its own (7th century) context.
4. An understanding/interpreting/applying relation between today's addressees and the Koran exists.[289]

Fazlur Rahman's approach is "*bütünsel ve tarihsel*—comprehensive and historical" in that it takes into account the inner structure of the Koran and its milieu. (p. 135) He arrives at his approach in four stages.

a. What kind of a book is the Koran?—It is "*Tevhide dayalı bir ahlak düzeni*—an ethical order [ORDO] based on monotheism."
b. In order to avoid subjective interpretation, we have to "*Metnin ortamına gitmek*—[mentally] go to the Text's [originally addressed] milieu."
c. In the light of both that °broad-range milieu *(geniş ortam)* and (each verse's) individual milieu, we are to understand the verses' intentions one by one.
d. Those intentions must be divided into °the general idea *(genel fikir*—intellectual background?) and the ethical objectives.

What Çiftçi provides here is in fact a more detailed reconstruction of Fazlur Rahman's first movement. Çiftçi then makes the observation that the first movement is inductive *(tümevarımsal)*, the second deductive *(tümdengelimsel)*. This is in Çiftçi's eyes the reason why Fazlur Rahman was able to call his approach "scientific/scholarly—*bilimsel*". (p. 135) According to Fazlur Rahman, for that second step to be applied correctly today it is necessary "to know and understand the present situation and all its components". (p. 136)[290]

Çiftçi now connects theological theology and ethics. Monotheism is not only a theological principle, it is at the same time an ethical principle, because from the idea of 'one God' one has to proceed necessarily to 'one humanity'. (p. 140) From this, Çiftçi deduces a pertinent point. The inter-

---

[289] This list will be discussed under *(I) Criteria and Presuppositions*, below, p. 132.

[290] We will return to this under *(J) Careful Study*, below, p. 132.

relatedness of the theological and the ethical is the reason for Fazlur Rahman's particular juxtaposition of object and subject. Rather than having the interpreting subject influence the subject matter, he sees the Koran's historicality as influencing the reader's historicality. (p. 140) That is to say, the Koran, though speaking in a different historical context, wants to change the world as it is today. Adil Çiftçi sees two reasons for Fazlur Rahman's juxtaposition, in other words, for his anti-Gadamerism. Firstly, the Koran is God's word; "*onun muradını bilmek için kendimizi ona yüklemek değil, onu 'dinlemek' zorundayız*—in order to know what it wants, we must, rather than impose ourselves, *listen* to it." (p. 140)[291] Secondly, Fazlur Rahman recalls that throughout the Islamic tradition "'wild'" interpretations have imported private prejudices into the text, and that happened not under the label of "application" but already on the level of [alleged] "understanding". Fazlur Rahman would, according to Çiftçi, not be in conflict with Gadamer as far as openness towards "all influences of one's own historicity" is concerned in application. But Fazlur Rahman sees no objective basis for such an application, if there is not, before the application, an objective grasp of what the Text means. (p. 140)

Discussion: Applying Mathematics, Laws, and Ethics

Among the studies to be presented here, Adil Çiftçi's is the most specialised in hermeneutics and methodology. Discussion will consequently also focus on hermeneutic questions. Firstly, we have to revisit Çiftçi's presentation of Gadamer, *(A)–(B),* then his discussion—and defence—of Fazlur Rahman, *(C)–(J).*

(A) The Power of Tradition

(Cf. above, at note 284 on p. 122.) Like Fazlur Rahman, Çiftçi refutes an allegedly Gadamerian position which Gadamer actually never held. (Cf. above, p. 118 on historical determinism.) Gadamer stresses that tradition is powerful, but he does not make it all-powerful. Çiftçi has in the course of his discussion silently introduced an interesting distinction which Gadamer would not have made. He strictly distinguishes text and tradition. Both are powerful factors for him. But while tradition is for him a retaining power, the text has, in his eyes, a reforming power. The advantage

[291] What is translated in this quote by "it" and thus taken to mean the Koran may also be referring to God.

of this view is that it describes well what happens ideally when one is rethinking. After all, his book is called "Rethinking Islam ...". The fresh look at the old text sets free a great power. Thus empowered, the text can change something today, because it is stronger than long held lore, which can thus be discovered to be false, illegitimately appealing to the text, and not binding. But Çiftçi did not consider these problems of his distinction, or separation, of text and tradition:

a. Does not the belief that one has immediate access to the text under evasion of tradition make you blind, and therefore helpless, towards the influence of tradition?
b. Should not any text—at least in its form—be seen as being itself the product of a tradition? Does that not render invalid the distinction between an ever fresh source point, the text, and the sticky tenacious stream of tradition?
c. Is it not our consideration of tradition—especially when we find it to have misunderstood the text—that makes us cautious about our present attempt to understand the text: it will also be discovered imperfect sooner or later.

(B) Objective Understanding

(Cf. above, at note 282 on p. 122.) Çiftçi's Gadamer justifies objective understanding because of the distance between subject matter and the reader. This is not Gadamer's own view, however. For him, the mere concept of 'objective understanding' betrays epistemological and hermeneutical unawareness. Objectivity is precisely the static ideal which Gadamer wants to overcome through his emphasis on the hermeneutical productivity of historical distance.[292] Possibly, but confusingly, Adil Çiftçi uses "objective" to mean 'with greater clarity'. This is probably due to the fact that in the Eng-

---

[292] Cf. the whole chapter: part 2, ii.1.c, where Gadamer says that it is the distance of "times" which provides safe criteria for interpretation: „Hier ist es nicht zuviel, von einer echten Produktivität des Geschehens zu sprechen. Jedermann kennt die eigentümliche Ohnmacht unseres Urteils dort, wo uns nicht der Abstand der Zeiten sichere Maßstäbe anvertraut hat." (p. 302) In 1985, Gadamer widened his concept of distance, in an "Attempt at Self-Correction", to mean not only temporal distance but also the distancing from oneself that takes place, e.g., in the conscious search for the common ground in a conversation: „Es muß sich nicht immer um einen geschichtlichen Abstand handeln, und es ist durchaus nicht immer der Zeitenabstand als solcher, der imstande ist, falsche Überresonanzen und verzerrende Applikationen zu überwinden. Der Abstand erweist sich sehr wohl auch in Gleichzeitigkeit als ein hermeneutisches Moment, z.B. in der Begegnung zwischen Personen, die im Gespräch erst den gemeinsamen Grund suchen [...]". (*Wahrheit und Methode*, vol. 2, p. 9)

lish expression 'objective understanding' the word 'objective' has a rather adverbial function (understanding objectively) and seems to mean: 'in striving to overcome one's false prejudice' (cf. ‚sachlich') whereas German philosophers—even though they may well accept that the human mind can have access to reality—have an allergic reaction to the expression because it sounds dogmatic to them: understanding the object as it is. Such a claim may imply one is missing that every access to reality is from a certain perspective.

(C) One World, Many Horizons

(Cf. above, at note 283 on p. 122.) It is not obvious that Çiftçi understood what Gadamer was describing in creating the image of the fused horizons. Gadamer's point was, here, not the otherness of the text's world *(alternatif bir 'dünya')*[293] but—while certainly admitting for the difference of perspectives—the discovery that one starts understanding a text when one sees that it is in fact talking about *the same things* which oneself has been wondering about: text and interpreter have a *common* area of experience![294]

Gadamer's description of understanding-agreement (‚Verständigung')[295] can be systematised as working in two steps. First, one should try to place oneself, as much as possible, into the other's *other* horizon.[296] But going there is only necessary to avoid *semantic* misunderstanding. It does not make for a real dialogue yet. Understanding takes place only when you return to your point of view and then no longer look at your partner's horizon but at *the objects* you are discussing.[297]

---

293 „Solche Anerkennung der Andersheit des anderen, die dieselbe zum Gegenstande objektiver Erkenntnis macht, ist insofern eine grundsätzliche Suspension seines Anspruchs." *(Wahrheit und Methode*, vol. 1, p. 309)

294 „Es gibt so wenig einen Gegenwartshorizont für sich, wie es historische Horizonte gibt, die man zu gewinnen hätte. *Vielmehr ist Verstehen immer der Vorgang der Verschmelzung solcher vermeintlich für sich seiender Horizonte.*" (Ibid., vol. 1, p. 311, Gadamer's italics)

295 In the translators' preface (p. xvi) of the revised translation of *Wahrheit und Methode* (cf. above, footnote 142), ‚Verständigung' is explained as: *coming to an understanding/agreement with someone.*

296 „Wer es unterläßt, derart sich in den historischen Horizont zu versetzen, aus dem die Überlieferung spricht, wird die Bedeutung der Überlieferungsinhalte mißverstehen." *(Wahrheit und Methode*, vol. 1, p. 308)

297 „Insofern scheint es eine berechtigte hermeneutische Forderung, daß man sich in den andern versetzen muß, um ihn zu verstehen. Indessen fragt es sich, ob eine solche Parole nicht gerade das Verständnis schuldig bleibt, das von einem verlangt wird. Es ist genauso wie im Gespräch, das wir mit jemandem nur zu dem Zwecke führen, um ihn besser kennenzulernen, d.h. um seinen Standort und seinen Hori-

(D) How Necessary Is Method?

(Cf. above, at note 253 on p. 113.) If we do not approach the Koran with method, we will lose the Koran, says Fazlur Rahman. But has he really argued convincingly for the necessity of method-in-reading? His argument depends on his shift of revelatory authority from the command to the intention. One needs a method to find the intention. This is prone to raise objections from right and left, so to speak.

Once one starts speculating about an ethical substructure of the Koranic commands, one risks losing the Koran altogether. One builds that substructure, and for that, one has to build a methodological scaffolding first. Why, instead of constructing rules for oneself, does one not simply apply the rules we already have: the Koran?

The above position supposes that one needs a method only if one wants to get beneath the surface commands. And in fact Fazlur Rahman seems to believe exactly this, since his call for methodology arises only out of his need to find out the ethics underneath. That however is what could be termed the fallacy of mathematical hermeneutics. When only completely artificial, abstract entities are involved, it may be clear which rule applies. In real life however, there are no unambiguous cases. Any rule is PER DEFINITIONEM an abstraction and generalisation. Why is it precisely this rule that applies now? What does it mean in this case? Which other rules come in? You cannot find (i.) a one-for-all-cases rule that would decide which rule applies for which situation and what that rule means in that situation, because you need rules for that one-for-all-cases rule's application, AD INFINITUM; nor can you (ii.) state individual rules for each case, because that would again mean that you would have to state rules AD INFINITUM. So, the hermeneutical problems do not start only when dealing with the Koran as a book of ethics (to use Fazlur Rahman's formulation); similar problems occur when seeing it as a law book.

(E) Being a Romantic

(Cf. above, at note 281 on p. 122.) Çiftçi wants to defend Fazlur Rahman against the accusation of being a Romantic. Çiftçi therefore quotes Fazlur Rahman as arguing against the attempt to understand God better than God understands Himself. That—is Çiftçi's implicit argument—would really be Romantic. But by saying that, Çiftçi only refutes one part of the

zont zu ermessen. Das ist kein wahres Gespräch, d.h. es wird darin nicht die Verständigung über eine Sache gesucht.“ (Ibid.)

accusation. Admittedly, that bit of Romantic hermeneutics (understanding the authors better than they understood themselves) does not apply precisely to what Fazlur Rahman does. But that is not only so because we have an omniscient author here, but also because God's authorship of the Koran is, according to Fazlur Rahman, far more indirect than in the case of human authors. And certainly Fazlur Rahman would agree with the formula 'understanding the Koran better than Muhammad understood it'. Fazlur Rahman has no awareness of effective-history, and does not want to have any. He operates in what is commonly called the Romantic pattern, and Adil Çiftçi has not disproved that claim. He might have discussed

a. whether the (pejorative) label 'Romantic' is useful in general, and
b. whether in the case of a text like the Koran, with Muhammad probably not at his everyday consciousness when proclaiming it, one can apply the same criteria as for a normal text, i.e., one composed consciously by an undisputedly human author.

(F) Two Historicalities?

(Cf. above, at note 285 on p. 123.) Nowhere in the text does Çiftçi criticise Fazlur Rahman's problematic view that one can objectively produce today the normative meaning of the past, i.e., in this case, of an ancient text. Çiftçi calls our contemporary conditions, which "influence" only the translation of those fixed meanings for today, "historicality". If those contemporary conditions can be seen objectively and, again, do not actively shape our view of any other period within history, it is an unnecessary and indeed confusing complication to call them "historicality". Talk of "historicality" (‚Geschichtlichkeit') implies that one is aware of the effects of history on one's own perception of it. Simply setting Gadamer's view besides Fazlur Rahman's contrary view, and even using the key anti-objectivism concept of Gadamer (and his predecessors) in the presentation, without bringing the two views into an argument is not taking philosophy seriously.

(G) A Guidance

(Cf. above, at note 286 on p. 123.) Fazlur Rahman has a strong case when he says the Koran is a book of ethics because it is "a guidance for human beings". He can adduce a Koranic self-definition. Still, three questions remain:

a. Is "a guidance for human beings" really a complete definition, which excludes the Koran's functioning in any other way; e.g., as a (strictly monotheistic) theology?
b. Does "guidance" mean what Fazlur Rahman wants it to mean: ethical doctrine? It may, clearly. But apart from the alternative option 'law book', which Fazlur Rahman sees, other possible ways of understanding *'hudā'* (guidance) should not be overlooked: 'The book which has come down as a guidance' need not refer to the *content* of the Koran but can refer, e.g., to the *historical fact* that Muhammad was preaching in God's name. Or, the guidance is not meant as stipulating by norms but by *predictions*: God controls all human behaviour and now tells people what He is going to ordain.
c. Is not a different kind of questioning that verse, and the Koran, also true to the text? E.g., what does the fact that God wants to guide human beings say about God and human beings? Cf. the discussion of an anthropology of obedience (above, p. 81) and the creativity of being guided (below, p. 189 (b.) and (c.)).

(H) Mental Reconstruction and the Applicability Dogma

(Cf. above, at note 287 on p. 123.) Çiftçi says, with Fazlur Rahman, that understanding the Koran is allocating a place for each Koranic command within the whole of the Koranic world-view; this world-view has to be re-expressed in every time according to each time's particular intellectual situation. Çiftçi has not pointed out the problems involved.
a. To understand understanding as giving to the individual phenomenon a place within the whole is a plausible, and indeed classical[298] view. However, if the whole is identified with the system the Koran constructs, that is a restricted form of understanding,[299] which should be termed mental reconstruction.
b. How can the dialogue between a contemporary world view and the Koranic intention work in an honest way? Would not benevolent modern readers impute to the Koran an intention which they find acceptable? The Koran could not defend itself, even if it actually intended to criticise an element of a modern world view. On the other hand, those modern readers will never criticise a Koranic intention, because the

[298] Cf., e.g., Wilhelm Dilthey, quoted by Hans-Georg Gadamer, *Wahrheit und Methode*, vol. 1, p. 202.
[299] At least if the Koran does not contain all the knowable truth about everything; Fazlur Rahman would not claim that either.

whole task of their reading is to re-formulate the Koran in a manner acceptable today. This goes back to what should be called Fazlur Rahman's applicability dogma. This is to say, he claims that "if the results of understanding fail in application now, then either there has been a failure to assess the present situation correctly or a failure in understanding the Qur'ān".[300] The third possibility, viz., that it is the Koranic intention which is wrong, is not even mentioned, because Fazlur Rahman presupposes that the Koran is God's will, and therefore infallible. Would it not be much more convincing to *establish* the Koran's ethical superiority rather than starting from it as an axiom unchallenged?

(I) Criteria and Presuppositions

(Cf. above, at note 289 on p. 125.) When asking himself on which criteria Fazlur Rahman relies for correctly drawing ethical principles from the Koranic legislation, Çiftçi produces a list of four points. It is an important list, the result of a considerable effort of abstraction. However, it does not provide criteria for correct understanding, but is a list of (some of) Fazlur Rahman's silent presuppositions. As such it is useful. It demonstrates that Fazlur Rahman's method depends on claims he never bothered establishing.

(J) Careful Study

(Cf. above, at note 290 on p. 125.) Çiftçi states that Fazlur Rahman's two methodological steps have an inductive and deductive character respectively. This is a correct observation. Then Çiftçi says that according to Fazlur Rahman, knowledge of today's conditions is necessary for an apt application of the norms found.[301] Fazlur Rahman writes: the application

---

300 Fazlur Rahman, *Islam & Modernity*, p. 7. Çiftçi quotes that passage on his p. 137. What is termed here Fazlur Rahman's applicability dogma seems to be his replacement for the classical dogma of the Koran's inerrancy, which is based on what the Koran says about itself. Cf., e.g., 2:2; 4:82; 16:102; 22:54; 39:28; 43:4. Fazlur Rahman's thought can be formalised as follows: (1) The Koran has been applied successfully in earlier times. (2) Therefore, it can be applied successfully today, (3) if only understood correctly. The problems within this train of thought are: a. Where do we get the criteria for "successful" application? b. (2) does not follow logically from (3). c. Or everything depends on (3) which however does not offer a criterion for "correct" understanding other than possibly 'what makes for successful application of the Koran today', in which case the whole train of thought is circular, a PETITIO PRINCIPII and of no argumentative value.

301 The reference Çiftçi adduces for that is *Islam & Modernity*, p. 6, where no such claim is made. It is supposed here that he is referring to the passage quoted in the text which is to be found ibid., p. 7.

of the general norms today "requires the careful study of the present situation and the analysis of its various component elements so that we can assess the current situation [...]". Fazlur Rahman's own words contain a key to criticise or develop his approach. In his formulation ("careful study [...] assess", rather than 'know and understand') he demonstrates his awareness of the difficulties involved in such an assessment, which will within history never be complete 'knowledge and understanding'. Now, if Fazlur Rahman is able to see that difficulty about objectively seeing our own situation, he could have been brought to a similar insight concerning the past. Neither the 7th century Arabian milieu nor the intention of the text will ever be understood conclusively as long as human history goes on. But since Çiftçi converted his Fazlur Rahman into an objectivist about the present, he deprived himself of the instruments which could have demonstrated, from Fazlur Rahman's own insights, the problems with an objectivism about the past.

Conclusion

Adil Çiftçi has produced a high level study on Fazlur Rahman. It does not restrict itself to translation and repetition but brings in other strands of scholarship. Thus Adil Çiftçi has made Fazlur Rahman's approach clearer. However, many of the problems with that approach which Fazlur Rahman did not see have not been tackled by Çiftçi either. In merely reconstructing the author's intention rather than also discussing in a new light problems which arise, Çiftçi's dealing with Fazlur Rahman is in fact similar to what Fazlur Rahman does with the Koran. But the achievement Adil Çiftçi has to contribute to Muslim theology should not be seen so much in a refinement of methodology, where he has left many questions open, but in his application of Fazlur Rahman's approach and thus his revisiting of Islam's core tenets as a modern thinker. Çiftçi's observations such as the ethical relevance of monotheism as uniting humanity (cf. above, p. 125) are important insights. But they are in danger of remaining hidden within a multitude of methodological musings.

Chapter 3
Ömer Özsoy: The Koran is What God Wants to Do

Ömer Özsoy was born in 1963 in Bünyan (Kayseri). He received his secondary education at Kayseri High School. Between 1980 and 1985 he studied at Ankara Üniversitesi İlâhiyat Fakültesi. He gained a doctoral degree from the Sosyal Bilimler Enstitüsü of Ankara University in 1991. From 1991 until 1993 he pursued further studies on Islam at the University of Heidelberg, Germany. His doctoral thesis, *God's Sunna. A Conceptualisation of the Koranic Expression,*[302] of 1994 is, almost a decade on, still a famous book. Apart from many articles in Koranic studies, he published, together with İlhami Güler,[303] a thematic arrangement of the Koranic verses;[304] he also produced a collection and translation of articles on the Koran by Rudi Paret.[305] Özsoy is a founding member of the journal İslâmiyât.[306] He is Professor of Tefsir at the Ankara Faculty of Theology.

1 De-historicising the Koran

In a 1997 issue of the Turkish journal *İktibas*, an interview with Ömer Özsoy appeared—"With Ömer Özsoy about 'Historicity'".[307] It is not usual to base a research into academic theology on published interviews. But one should not miss the advantages of using that type of source material, too. Firstly, the spoken word allows for a glance over the scholars' shoulders while at work. Even mistakes, misunderstanding, self-corrections can be important clues. Secondly, much more than the monological writing situation, a live dialogue forces the participants, if they are not of the same opinion, to present opposing positions fairly and to take adverse arguments seriously. Thirdly, the greater circulation and accessibility of the

---

302 *Sünnetullah. Bir Kur'an İfadesinin Kavramlaşması*, Ankara 1994.

303 Cf. below, p. 165.

304 *Konularına göre Kur'an. Sistematik Kur'an Fihristi*, Ankara 1996 (Turkish–Arabic).

305 Rudi Paret, *Kur'an Üzerine Makaleler*, Ankara 1996.

306 Cf. above, p. 60.

307 "Ömer Özsoy ile "Tarihsellik" Üzerine," *İktibas*, September 1997, pp. 24–33. In the above text, page references will be to that article. The terminological usage 'historicality' will feature in the interview. Since however Özsoy stresses the interference of 'historicity' and 'historicality' in several Turkish words, our translation will for the time being stay with the widest possible rendering of *'tarihsellik'*: 'historicity'.

genre gives the foreign scholar a chance to follow up theology's repercussions in the wider public of Turkey. And the present interview is not simplistic journalism. It is of great conceptual ambition. But, naturally, it is rather jerky. Not everything will be immediately clear. Therefore, in the present case, points of comment and discussion cannot be outsourced to the end of each section. Rather, the dialogue's course must sometimes be interrupted for distinctions, clarifications and other additions. In order to distinguish presentation from discussion typographically, the present author's remarks will be indented.

1.1 *The Experience of the Koran*

1.1.1 *Being Historical*

The conversation goes straight IN MEDIAS RES: "Mr. Özsoy, our first question will be of conceptual content. What does, in your opinion, *'tarihsellik*—historicity' really express? Is it merely a method or is it a modern mentality with paradigmatic ramifications?" Özsoy's answer restricts itself to distinguishing between *'tarihselcilik'* (which he considers to be synonymous with *'tarihçilik')* and *'tarihsellik'*: 1. *'tarihsellik'* is the property of (a.) being an historical fact and (b.) being limited by history, not transhistorical. 2. *'Tarihselcilik'* designates the property of reflecting the original conditions, which need to be taken into account when interpreting. (p. 24)

> Why does Özsoy use the same Turkish word for his meanings (1a.) (1b.)? The common German philosophical distinction between ‚Historizität' and ‚Geschichtlichkeit' draws the line between 'has taken place' (which is Özsoy's (1a.)) and 'exists temporally' (which has to do with Özsoy's (1b.) and (2)).[308] He thus sacrifices a possible distinction in Turkish. But Özsoy's definitions are clear. They only have no equivalents in Western philosophical traditions and are not shared by many Turkish authors, either.[309] In order to explain his usage of *'tarihsellik'*, Özsoy took Jesus as an example. He wanted to say both 'he actually existed' and 'he was a real human being'. This may be the reason why these two meanings came under the same Turkish word.
>
> Özsoy was on the panel when one of his colleagues suggested a useful differentiation. On the 1996 Symposium held at Bursa under the title "The problem of historicity in understanding the Koran", Alparslan Açıkgenç gave the fourth and final main paper (after Mehmet Paçacı, Yunus Vehbi Yavuz and Ali Bulaç), headed

[308] Cf., e.g., Leonhard von Renthe-Fink, "Geschichtlichkeit", *Historisches Wörterbuch der Philosophie*, vol. 3, Basel 1974, cols. 404–8, col. 405.

[309] Mehmet Paçacı however explicitly states that 'the Koran is historical' means for him: an interpretation of the Koran must take the historical setting of 7th century Arabia into account. (Cf. above, at note 173 on p. 81.) Thus, his usage is in line with Özsoy's.

"An approach to historicity in the context of the concept of science in the Koran, and its contribution to exegetical method".[310] In his paper, Açıkgenç distinguishes three meanings of "*tarihsellik* (historicity)" (p. 184): "Firstly, 'scientific historicity *(bilimsel tarihselcilik)*,' which Collingwood[311] tried to achieve. Secondly 'anticipatory historicity *(öngörüsel tarihselcilik)*,' of which—according to Popper[312]—Hegel, Marx and Comte are protagonists. And thirdly the understanding which we will call 'interpretative historicity *(yorumsal tarihselcilik)*,' which concerns us here." Açıkgenç then offers more detailed explanations for his distinction. Collingwood's scientific historicity is summed up as "the view that history °as a scholarly discipline *(bilim olarak)* is more comprehensive than all other disciplines and includes even philosophy". (p. 184) His second type, anticipatory historicity, is explicated with a vague reference to Karl Popper's *The Poverty of Historicism* as "a kind of conceptual historical determination *(belirleme)* of the future, which takes as its foundation the principle of the prediction *(önceden görme)* of the future, arising form the general concepts of the social sciences which are formed from past historical events". (p. 184) The third concept, which he wants to use, interpretative historicity, is defined by him as "the view that some events are valid only within history, for a certain time and place". (p. 184) So, his concept of historicity is one of strict historical relativism. Özsoy is not that radical when stating the possible meanings of *'tahrihsellik'*.

1.1.2 Explaining Muhammad, and Understanding Muhammad

The interviewers rephrase their original question, now using *'tarihselcilik'* instead of *'tarihsellik'*. Özsoy replies, historicity is not a method but an approach, a mind-set. He supports that by considering Western Islamic studies. According to his observation, 20th century orientalists have shifted their perspective from 'Was Muhammad right?' and 'Where did he get it from?' to 'What did Muhammad want to say?'. (p. 25) But Özsoy adds that a psychological approach, which treated the Koran as Muhammad's autobiography, also became modern.

Without explicating it, Özsoy is making an important point here. The delimitations of Islamic theology and Islamic studies are being blurred when Islamicists become interested in understanding (rather than only explaining) Muhammad, and—though Özsoy does not say that—when Islamic theologians become interested in history, just as scholars like Ömer Özsoy himself are. But there were

---

310 Alparslan Açıkgenç, "Kur'an'da İlim Kavramı Çerçevesinde Tariselliğe Bir Yaklaşım ve Bunun Tefsir Yönetemine Katkısı", Muhammad Abay (ed.), *Kur'an'ı Anlamada Tarihsellik Sorunu Sempozyumu*, Istanbul 2000, pp. 183–93.

311 Açıkgenç is obviously alluding to Robin George Collingwood, *The Idea of History*, Oxford 1946.

312 He is obviously alluding to Karl Raimund Popper, *The Poverty of Historicism*, London (^{1}1944:) 1957.

Western scholars already a century ago—especially in Scandinavia—who attempted to *understand* Muhammad.[313]

1.1.3 *Why the Koran is Original*

The interview now focuses on the question: does the Koran have an "*özgünlük*—originality, exemplary character" for all times? Özsoy interprets the word in question as: "being adequate to the origin—*asla (orijine) uygunluk*". This concept brings him to speaking about the other monotheist religions.

How does he get from originality to monotheism? The link probably works thus: 'originality' was meant as its irreplaceable content; 'original adequateness' implies that a core message (which may also—though in differing versions—be passed on through other monotheist traditions) was brought into 7th century Arabia through Muhammad. If that is right, what Özsoy is saying here amounts to stating that the Koran is original because it is not original. In other words, the Koran has a universal message because it preaches what others also preach. But he could imply that the Koran is particularly faithful to the basic monotheist intuition.

1.1.4 *In Favour of Tradition*

The interviewers now turn towards the question of objectivity. (p. 27) Özsoy's response starts from the uncontroversial observation that the Koran was proclaimed in a certain "history", for human beings, with a language used by human beings. The many passages which refer to particular moments of Muhammad's life already demonstrate the necessity of reading the Koran "within" its own history, he says. And Özsoy goes on by introducing one of his core categories. The Koran provides us with an *experience* whose example we are to follow. One must not claim that God's intention is the same for everyone and for all times. What saves us from an arbitrary, distorting interpretation is the guiding question: what did the first addressees understand? But—the interviewers object—if one claims that each Koranic verse can only be understood out of its original situation, then there will always be dispute about which situation belongs to which verse. "I think we cannot speak of a level of understanding that is independent of history and tradition", is Ömer Özsoy's reply. There has been the claim to understand the Koran outside of its historical material. This position is called "*mealci*—'contentist'". And the historical context of the Koranic texts, at least their designation as 'Meccan' or 'Medinan' re-

---

313 Cf., e.g., Frants Buhl, *Muhammeds Liv*, Kopenhagen 1903, translated into German by Hans Heinrich Schaeder.

spectively, have always been a subject of investigation, just as historical research was necessary when trying to solve semantic problems. But—interfere the interviewers—if history and tradition are so important for a contemporary interpretation of the Koran, why is tradition at the same time criticised so strongly by those contemporary interpreters? Özsoy's answer is a reflection on the interaction between history and human beings. Human being is conditioned by history. At the same time, it is human being which makes history. And two people starting from very similar conditions can still come to completely different conclusions.

One may wonder why this is an answer to the question posed. It seems that Özsoy has fallen into a—possibly unintended—trap of his interviewers here. The train of thought was this: a. History/tradition is a key to understanding a text today. b. How can you be so much in favour of tradition suddenly, when you are a modernist? c. What is not distinguished here, but should have been, is "being in favour of". Özsoy does not want to *accept* the traditional position because it is traditional. Here, he was using traditions only as stage properties to understand what is being played. d. Özsoy, rather than discovering the conceptual confusion, continues by taking over the interviewers' meaning of "being in favour of" and thinks he is obliged to take his point back half way: tradition is something ambiguous, you can use it this way or that (so tradition *can* be something good). That is a valid point. But it is unnecessary to leave the interviewers with the impression that Özsoy has admitted an inconsistency in his stance towards tradition.[314]

1.1.5 Criteria of Criticism

The interviewers now pick on the question on what grounds Özsoy is able to criticise tradition.

This is interesting because he was implicitly saying that you can make good or bad things out of tradition. A call for understandable criteria is in place.

Özsoy replies: the criticism of tradition is fed from other, now weakened, strands of tradition. (p. 28)

Here, the interviewers could have responded: and on what grounds do you choose one strand rather than another? Thus they could have shown that Özsoy, once he has gone into the trap, is caught in circular traditionalism. Özsoy would have avoided that trap if he had made clear earlier on that the criticism of the tradition can well, and without detrimental effects on tradition itself, flow from arguments based on logic and the contemporary state of human knowledge.

---

[314] A distincition made above (p. 126) concerning "tradition" supports the differentiation which is necessary here. Being aware of a text's effective-history does not make one a traditionalist helplessly given into the hands of tradition but quite on the contrary enables one to see and handle the otherwise hidden power of tradition.

1.1.6 *Clothes and Wind*

We cannot rid ourselves from tradition. Therefore we have no choice but to criticise traditions with traditions: "Do you want to say that criticism of the tradition requires tradition again?—Özsoy: Absolutely; because it is not clothes we can take off." (p. 28)

> This is an exaggerated conclusion. Even if the Gadamerian point[315] is accepted that traditions are omnipresent and have their effects on our way of thinking, speaking, asking questions, etc., that should not be taken to mean that there cannot be any new arguments, new insights. After all, it is especially Gadamer who points out that tradition and we can both look at one and the same world.[316] If on a bicycle tour you cannot escape the wind, still not all movements on your trip need to be wind-powered.

1.1.7 *The Founder of Textual Criticism*

The point of reference for criticising tradition is "the criticism of the text—*metin tenkidi*".

> 'Textual Criticism' is normally used for the study of the history of a written text once it has been copied, corrected, codified, etc. Özsoy's understanding is different here. What is being criticised in his "criticism of the text" is either the content, or the divine origin of a text.

Özsoy illustrates his point with ʿĀʾiša. "The first founder of it [scil., criticism of the text] is ʿĀʾiša".

> He is obviously alluding to the ironic comment Muhammad's favourite wife made on 33:50–1. The verses give exceptional privileges to Muhammad in matters matrimonial. ʿĀʾiša's reaction upon hearing the proclamation was: "God hurries to do your will!"[317]

---

315 Cf. above, p. 117.

316 Cf. above, at note 297.

317 Cf., e.g., Rudi Paret, *Mohammed und der Koran*, p. 66. Paret refers to Ibn Saʿd 8,141, Buḫārī's *Tafsīr* 33,7 and aṭ-Ṭabarī's commentary 22,17. He judges the remark likely to be historical. He has a good case here, because, in the language of New Testament criticism, which is helpful in this question, he could invoke the *criterion of embarrassment.* It pinpoints *sīra* material that would hardly have been invented by the early umma, since such material created embarrassment or theological difficulties for the first Muslims.

1.2 *The Practice of the Koran*

1.2.1 The Significance of Sunna

Understandably, the interviewers insist even in ʿĀʾiša's case on a criterion for criticising the Koran. Özsoy says, the criterion is "the Prophet's Sunna," and he explains 'Sunna' as "the first experience". (p. 28) "Sunna gives us the direction (*istikamet*) of the words to be found in the Koran. Once we have set fire to the gun, the missile can get anywhere. But if we have a particular aim, if we want to make clear our direction, we have to aim at our target exactly. [...] The "first practice" gives a direction to the words. Muhammad had a personal life-style, just as [he had] the experience of revelation, and there was a correction of what happened [in his life]; but apart from this, he also made *iǧtihād*, if necessary." (p. 29)

Does that mean, Muhammad's way of understanding and living is made into a principle? No, says Özsoy, one cannot reach a general principle, because Muhammad lived in a certain "combination of circumstances—konjonktür",[318] and what he said referred to those circumstances. Here, Özsoy introduces another distinction. Is Islam as exhibited in Koran and Sunna "a standard STATUS QUO *(standart bir durum)*—or, rather, a stance *(duruş)* taken towards a certain historical STATUS QUO? If we perceive Islam as a STATUS QUO, we will strive for °a wholesale re-actualisation *(blok olarak yeniden gerçekleştirmeye)* of that STATUS QUO in all historical layers. If however we perceive it as a stance, our question will be: what can the relation[319] of that stance, which exhibits the Arabian combination of circumstances in the 7th century,[320] be in this [today's] combination of circumstances?" In answering this question, the "categorical distinction between Koran and Sunna must not be overlooked".

> The argument has to be reconstructed here. The Koran is, for Özsoy, ambiguous. It can be heard to say various things, also wrong things. It is not evident from the interview whether Özsoy thinks that this is true of all texts ("words") or not. At least in the case of the Koran he presupposes that the text is not clear. But clarity can be gained through the interpretative instrument which comes along with the Koran. This can of course not be another text. Otherwise the same problem could occur. It is the experience with the Koran put into practice, in other words, the reaction to the Koran. A new interpretive tool is offered: the first believing

---

318 Cf. below, footnote 337.

319 The text has *"açılımı"* which is 'astronomical declension; i.e., distance from celestial equator'. If not actually another word (e.g., *'açılması'* ('solution') or *'açımı'* ('commentary')) was meant, 'declension' may be used here as a metaphor for 'relative position towards—'.

320 The text has "17th century".

addressees' comportment. Özsoy certainly offers an inspiring new solution to a vexing problem. And it is courageous to say that the Koran is not in itself clear. These points should however be considered: (1) The relation between text and the extratextual tool (Sunna) is not clear. Can there be instances in which the first addressees' reactions to the Koran were wrong (e.g., due to misunderstanding or disobedience)? If it is possible to say that, then either a third criterion besides Koran and Sunna is involved (but not mentioned), or the Koran is actually clearer than Özsoy presupposed. Can the Koran judge Sunna or not? Or, can one today, with Koranic criteria judge Sunna or not? If Sunna is infallible, then one will either have to exclude some of the first addressees' actions from Sunna (but on which grounds?) or one has canonised even very problematic actions. (2) To say that the necessary interpretative tool for the Koran is Sunna, i.e., a certain practice, implies that the Koran is only about action. That would amount to what has been called ethical reductionism above. (p. 84) (3) Although Sunna is observable action, a person of today can, of course, not observe the Koran's first addressees. Today, Sunna can only subsist in indirect forms, viz., in action according to Sunna or in texts (oral or otherwise). With all these forms of subsisting one has the same interpretative problems as were claimed to be in the way of unambiguously understanding the Koranic text. (4) Can there not be people in later centuries who live the Koran just as correctly as the actors of Özsoy's Sunna but can be understood and imitated better? In his discovery of the hermeneutic importance of tradition Özsoy is, so to speak, taking a Catholic stance, because he leaves Reformation's principle of SOLA SCRIPTURA. But then again, he restricts the time during which relevant tradition happened to a very short period of history.

1.2.2 The Dialectics of Commandments and Circumstances

Özsoy stresses the importance of the connection between the concrete Koranic *propositions* and the *principles* which are illustrated by those propositions. "If, when speaking about the Koran's universal principles, something independent of the individual commands directed towards the circumstances would be meant, that would be a groundless abstraction." (p. 29) One has to see the "dialectics" between the circumstances and the formulation of a commandment.

Özsoy may be thinking of up to four types of dependence in a relation of reciprocal mediation, which justifies the usage of "dialectics". (a.) Koranic commandments depend on events in the life of Muhammad. (b.) Certain persons' courses of action depend directly, via obedience to the proclamation, on Koranic commandments. (c.) Muslims' general ethical principles depend on individual Koranic commandments. (d.) The Koranic commandments depend on the ethical norms they manifest.

Even ʿUmar made *iğtihād*; but before that, "during the coming down [scil., of the Koran], we cannot observe a distinction between °meaning and wording *(maksat ve hitap):* at that time, the two were °mutually implicit (*içiçe*)." (p. 29) The famous case, when ʿUmar abolished the Koranic sanction of theft during a period of hunger, is not a case of adapting Koran to another time, says Özsoy. And he adduces this justification: because taking away food in a period of hunger isn't stealing. Another example is ʿUmar's practice of not complying with clear Koranic commandments, in order to gain the hearts of recently converted Muslims. (p. 30) That was necessary, says Özsoy, when Islam still had problems in getting a "lobby". (Ibid.) Nowadays, there is no more need for such tricks. Özsoy admits that ʿUmar's situation was special. He had the self-confidence to say "I have understood what kind of a society God wants. I know what God and the Prophet want to do." He was able to say so because he had in his memory his own life experience of the Koran's proclamation and the Prophet's actions. "Therefore, Fazlur Rahman stresses the concept of Living Sunna." (p. 30) But why did the Caliphs start collecting a written Koran so soon after Muhammad's death? The Koran was recited even before it existed as °a physical book *(muṣḥaf)*. It was not in order to have a reference text that the first companions of the Prophet collected the Koran. God has not sent down a book to be passed on between two covers from generation to generation. Rather God "revealed in order to create a congregation, exemplary to humanity". (p. 30) When the interviewers ask whether God's priority was to found a community—rather than to reveal a book—Özsoy does not reject that. The next question is: "Is then inevitably in addition to the Koran the foundation of a community necessary which understands, perceives that Koran?" (p. 31) Özsoy replies affirmatively, justifying his response with the thought that a merely text-based behaviour always needs a criterion to decide how to apply the text.

This is a step forward in Koran hermeneutics. Özsoy has entered an Islamic ecclesial hermeneutics. But it is unfair to christen his insight with such charged terminology. Özsoy says that God's revelation is not words but a group of people. With that, he has implicitly left Fazlur Rahman's claim that the Koran and its context, and thus its meaning, can be sufficiently objectively ascertained,[321] which does not seem to require the criterion of a congregation.

321 *Islam & Modernity*, p. 8.

1.2.4 Epistemology and Ethics

But as Özsoy admits, after Muhammad's death the congregation immediately started to "soil" (p. 31) the purity of the original doctrine. Is that to say, there is no way to live according to religion? It is, in spite of our historical distance, possible to get hold of the Koran's will for humanity. "God's contribution *(katkı)* to human beings is according to this understanding not an epistemological but an altogether ethical one."

Özsoy is distinguishing here between information and instruction. And "ethical" means for him 'common sense'. And there is nothing new to be learnt from the Koran's instruction, as will become clear in the following paragraph. So what Özsoy is stating again (as under *1.1.3*, above) is that the Koran has no original contribution to make.

1.3 The Message of the Koran

1.3.1 New Information in the Koran?

"*Kor'an insana bilmediği birşeyi anlatmıyor*—the Koran does not explain something to human being[s] which they had not known before." Here, the interviewers interfere. No, they say, there is for example new information about Jesus's death. Therefore the interviewers change to the subject of the historicity *(gerçeklik)*, i.e., the historical actuality of the Koranic narratives.

Because of this shift of perspective the expectable and interesting question was not asked let alone answered: 'If the Koran has not brought anything otherwise unknown, why was it sent in the first place?' Possible replies to this would be that the Koran's contribution is irreplaceable because (a.) it is (though not of high ingenuity) of the highest possible *intensity*; (b.) it addresses that particular group of human beings which had *forgotten* what otherwise everybody knows; (c.) it created an exemplary society which serves as proof for the possibility of ethics to reign or as a model to be followed. Ömer Özsoy's own answer would certainly go along the lines of the last reply (c.). Here, one may ask if other instructions comparable to the Koranic event not also create exemplary societies, e.g., Ancient Israel?

1.3.2 Disagreeing About Facts

In speaking about historical actuality, Özsoy gives two examples. Whereas the Koran considers the Christian Trinity to contain Mary, Christians claim that to be no Christian position. Whereas the Koran considers the Jews to hold Ezra to be the Son of God, Jews claim they have never held that.

Özsoy is alluding to passages concerning Maryam like 5:116, and the verse concerning ʿUzayr, viz., 9:30.

These two examples, together with the question whether Jesus died on the cross or not, bring him to the conclusion that there is disagreement.

As a reaction to the interviewers' suggestion of turning to the problem of historicity, this may amount to admitting one of two things. Either (a.) there are historical mistakes in the Koran; or (b.) one will never be able to settle debates on what actually happened.
But disagreements may originate not simply in different textual foundations, as Özsoy says, but in equivocations, which can be clarified. The passage about Mary, e.g., may either refer to a heterodox 'Christian' teaching, or it may well be based on, and directed against, Christian *practice.*—The debate will probably never end within history. But to conclude "so there is disagreement" and then stop the debate is avoiding to be touched by the power of arguments. One should still keep exchanging arguments about which possibility has the better claim at historicity.

1.3.3 The Koran as an Historical Source

The discussion now focuses on [Muḥammad Aḥmad] Ḫalaf Allāh.[322] The interviewers summarise his position thus: "The Koran does not talk about one [single historical] fact." (p. 32) Özsoy however refutes that summary. He says Ḫalaf Allāh's view was that the Koran "preferred, in order to give historical information, not to enter into a confrontation of the addressees' culture and history." (Ibid.) That is to say, Ḫalaf Allāh–supported by Özsoy–believes that the Koran simply used the stories in the air to make its point. But then Özsoy himself says that the Koran upon telling stories does not claim to be telling history. "Reading the Koranic passages that relate to the universe and the creation as if they were scholarly information is a mistake." (p. 32)

Here, Özsoy is touching upon a relevant point not discussed much in recent Koran exegesis. Besides a juridical usage of the Koran some reflections on the Koran's—implicit or explicit—theological theology and anthropology[323] have been undertaken. Likewise, aesthetic questions have triggered recent scholarly interest.[324] The early modern question of the Koran's scientific value is in most scholarly circles settled, e.g., by claiming that the Koran does not want to make scientific statements, or by saying: the Koran is adapting its world view to the

[322] Cf. above, p. 42.
[323] Cf., e.g., Fazlur Rahman, *Major Themes.*
[324] Cf. Navid Kermani, *Gott ist schön. Das ästhetische Erleben des Koran*, Munich 1999.

mind set of 7th century Arabs. But here Özsoy inquires about the *historical value* of the Koranic narratives.[325] A distinction is due. Is Özsoy rejecting the view that

a. the Koran wants to make historically correct statements;
b. the Koran does in fact make historically correct statements;
c. the historical correctness or incorrectness of Koranic statements can be ascertained; or
d. the Koran can be read as a source for historical knowledge?

1.3.4 What God Wanted to Do

If it is the aim of the Koran to make a scientific contribution, then God told a lie, Ömer Özsoy says. "As a Muslim, °I try to understand what He wanted to do *(ne yapmak istediğini anlamaya çalışıyorum).*" (p. 32)

The GENUS VERBI of *'yapmak'* is surprising. If, as Özsoy pointed out, (p. 31) the Koran is to be read as an ethical book, why did he not say that he tries to understand what God wants *to be done (ne yapılmak istediğini)?* It would be too easy to split up the areas of subject matter of a text into ethical, historical and scientific, and then claim that the text wanted to make propositions only of the first type. Why should a text not want to make other claims? Because in the other areas it is proven erroneous? This is a common trick, not only in Islam. But it is inconsistent, arbitrary and a fatal curtailment. And it does not shed a good light on ethical exegesis because it starts from the rather weak presupposition that the text may be wrong in all areas—only in ethics, it isn't. Now, since arguably, general ethics is the least controversial of all subject matters mentioned, this strategy is bound to be seen as total surrender. It is retiring from all public strongholds to some shaky cottage which nobody will attack because everybody can easily build their own.

If however Özsoy really meant the active voice here, then he made an interesting statement which opens up a new type of questioning. His view then triggers the following comments. (1) If the primary question for understanding the Koran is 'What God wanted to do', the implication is: God wanted/wants to act through the Koran. This sheds new light on God's way of acting. (At least one type of) God's action is then suggestive, rather than °Self-asserting and Self-imposing Himself (‚sich durchsetzen'). This can be seen as a restriction of God's omnipotence. It can however also be understood as affirming God's deliberate renunciation of power. In other words, if Özsoy asks what God wants to do through the Koran, then he raises the question whether God's will is necessarily fulfilled or is, rather, an ethical intention which is proposed to free beings. (2) "Wanted to do" does not necessarily imply '… but did not succeed in accomplishing'. (3) If the Koran is understood as the expression of God's will which was actually fulfilled,

[325] Ömer Özsoy knows well, and is clearly influenced by, the work of Rudi Paret. Paret wrote an article in 1960 titled, "Der Koran als Geschichtsquelle", *Der Islam*, vol. 37 (1961), pp. 24–42, which was reprinted in IDEM (ed.), *Der Koran*, Darmstadt 1975, pp. 137–58. Paret's result was that "one can learn next to nothing about the external course of history from the Koran". (p. 148 in the 1975 edition)

the attention of those who want to understand God's will widens: from a textual fixation to a consideration of the actual practice of the community which God founded by the Koran. And this is precisely Özsoy's congregational hermeneutics. (4) It is however (especially for this type of hermeneutics) unnecessary and dangerous as an exegete of the Koran to abandon the field 'what God did' completely, and only defend 'what God wanted to do'. Because (a.) 'what God wanted to do' contains itself an historical claim, which must, just as 'what God did', be established historically; therefore, if one holds that one cannot read 'what God did' from the Koran, one cannot read 'what God wanted to do' from it, either; (b.) if the precise content of 'what God wanted to do' is to be understood not from the Koran but only from its complement, the Sunna, then one has to rely on Sunna historically while one has just declared the Koran to be historically unreliable; this is operating with double standards. (5) Since 'ne yapmak istediği' can be translated in the past and the present tense, the formula even offers a useful question for applicative interpretation today. What does God want to do with us now reading the Koran?

1.3.5 What God Has Done

The function of the Koranic narratives is not to give historical information. Rather, the intention of, e.g., the narratives about earlier prophets is a psychological one. We are to understand the parallel between what happened to those prophets and Muhammad.

Özsoy is overstating Ḫalaf Allāh's position. In Ḫalaf Allāh's eyes, the Koran cited what *actually happened* as narrated by the ancient Arabs, i.e., with heavy legendary embroidery.[326] For Özsoy however the narrative bits of the Koran work exclusively as parables. This implies a huge claim. It is the surrender of history of salvation. God says (and perhaps does) through the Koran what He wants to do, but He does not say what He has done. One might want to qualify this statement and say: 'But at least the Koran mentions the *types of things* God does, if not the individual events, because even though the individual stories about earlier prophets are not historically true, they are *generally* true; *things like that* happen in history.' The problem with that view is however that it has reduced history from an actual string of events to a theory. If the theory cannot be corroborated by actual events, it is thin air. And if theology cannot name which concrete things God actually brings about, it is not talking about God in power, and therefore not about God.

[326] Cf. above, p. 42.

1.3.6 Credulity vs. Scepticism

The interviewers criticise Ömer Özsoy's method as flawed from the outset, because he "breasts the critiques [forwarded] from the West, in the same Western patterns". (p. 32) In answering this accusation, Özsoy takes a moderate stance: the criticism Islam receives may have scholarly value. But one need not therefore defend Islam by accepting the critic's presuppositions wholesale. The interviewers' concern is that by accepting historical criticism the Koran may be shown to contain historical incorrectness and thus lose its authority as "absolutely right". (p. 32) Özsoy establishes his view that the Koran does not intend to contribute anything to its addressees' historical knowledge, by stating that what the Koran says about the past was known to them anyway. The Koran is using its addressees' language, not worrying about the historical or scientific correctness of the conceptions that language implies. There actually were people who believed what the Koran says about, e.g., Jesus's not dying on the cross. But the Koran is not giving any information about Jesus's death, it simply takes up people's beliefs in order to fulfil its specific function. At this point, the interviewers come up with the wish to read the Koran with all the questions (scil., about history) left aside. That, concludes Özsoy, would amount to giving up the endeavour to understand the Koran.

> In that, Özsoy is right. Closing one's eyes to certain types of questions will never lead one to a belief one can hold with full conviction because one knows there are problems which one has simply decided not to tackle. One's views do then not deserve the name 'understanding'. Özsoy's position and his interviewers' position have pushed each other into opposing ditches, and unnecessarily so. The *İktibas* team says, we want historicity for our faith. That is a reasonable claim. Özsoy says that the Koranic legends do not offer historicity. That, too, is to a large extent reasonable. But now both feel crashed into their ditches. The *İktibas* team then says it will stop asking about history and simply believe it to have happened as the Koran says. This is an odd concept of believing, and not a rational position. But likewise Özsoy is overstating his case when he says there is no history in the Koran. The Koran's historical value—in the sense of a document providing information about what happened—must be seen especially in what it says about the first Muslims. They saw God at work in their own history. Özsoy was about to say that. Why has he not completed his train of thought? It is a valuable insight which can lead Koranic theology on, to say that a history of salvation must start with Muhammad and his companions. Surely, not many doubt *their* historicity.

2 Historical Proclamation and Objective Understanding

The 1996 volume of the journal *İslâmî Araştırmalar*[327] is a 300 page collection of articles headed *Kur'an'ın Anlaşılmasında Yöntem Sorunu*, i.e., The question of method in comprehending the Koran. Ömer Özsoy contributed an article to it titled "*Kur'an Hitabının Tarihselliği ve Tarihsel Hitabın Nesnel Anlamı Üzerine*" (On the historicality of the Koran's proclamation and the objective understanding of the historical proclamation).[328]

2.1 Untexting the Koran

2.1.1 Message and Manner

Özsoy starts from the observation that widely—and fatally—two positions are identified, viz., the positions 'I believe in the Koran' and 'I take the Koran as a transhistorical, universal text'. Özsoy is unhappy about that identification. He sees its root in the confusion of 'the Koran's message *(mesaj)*' and 'the Koran's °diction/manner of speaking *(hitap/söylem)*'[329]. (p. 135) He consequently sets out to demonstrate that even classically there have been tendencies in Islamic thinking against pigeon-holing the Koran as a text, i.e., as only allowing for literal application. It has also been treated as an historical proclamation. (p. 136) Özsoy distinguishes between the theologians' and the lawyers' dealing with the Koran: "The theologians were looking for a coherence *(insicam)* not only in the totality of the verses' content but even in the sequence *(ardarda geliş)* of the Suras." Here, Özsoy

---

327 Cf. above, p. 61.

328 pp. 135–43. Page numbers in the text above refer to that article.

329 What does Ömer Özsoy mean by *"hitap/söylem"*? Further down in his article, (p. 137) he himself offers a translation. That may demonstrate that the Turkish wording isn't clear. However, the translation isn't, either. What he suggests further down is "discourse". *'Ḫiṭāb'* is common in *Arabic* for 'discourse' in Michel Foucauld's tradition. (Cf., e.g., Naṣr Ḥāmid Abū Zayd, *Naqd al-ḫiṭāb ad-dīnī*, Kairo 1992: "Critique of the religious discourse".) Is Özsoy, therefore, referring to Foucauld's fashionable ‹discours›, i.e., a territory of evidence in its own right? Or to Karl-Otto Apel's and Jürgen Habermas's ‚Diskurs', i.e., critical communication on validity claims? Since Özsoy is not discussing epistemology but general linguistics here, it is more likely that he uses it in the ordinary sense of 'speaking'. Cf. below, footnote 333, and Helmut Peukert, "Diskurs, Diskurstheorien, diskursiv", *Lexikon für Theologie und Kirche*, vol. 3, Freiburg ³1995, cols. 263–5, col. 264. (*Historisches Wörterbuch der Philosophie* has no entry ‚Diskurs'.) See also Geoffrey Lewis's critical comment on the ambiguous and—in his eyes—superfluous neologism *'söylem'* in: *The Turkish Language Reform*, pp. 145–6.

mentions the Arabic term '*tanāsub as-suwar*'.[330] On the other hand, Özsoy presents the lawyers' method.

2.1.2 First Practice

According to Özsoy, the lawyers wanted to use the Koran as a "source of practice". Therefore, "before disclosing how it may be put to practice, they stressed its first practice". This is to say, they were interested in the Koran's original understanding and application. "That means they were able to go beyond the available textual structure and to handle it from an historical viewpoint." (p. 136) Özsoy uses the word "historical" in the sense of 'diachronical' here. That becomes clear when he says: "From the point of view of jurisprudence, [the categories of] °*nāsiḫ/mansūḫ*, Meccan/Medinan and the occasions of revelation' [i.e., the questions of a later verse abrogating an earlier, of chronology and context of proclamation] gain special importance as elements which add an historical dimension to the Koranic text." (p. 136) Özsoy now asks the pertinent question whether the Koran was originally meant to be a text. "The weaknesses the Koran displays according to the criteria of literary textual criticism[331]—°lack of unity, contradictory expressions, repetitions *(bütünsüzlük, çelişik ifadeler, tekrarlar)* etc.—demonstrate that from an historical point of view, the Koran was not originally conceived as a text." (p. 137)[332] But in the next paragraph, (p. 137) Özsoy points out that it is unhistorical to consider the Koran to be

330 Özsoy is not adducing a reference for the term. But the usage of the concept and even more so the theme are classical. The concept appears in the Koran commentary of al-Qurṭubī (d. 1272). Al-Qurṭubī, when trying to explain the inimitability of the Koran, enumerates ten characteristics of the Koranic text, the last of which is its "*tanāsub*", i.e., the state of being free of contradictions (cf. Roger Arnaldez, "al-Ḳurṭubī", *EI*², vol. 5, Leiden 1986, pp. 512–3, p. 513). Al-Qurṭubī's term comes in an old tradition: Sulaymān al-Ḫaṭṭābī (d. 998), al-Bāqillānī (d. 1013) and al-Ǧurǧānī (d. 1078), when considering the inimitability of the Koranic structure (*naẓm*) discussed the interrelation of words and phrases in the Koran (their *munāsaba*). Later classical commentators like az-Zamaḫšarī (d. 1144) and especially ar-Rāzī (d. 1209) extended their scope of structural research, considering also the relationships among verses, groups of verses within the Suras and groups of Suras within the Koran. (Alford T. Welch, "Sūra", *EI*², vol. 9, pp. 885–9, p. 888) In all the commentaries mentioned, the synchronic search for a meaningful system behind the order of the Koranic passages as they stand in "ʿUṯmān's" text has had the dogmatic interest of establishing the Koran's unique—and ergo revealed—form.

331 Özsoy is here not talking about textual criticism in the terminological sense of the history of a text from its earliest written forms until today. His *"edebî metin tenkidi"* (literary text criticism) could just as well have been *'edebî tenkit'* (literary criticism). Cf. also above, p. 140.

332 His usage of 'text' will be considered below, on p. 155, under *(A) Not a Text*.

an *inconsistent* entity. If it were one, that would have been the first thing to pick on °for anti-Muslims of Muhammad's time (*nüzul dönemindeki İslam-karşıtlarınca).* So, *is* in Özsoy's eyes the Koran a consistent entity after all? No. His argument E SILENTIO ADVERSARIORUM, the opponents' silence on this point, is an element of Özsoy's historical proof which runs, if schematised, this way:

a. There are contradictions in the Koran as we have it.
b. The earliest adversaries of Islam did not find them problematic.
c. Therefore, the Koran was not originally understood as one systematic whole.

Now Özsoy is ready for offering a description of what the Koran is: "Nothing but a collection of passages, independent of each other, revealed in connection with different events and developments in twenty-something years." (p. 137)

2.1.3 The Koran: Oral Or Literal?

Subsequently, Özsoy brings in the distinction *söz—metin* (speech vs. text), which rests, as he says, (p. 137) upon two pairs of linguistic categories, viz., oral vs. written *(sözlü—yazılı)* and speech vs. language *(söz—dil).*[333] Writing can only convey the meaning transported in the speech act, the NOËMA, not the speech act itself. (p. 137) "What the text says becomes more important than what the author wants to say, because in writing, the non-verbal processes, which are helpful in understanding speech—intonation, manner of speaking, mimics, gestures—cannot be documented."[334]

Applying his distinction to the Koranic text, Özsoy says the Koran is *written speech*. He concludes that in reading the words of the Koran, we are lacking information necessary for understanding those words. (p. 138) But, he observes, the Koran itself was while taking shape aware of the addressees' role as "contribution and influence". (p. 138) He demonstrates this

---

333 Özsoy offers in fact three categories, *dil/söz/söylem* and gives English (?) equivalents for them: language/parole/discourse. He refers to Paul Ricœur as the origin of those categories. Ricœur is explicitly taking over Ferdinand de Saussure's distinction of
‹langage› the whole phenomenon of language;
‹langue› the established institution of a language;
‹parole› an act of speaking.
(Paul Ricœur, *Hermeneutik und Strukturalismus*, Munich 1973, p. 42.—Ibid., p. 101 (cf. already p. 67), Ricœur introduces a fourth category,
‹discours› a speech.)

334 Özsoy's distinction will be discussed under *(B) Discourse and Distance*, below, p. 156

claim by quoting a passage from 5:101.[335] "Don't ask questions about themes which will, once they are being explained, make you sad. If you ask about them while the Koran is being sent down, those themes will be explained to you." Özsoy's point is that a passage like the one quoted implies, indeed explicates, that there is "a process of open dialogue between the immanent and the transcendent". An example to which Özsoy alludes is the case of the holy months.[336] Özsoy calls the answer reported in the Koran "political, and therefore accidental[337]".

2.1.4 The Koran As Commentary

How can these occasional statements gain the status of an inspired text? Özsoy introduces the concept of approval (*onaylamak*: to approve). It works, again, in the form of an E SILENTIO argument. While Muhammad's and the Muslims' wrong decisions were criticised, corrected, cancelled, the right ones were not. This slightly circular sounding statement is clarified thus: God's approval is that the Koran did not reject it. (p. 139) Thus, history—in the sense of *action* over against *word*—gains a role congenial to the text. Indeed, Özsoy's model implies that the revealed text is a commentary: the decisive commentary on the actions of its first hearers.

Özsoy introduces a terminological distinction between two Arabic words, *ad-dīn* (religion) and *tadayyun* (religiosity). By "religion" he means the Koran's "religious substance", which is the same as that of other prophets, whereas "religiosity" is any possible "immanent—i.e., temporal—manifestation of religion". (p. 139) Applying his own[338] distinction, Özsoy is now able to state: "The Koran is religion's °final reflection/mirroring *(son yansıma)* on the human level; [the Koran is] not religion itself." (Ibid.) Treating the Koran as the religious essence itself amounts

[335] Özsoy has not stated the reference.—The text given here translates Özsoy's Turkish translation.

[336] 2:217: "You are being asked about the holy month, [that is] whether [it is allowed] to fight in [the holy month]. Say: Fighting in it is a grave offence. But keeping [others] away from God's way, and not believing in God, and keeping others away from the holy place, and expelling its inhabitants—[all these offences] are graver." According to aṭ-Ṭabarī's commentary in loc., the verse refers to the incident when Muslims before the end of the holy month of Rağab (in the second year after the Hiğra) attacked a Meccan caravan. During the attack an "unbeliever" was killed by a Muslim. Cf., e.g., Rudi Paret, *Kommentar und Konkordanz*, p. 46.

[337] Konjonktürel—situational, occasional. The word is given in the Turkish dictionaries only with its economic meaning. But the context demonstrates that it means "influenced by the circumstances (‹conjuncture›) and therefore contingent" here. Thus, "accidental" seems to capture the idea well.

[338] He quotes Tahsin Görgün as an earlier user of the word *'tadayyun'* in this sense.

in Özsoy's view to "raising what is factual to the normative level". (p. 139)[339] And that, again, would mean in the last analysis understanding that the Koran does not want us to become Muslims, but °to become Arabs (*Araplaşma*). (p. 139)

2.1.5 Finding the Koran's Objective Meaning

In front of this conceptual backdrop, Özsoy is now able to turn to the important hermeneutical question of a text's *objective meaning.* Under the witty[340] headline "The objective meaning and its enemies", (p. 139) he defines 'objective meaning' as "the meaning of the spoken speech—*sözlü söylemin anlamı*" and again as "the original meaning which the speaker will have intended—*mütekellimin*[341] *kastetmiş olabileceği özgün anlamdır*". (p. 139) The simplest method of finding out the "objective meaning" is to "transfer the written speech back into the original word-milieu and to re-set/re-imagine the speech act—*yazılı söylemi yeniden özgün söz ortamına taşıyıp, söz-eylemi yeniden kurmak/kurgulamaktır*".[342]

In order to prove that there has been a consciousness in Islam for the objective meaning of the Koran, he reminds us of the lawyers' distinction of adequate and false interpretation. On the other hand, he cites as the oldest anti-objectivists the *ẓāhirī* approach (as opposed to the *bāṭinī* approach). These are two Koran hermeneutical positions. The former claims that only the plain wording *(aẓ-ẓāhir)* can be the basis for an application. The latter presupposes a hidden *(bāṭin)* meaning to be discovered beneath the surface semantics (the PRIMA FACIE meaning) of the Koranic words. "By approaching religious texts—and also the language event—from the surface wording, the *ẓāhirī* approach misses language's indirect ways of communicating, the most important of which is the metaphor." (p. 140)[343]

In Özsoy's diagnosis, today's greatest negligence of "objective meaning"—the severest hermeneutic disease of Islam—is the anachronism which wants the Koran to have literal answers for *today's* questions. "In order to read the Koran "as if it had come down today", or to ask the Koran constantly in order to understand it: "what am I being told here?"—

---

339 This point will be discussed under *(C) The Factual Turned Normative*, below, p. 157.

340 Özsoy seems to allude to Karl R. Popper's *The Open Society and Its Enemies*, and its companions.

341 Rather than the text's *"mütekkellimin"*.

342 "Objective meaning" will be discussed under *(D) The Speaker's Objective Intention*, below, p. 157.

343 These traditional linguistic and exegetical categories will be reconsidered under *(E) Traditions of Objectivism*, below, p. 158.

without seeing all those [scil., hermeneutical] difficulties—one has to remove the [concept of] objective meaning." (pp. 140–1).[344] The question remains: how can Muslims,[345] once they have seen the Koran's contextual dependence make it speak into today's context? Özsoy sets out to answer this with an analysis of modernity. Its self-perception includes not only its being different from all other eras, but also its superiority. And even post-modernism, he says, is not different from modernity's overestimation of its own capacities by offering what it calls the only possible solution. The Muslim reaction to this is to "look for the solution of these problems in the Koran, or, rather, produce solutions adequate to the Koran". (p. 141) So, the difference which Özsoy seems to see between the Muslim and the modern attitude is that of the source of solutions. While modern approaches are constrained, according to Özsoy, to search *within themselves* for a way out, Muslims have the Koran, something like an Archimedean point outside of themselves, to move the world.

2.1.6 *Analysing the Koranic Context, and Ours*

He describes the Muslim approach in Fazlur Rahman's terminology (cf. above, p. 76) as a "double movement" of understanding and interpreting. He cites Amīn al-Ḫūlī[346] as his ally in designating the first movement (understanding) as objective and the second (interpreting) as subjective. He justifies this distinction thus: "While there is no problem in analysing the historical and local dimensions within a Koranic passage, it is not always possible to analyse with the same accuracy the situation given now, which is, after all, also °a 'historicality' *(bir 'tarihsellik')*".[347]

Özsoy ends his essay with a fundamental reflection. He observes that there are universalising and historicising camps not only in Islam but also among Kemalists, Marxists, and adherents of other world views referring to texts. The basic difference between the two camps is according to Özsoy their concept of history: "Those who prefer a 'historical reading' feel the necessity to appreciate every new situation within its own conditions be-

[344] This criticism will be reconsidered under *(F) The Heuristic Power of Anachronism, below*, p. 159.

[345] In an incidental remark, Özsoy gives a noteworthy definition of 'Muslims': human beings who want to be addressed by the Koran's message. (p. 141)

[346] Cf. above, p. 42.

[347] Like Mehmet Paçacı, Ömer Özsoy is using *'tarihsellik'* (at least sometimes) to mean 'individual historical situation', otherwise he could not use it in combination with '*bir*—one'. Özsoy's idea of analysing the past is being discussed under *(G) Understanding Past Events*, below, p. 159.

cause of the movement which makes each historical event unique and unrepeatable; the opposite camp does not betray such a sensitivity." (p. 143)[348]

2.2 *Discussion*

(A) Not a Text

(Cf. above, at note 332 on p. 150.) Özsoy's distinction of text and speech sounds confusing, because dealing with a communication as a text does not necessarily imply dealing with it un-historically, nor does 'text' necessarily imply 'systematic structure'. But 'text' has acquired that contrasting image of petrified words in Özsoy. Why did he not use 'book' *(kitap)* instead of 'text' (*metin*)? Wouldn't that have conveyed better its once-and-for-all-time character? Two answers must be given:

1. That is probably not the Koran's own understanding of 'book'. Daniel Madigan's study in the Koranic usage of the word 'book' *(kitāb)*[349] is elucidatory. *'Kitāb'*, he demonstrates from the Koranic wording, need not mean a physical object; it can be the act and content of a stipulation. That would be very much in line with what Ömer Özsoy wants the Koran to be.
2. *Matn/metin* is, apart from simply meaning 'text', the technical term for a literal formulation of Koran or Hadith serving as the basis for legal argumentation. So, 'metin' seems to have a systematic ring, which is precisely what Özsoy needs, because he wants to reject it.

Özsoy's remark that the Koran was not originally intended to be (used as a written) text is excellent and deserves further establishment. For additional corroboration of the thesis one could e.g., adduce the fact that there was among the early Muslims no unanimity about the choice and arrangement

348 Özsoy's "camps" will be reconsidered under *(H) Artificial Adversaries?*, below, on p. 160.

349 Daniel A. Madigan, *The Qur'ân's Self Image. Writing and Authority in Islam's Scripture*, Princeton 2001 (cf. already: IDEM, *"The kitâb about which there is no doubt ...". Books, Writing and Canon in the Qur'ân's Understanding of Itself*, (Columbia University Dissertation) Ann Arbour 1997, and now IDEM, "Book", Jane Dammen McAuliffe (ed.), *Encyclopaedia of the Qur'ān*, vol. 1, Leiden 2001, pp. 242–52). Otto Pretzl, not very optimistic about the quality of the Koran's transmission, pointed out already in 1940 that the Koran has never been a "book" in the strict sense of the word: Otto Pretzl, "Aufgaben und Ziele der Koranforschung", Rudi Paret (ed.), *Der Koran*, pp. 411–2, p. 411.

of the Suras,[350] because there was no revealed or Muhammadan regulation for it.

(B) Discourse and Distance

(Cf. above, at note 334 on p. 151.) Özsoy distinguishes between oral and written. While written communitcations convey only the NOËMATA (the *söylenen*, i.e., that which is intentionally said), oral communications also convey other data relevant for the interpretation, he says. Özsoy's distinction is important but in need of these specifications.

1. The distinction he actually envisaged is that of real-time, face-to-face communication over against lagged, distanced communication; in other words, the difference of time and place. This should not be pinned down to the dichotomy of oral and written. Take audio-taped messages: they are oral but can be remote in time and space; or writing-conversations: the partners can be present in one place although the messages are being written. The relevant parameter is *spatiotemporal distance*. If one specifies Özsoy's distinction according to this parameter his observation becomes pertinent. The former type of communication (spatiotemporally close contact) provides plenty of unsaid data, which one might call the speech context.
2. Even a spatiotemporally remote message can provide *other data* than only NOËMATA. E.g., subconscious and automatic choices like the selection of language (Arabic, or Aramaic?), of linguistic level (standard language, or dialect?), of individual words *(wāḥid, or aḥad?)* are themselves data.
3. When Özsoy enumerates the "processes" not conveyed in literal communications, he lists only behavioural elements of the speaker like accentuation and mimics. It would however have been more to Özsoy's own point, if he had also listed aspects concerning the speech *context* like: when was it said, which was the question, who was listening, what happened afterwards? They are not transmitted in the written text, and they are vital for interpretation.

[350] Theodor Nöldeke and Friedrich Schwally, *Geschichte des Qorān*, vol. 2, esp. pp. 42–6.

(C) The Factual Turned Normative

(Cf. above, at note 339 on p. 153.) Özsoy is using yet another conceptual pair—factual/normative—for an idea which we have already met in the other authors analysed here. The Koran is an exemplary application for something else, which is the message proper. He has not yet stated

1. *why* that application is the decisive one;
2. how to get from the application to the norm, or, in order to elaborate Özsoy's imagery, from the reflection to the archetype;
3. how the behaviour of Muhammad can be declared to be merely factual *(olgusal),* not by itself normative, if the Koran itself declares Mohammad to be an example *(uswatun ḥasanatun*, 33:21), which is most likely to refer to Muhammad's *exemplary actions*;
4. what type of propositions are to be included under the vague word *'ad-dīn'*[351], and which not: is *ad-dīn* merely action guiding, or does it include other communications?

(D) The Speaker's Objective Intention

(Cf. above, at note 342 on p. 153.) Özsoy defines a text's objective meaning as "the original meaning which the speaker will have intended". There are a couple of problems with the terminology of "objective meaning" to be noted here.

1. As already the POTENTIALIS in Özsoy's definition *(olabileceği)* implies, there is no easy, uncontroversial access to the original speech-intention. There can only be suppositions. Then however 'objective meaning' promises a clarity which it cannot keep.
2. Who is the speaker in the case of the Koran? In other words: whose intention betrays the objective meaning? There are three possible answers to this question: God, Muhammad, or Muhammad-inspired-by-God. If the answer is Muhammad, then one is confronted with the difficulty that the historical Muhammad might well be shown to have had intentions which we see today as limited or even inappropriate. The problem with the answer 'God' is that one will hardly be able to understand, let alone verbalise God's intention behind a certain verse. Because if it is according to God's will that the Koran is being used today and in many generations to come as a reference, God's intention must be much

---

351 "The word *dīn* has never become a theological term. That was probably due to the fact that it was not sufficiently unequivocal." Josef van Ess, *Theologie und Gesellschaft*, vol. 4, p. 567. Cf. van Ess's comprehensive discussion of the word, pp. 565–7.

more than the original, i.e., mono-situational, intention to be deduced from a verse's historical context. So, one has either to know all situations the verse in question will ever be meant to regulate. Or one abstracts the intention, and is, then, back to the problems of applying rules.[352] Lastly, one might proffer the *inspired Muhammad* as the subject of the Koran's intention. But this answer contains the difficulty that Muhammad will, in spite of being inspired, not have known the reason (or, all the reasons) why a certain proclamation was in place when it was to be pronounced. So, Muhammad's intention can in fact be irrelevant. Umberto Eco thinks that he knows a way out of our trilemma. Rather than being interested in the author's—let alone, the reader's—intention, he proposes to look for *the text's* intention.[353] That however is the position diametrically opposed to Ömer Özsoy's, who wants, so to speak, to un-text the Koran by re-speeching it.

(E) Traditions of Objectivism

(Cf. above, at note 343 on p. 153.) Concerning Özsoy's glimpse into the history of the idea of objective meaning in Koran exegesis, three comments are in place:

1. He is right in claiming that the lawyers' distinction between correct and wrong interpretation of the Koran implies the view that a text has an inter-subjectively accessible decisiveness. But: (a.) Can any possible interpretation be judged (objectively) as either right or wrong, or are there *undecidable* interpretations? (b.) Is it necessary for the lawyers' qualification of certain interpretations as inadequate, that the objective meaning of the text itself *can be worded?* (c.) Are the lawyers—actually or necessarily—*unanimous* concerning the correctness of interpretations?
2. To say that starting from the PRIMA FACIE meaning of a text is not to understand how language works, is an interesting and pertinent commentary on a major problem of *ẓāhirī* semantics. But as long as one does not substantiate such an objection with examples from exegeses (claiming to be) working strictly with *aẓ-ẓāhir*, the argument does not go down.
3. Özsoy does not name the problem in *bāṭinī* exegesis, whereas he pertinently lays open the problem in the *ẓāhirī* approach. He might have

[352] Cf. above, at notes 28 on p. 25 and 153 on p. 74.

[353] In the 1990 Cambridge Tanner Lecture published as: Umberto Eco, *Interpretation and Overinterpretation*, Cambridge (U.K.) 1992, p. 25: INTENTIO OPERIS, rather than INTENTIO AUCTORIS or INTENTIO LECTORIS.

said, along his line of "objective meaning", that while a *ẓāhirī* exegete does not know how *meaning* works, the *bāṭinī* interpreter has an unnecessary problem with *objectivity*.

(F) The Heuristic Power of Anachronism

(Cf. above, at note 344 on p. 154.) In Ömer Özsoy's eyes, as-if-today approaches are anachronistic and therefore illegitimate. Certainly, they betray a certain naïvety and leave the whole hermeneutical problem simply aside. But one should not undervalue the heuristic power of free associative and merely reader-contextual readings.[354] Of course other (e.g., historical) criteria will subsequently judge, in their own terms, about those interpretations' adequacy.

(G) Understanding Past Events

(Cf. above, at note 347 on p. 154.) Özsoy says, in understanding a text one can be objective; but in interpreting a text one has to be subjective, because it is impossible to analyse today's situation completely. Özsoy's position is problematic but elucidatory. It makes a silent presupposition which is worthy of consideration. One can easily see why it should be difficult to analyse the present, because much of what is going on presently has not reached its result and is therefore open to the future, which will eventually reveal the present's true meaning. So, what Özsoy calls "analysing" is in fact "understanding". But Özsoy now says: It is impossible to understand the present, but it is possible to understand the past. This implies that all elements of the past are *finished*, which again means that later times are not influenced by previous events and cannot shed new light on them. If Özsoy rightly sees (i) that we cannot understand fully what the present means in all its ramifications; and (ii) that a past event has effects on the present (Özsoy is referring to the Koran as a source of solutions for today!), then he should have seen (iii) that it is, within history, also impossible to understand the past fully.

[354] Cf. also above, p. 147.

(Cf. above, at note 348 on p. 155.) When observing how people handle history, Özsoy makes out two camps, viz., universalisers and historicisers. His description of historicising or, indeed, of having an historical consciousness is perceptive: valuing each situation anew. But like the other authors presented here it is doubtful whether Ömer Özsoy is doing justice to his (universalising) opponents by refuting a principle without showing us that and how the alleged opponents use it. *Who is* a universalist?[355] Do they claim context independence? For all historical events or only for the formative one? (There may be *arguments* for a certain event to be de-particularised!)

3 Conclusion: Revisiting History

There is one final point in need of discussion here: Ömer Özsoy, and with him other Koran interpreters designating themselves as historicalists,[356] happily take over a central concept of European thought, *history*. European thinkers will generally welcome such a usage. But one should at the same time observe what happens to the concept on its journey. Ömer Özsoy and the other Turkish authors studied here frequently use the word 'tarih' and its derivatives, and it has been translated by 'history' and its derivatives in the present study. The translation seemed to work, which suggests equivalence of the words. But the English word 'history' itself carries an ambiguity which has so far not been commented upon. British authors like Collingwood define 'history' as the methodical collection of past events.[357] We shall for the moment call this meaning the 'events discipline'. It is easy to deduce from that definition of the scholarly discipline the subject matter of history as being *what happened*, which is a possible second usage of the word 'history'. Let us call that second meaning 'events past'.[358] For many scholars in the continental European tradition, it is a grave underrating of the concept of 'history', if it is understood merely as 'events discipline' and 'events past'. German terminology has tended to use the (otherwise uncommon) word ‚Historie' for 'events past' and especially for the

---

[355] Cf. above, at note 139 on p. 68.

[356] Cf. above, footnote 139.

[357] Collingwood, *History*, p. 3. He can adduce Herodotos (i.1) with his understanding of 'ἱστορεῖν/*historeîn*' as an ally.

[358] A similar, but triple, distinction of 'history' is made by Albert Veraart: (a.) RES GESTAE; (b.) their presentation; (c.) their scholarly study: "Geschichte", *Enzyklopädie Philosophie und Wissenschaftstheorie*, vol. 1, Stuttgart [1b]1995, pp. 750–2, p. 751.

'events discipline'.[359] So, what is 'history' in its authentic meaning, what is ‚Geschichte' for them? It is a concept which developed on the background of the Biblical understanding of events past.[360] Although the term has been secularised, the idea is a religious one. Israel tried, in the religious thinking witnessed in the Bible, to keep track of *God's unpredictable but understandable actions*. 'Unpredictable' includes here the insight that what happens is ever new, rather than running in preset recurring patterns. That would be the position of non-historical (not ‚geschichtlich'), mythical world-views. 'Understandable' includes the idea that the course of events comes to a fulfilment which reveals the meaning of all events. Israel saw the chain of events like Exodus and Exile in the context of their own obedience and disobedience as God's calling, liberating and judging action. From the concept of "the Lord's deeds", the idea of history developed. Issuing commandments is only one, and a subordinate, element of divine action. History is, for Israel, not merely a prop of God's legislation but the so far unfinished totality of God's acting in the world. What about human action? Human beings position themselves towards God's action, God's election and judgment, by accepting or rejecting it. But their free actions can again be integrated by God into the meaningful whole, so that everything can be understood as God's action. History was thus discovered by Israel as the totality of reality, and the totality of reality as history. Although the concept has—starting with Voltaire and Vico—been secularised in that it was now the human beings who became the subject of history, 'history' (‚Geschichte') keeps including the dimensions of comprehensiveness and therefore understanding, for many contemporary continental theorists.[361]

---

359 Hans-Walter Bartsch, "Geschichte/Historie", *Historisches Wörterbuch der Philosophie*, vol. 3, Basel 1974, cols. 398–9, remarks that the distinction goes back to Friedrich von Schlegel (d. 1829) but was welcomed especially among Christian theologians, starting with Martin Kähler in 1892. Cf. however Søren Kierkegaard's terminology which uses similar words but draws another distinction, which comes close to the English distinction between 'historical' and 'historic'. (Richard Schaeffler, "Geschichte, Geschichtlichkeit", *Lexikon für Theologie und Kirche*, vol. 4, ^{3}1995, cols. 553–7, col. 556.) Cf. also Georg Wobbermin, *Geschichte und Historie in der Religionswissenschaft*, Tübingen 1911.

360 Demonstrated e.g., by Karl Löwith, Gerhard von Rad and Mircea Eliade, but already observed by Wilhelm Dilthey, cf. Trutz Rendtorff, "Geschichtstheologie", *Historisches Wörterbuch der Philosophie*, vol. 3, Basel 1974, cols. 439–41, col. 439, and especially, Wolfhart Pannenberg, "Heilsgeschehen und Geschichte"; IDEM, *Grundfragen systematischer Theologie*, vol. 1, Göttingen 1967, pp. 22–78, p. 36, IDEM; *Anthropologie in theologischer Perspektive*, Göttingen 1983, chapter 9.

361 Cf., e.g., Jürgen Habermas, *Zur Logik der Sozialwissenschaften*, Tübingen 1967, p. 166, and Pannenberg, "Heilsgeschehen", p. 36.

When Ömer Özsoy hands out a thirty-five title reading list on "Koran and History", his students find on it one Western author explaining to them the concept of history: Collingwood![362]

The scholars whose Koran exegesis we have encountered in the present study focus on history in a limited context. Their first and foremost interest is divine legislation. In order to understand and interpret it, they are interested in two sets of circumstances: those contemporary to the Koranic proclamation and those contemporary now. For these authors, history is not a chain of events, of divine action, human response and divine integration of what happened; it is not a course of always new incidents which can subsequently be understood as revealing God's being. Rather, history is for Ömer Özsoy and his colleagues a set of conditions to which the divine imperative reacts with the intention to transform these conditions. They use the word "conjuncture", and sometimes "history" is for them a synonym of "historical situation at one particular moment".

Theology of history would see 'history' in its breadth. An hypothesis may be ventured here. Can a *loss of history* in Islam be diagnosed? Two questions arise immediately from the hypothesis, which may be held for a moment for its heuristic value. They question the designation 'loss' from different angles: is it problematic?, and is it Koranic?

1. Is it not acceptable to take a word from one cultural context and import it into another with some conceptual changes introduced on the way? It certainly is. But the point to be made is the following. 'History' in what is claimed here to be part of the occidental understanding of the term might prove a useful concept in Muslim theology, too. These advantages should be considered:
   a. Religion can, if it does theology of history, offer an answer not only to the question 'What are we to do?' but also to the question 'What does it all mean?'.
   b. An Islamic theology of history need not be bound to look only to one moment in history, 1400 years back, when in search of Muslim identity. The whole story of Islam could become thematic, and why-questions like 'Why were the gates of *iğtihād* declared to be closed?' could yield theological fruit, pertaining to questions like 'What is it to be a human being?' and 'What is the point of being a Muslim?'. Thus, ethics and legislation could have a different starting point. Rather than being tied by ancient commands as the core content of

362 Ömer Özsoy, "Kur'an ve Tarih. İçerik ve Kaynakça", (one page photocopy). He lists, as no. 2, Collingwood's *Idea of History* in its Turkish translation *Tarih Tasarımı*, translated by Kurtuluş Dincer, Istanbul 1990.

the foundational event, Muslim theology could deduce guidelines for action from an Islamic anthropology, from an understanding of the present in the context of God's guidance and a sense of the vocation Islam has for today.[363]

c. Deontic ('thou shalt') propositions and scientific statements made in an ancient text can easily be superseded by the cognitive progress of ethics and the natural sciences. Even a text's historical *claims* are open to historical criticism. But the methods of historical criticism can make an ancient text provide information about historical facts. It is this factual content of a text which makes an ancient text an irreplaceable witness. (The status of what is called facts of history is, of course, hypothetical. As long as scholarship continues, absolute certainty cannot be reached. But one can secure data with a high degree of probability.) If a sense of history as an ongoing and meaningful process is lost, the ancient text loses its value as testifying to a unique event. It is therefore bound to lose its universal significance.

2. What is the concept of history in the Koran? There are, it seems, three different theologies of history, i.e. outlooks on the whole course of events, in the Koran:
   a. Ethnic parallelism. All peoples have their divine messengers;[364] all those messengers have similar messages to bring and similar fates to endure. Within this type of historical outlook the various peoples all have their individual histories. A future historical interplay or even unification of the peoples is not envisaged.
   b. Criteriological unification. The message Muhammad brings is seen as judging about the truth or transmissive accuracy of all other prophetic messages. With the criterion of the Koran at hand, the present is seen as the KAIROS of world wide relevance. The meaning of history is Muhammad's bringing together all peoples.[365]

---

363 The last point is touched upon by Mehmet Paçacı, cf. above p. 66. But not even Paçacı sees each historical era as offering new, revealing material for a comprehensive interpretation of the course of events.

364 Cf. *"li-kulli ummatin rasūlun"* 10:47.

365 At closer consideration, already the first model contains a unifying outlook on history. The message brought by the different messengers includes the announcement of an eschatological judgement of universal comprehensiveness. Everyone will be judged by the same judge and, consequently, according to the same criteria. Therefore, even the various lines of this model, though parallel in history, meet at the day of resurrection. Thus, any universal eschatology implies an integration of history in its totality.

c. Confirmative intervention. The Muslims' military successes are seen as God's confirmation of Muhammad's prophetic mission.[366] Now it is human action, not only regularly recurring or exceptional events in nature,[367] that can be seen as *signs*, i.e., as of revelatory character. In this strand of theology of history however defeats have not been seen as equally speaking events.

If the observations expressed here hold true, there are starting points of a theology of history in the Koran, in the unifying task of the Koran and in the understanding of—at least some—events as divine action.

366 Cf. also: David Marshall, *God, Muhammad and the Unbelievers. A Qur'anic Study*, Richmond (U.K.) 1999. Marshall cites verses like 8:17 to substantiate his thesis that Medinan Koran passages interpret the early umma's military successes to be God's punishment of the unbelievers, foretold by the Meccan punishment narratives: "It was not you [believers] who killed them [the unbelievers who were killed at Badr], it was God. It was not you [Muhammad] who threw [or: shot], it was God."

367 In enumerations of God's creative actions, listing "heaven and earth; the sequence of day and night" etc., the Koran can also mention human-made objects like "the ships" as God's creatures. (2:164) This may be seen as radical creationism: booking human acts not on human beings' but on God's list of achievements. But such verses could also shed light on what the Koran means by 'creation'. God's actions and other agents' (e.g., human) actions need not be seen as mutually exclusive. Everything that happens is God's history. Richard Schaeffler has remarked that Semitic languages provide a particularly apt way of expressing God's making-by-letting things happen, viz., the causative conjugation. Richard Schaeffler, "Sprache als Bedingung und Folge der Erfahrung. Das religiöse Wort als Beispiel für die Geschichtlichkeit des Verhältnisses von "Sprache" und "Rede"", Wolfgang Beinert (ed.), *Sprache und Erfahrung als Problem der Theologie*, Paderborn 1978, pp. 11–36, p. 29. Does what Schaeffler says about Biblical divine causatives not offer a key to some Koranic formulations? E.g., God "lets" certain people "go astray": *yuḍillu*, 4th form!, 14:4parr.

Chapter 4
İlhami Güler: Contingent Koran, Absolute Contents

İlhami Güler was born in 1959 in Tortum (province of Erzurum). In 1980 he started his theological studies at Ankara University's İlâhiyat Fakültesi and received his Licentiate in 1985. Between 1985 and 1991 he worked on his doctoral thesis at Ankara University's Institute of Social Studies.[368] His thesis discusses the relation between ethics and eschatology in the Koran. From 1992 to 1993 he was at the University of Cairo for post-doctoral studies. Güler has published several books[369] and many articles, notably in *İslâmî Araştırmalar* and *İslâmiyât*. He is now Professor of systematic theology (Kelâm) at the İlâhiyat Fakültesi of Ankara University.

At the 1997 Koran Symposium, during the Third Koran Week in Ankara, İlhami Güler contributed a paper headed: "The transformation of a free will—God's will—and of a contingent history—610–632 [C.E.]—into 'the Eternal Word' and into 'Necessary History'".[370] The paper should be considered as an essay, i.e., as experimental. That should make us careful about jumping to conclusions on its author's intellectual qualities. If in discussing his essay we will find arguments refuting Güler, that does not mean that his thinking has failed. It means rather that he succeeded in triggering a good discussion.

The paper treats the hermeneutical question in a systematic theologian's perspective. It tackles a problem which has proved crucial in the present

---

368 Ömer Özsoy, too, earned his doctorate at that Institute, cf. above, p. 135.

369 *Allah'ın Ahlakîliği*, Ankara 1998, *Sabit Din–Dinamik Şeriat*, Ankara 1999, and, in 1996, together with Ömer Özsoy, a Turkish index to the Koran.

370 İlhami Güler, "Muhtar Bir İrade (Allah'ın İradesi) ve Mümkün Bir Tarihin (610–632) 'Kelam-ı Kadim'e ve 'Zorunlu Tarih'e Dönüşmesi", Osman Kayaer (ed.), *III. Kur'an Haftası. Kur'an Sempozyumu. 13.–19. Ocak 1997*, Ankara 1998, pp. 211–27. The title could also be rendered: "A free will (God's will), and the transformation of a contingent history (610–632) into 'the Eternal Word' and 'necessary history'". The translation of *'mümkün'* by 'contingent' rather than by 'possible' is justified by the facts that (i) Redhouse—not Steuerwald though—offers 'contingent' as a second meaning of *'mümkün'*; (ii) it is, in European languages, unusual to call non-necessary events which *have* actually taken place still 'possibilities'. The question how contingent history becomes eternal truth was a guiding question already for Gotthold Ephraim Lessing. (*Die Erziehung des Menschengeschlechts*, Berlin 1780; cf. also IDEM, *Über den Beweis des Geistes und der Kraft*, Braunschweig 1777, p. 12: „Zufällige Geschichtswahrheiten können der Beweis von nothwendingen Vernunftwahrheiten nie werden.")—Page numbers in the text above refer to Güler's article.

study,[371] viz., the tension between the accidental status of the individual Koranic rulings at the time of their origin and their normative status for Islam. Güler introduces his contribution with detailed reflections on principles of theology.

Güler: The Necessity of Historicity

Güler's first reflection is a lengthy plea for dealing with tradition *historically*. So before dealing with necessary (i.e., could not not-have happened) history he deals with necessary (i.e., must be done) historical studies. He starts by explaining two different concepts *involved when dealing with history, viz., "Historicism*—tarihselcilik yani Historisizm" and "historical scholarship—*Tarih Bilimi*". Studying a tradition historically means for him the discussion of the successes and the failures of that tradition. And that is what he wants to do. "But Historicism, i.e., *tarihselcilik*, which has existed since the 16th and 17th centuries and has its extensions [still?] also to some degree in the West and which attributes a task *(misyon)* to history and °is in a leading role for history *(tarihe ön deyide bulunan)*, has no connection with the great-big theories of history, which say that history is moving from the primitive to perfection or which say that the direction of history is to this or that side." (p. 211) It seems that Güler is trying to say that 'historicism' can be kept free from associations with what might be called a strong developmental[372] concept of history. In present-day reflections about history, the Koran comes into the discussion as the foundation of Islamic thought. (p. 211) Güler wants to challenge this exploitation of the Koran and asks: what is the point of historical criticism? His answer takes an unexpected turn: "Neither the world of Islam nor the world's humanity in general are happy with the 1997 condition we are in. What is the reason for that?" (p. 212) Güler, in his response, brings in the history of 'Enlightenment vs. religion'. Of course, he says, there are the anti-religious strands implied in Enlightenment thought; but he sees yet another factor at work. There was a fatal incapability in medieval religion, on the Islamic as well as the Christian side, an incapability originating precisely in the divine origin which

[371] Cf. above, pp. 112 and 152.

[372] Almost everyone would accept developments in history with 'development' meaning: a course of events in which the result is caused by previous events. However, *strong* developmental theories would hold that all dispositions are already present—pre-programmed—at the beginning of the time under review like seeds whose contents only have to be brought to light in the course of what is then called the 'development'. Cf. also Klaus Weyand, "Entwicklung", *Historisches Wörterbuch der Philosophie*, vol. 2, Basel 1972, cols. 550–7, col. 551.

both claim. "If those two religions had been able to incorporate *(barındırabilselerdi*—lit.: if they had been able to give shelter to) liberal and critical organs, that is, if they had been able to transform history according to God's will in the direction of their own progress, then the world's condition in which we are now would not have come about." (p. 212) And that means for İlhami Güler, secularisation would not have taken place. (p. 212) One may sum up his position in the following way: because our religious forbears were not flexible enough to deal with their history historically—i.e., as something to be adapted in each era—history became, for many, *history* (in the vulgar sense of 'irrelevant past'). Güler's thought implies a dialectic which can be explicated thus. Tradition meets Enlightenment; tradition can either react in a traditionalist manner by exiling Enlightenment, which leads to Modernity's sick dichotomy of weak religion and Satanic (cf. p. 212) secularism; or it can react through self-critique, thereby transforming itself into an adequate contemporary religion in which Tradition and Enlightenment are reconciled.[373]

İlhami Güler criticises several criticisms advanced against historical critique. The first criticism questions historical critique's legitimacy. Since it takes its values from Modernity and since Modernity is, according to its critics, Pharaonic (which seems to mean, for him, 'foreign, unbelieving, tyrannical and evil'), (p. 212) it has no place in Islam. Güler responds by producing a long list of examples demonstrating the Muslim world's backwardness and concludes: "That is to say that the condition in which the world of Islam is today makes it necessary to be governed by Modernity." (p. 213) The second criticism questions historical critique's feasibility. The critics are themselves parts of the history they criticise and therefore have to use in their criticism precisely the concepts they want to criticise. Güler says he takes this objection seriously. "But the fact that this criticism is justified does not give us the right not to start with the critique or to postpone it." (p. 213) A third point should also be counted as a possible criticism of historical critique, although Güler simply professes to be mindful of it: historical critique's hidden political interest directed against the Muslims.[374] The critique is influenced by "the Modernity in which we live" (p. 213) just as "revelation is, as long as it is within history, influenced by historicity and sociality *(toplumsallık)*".[375]

373 These dialectics will receive a short remark under *(A) Enlightenment*, below, p. 168.

374 Güler's responses will be reconsidered below under *(B) Sources of Critique*, below, on p. 169.

375 A reflection on Güler's 'sociality' can be found under *(C) Sociality*, below, p. 169.

Does one have to reject absolute standards when one does historical critique? In other words, is historical criticism relativistic? No, says Güler.[376] He goes on to identify historical criticism and historicity, the latter being, for him, the opposite of what he calls "anachronism—*anakronizim*"[377]. "[...] another name of historical critique °is historicity *('historicite'dir)*[378]: to give to events and thoughts a place in history. That is, to accept a before and after, to accept a movement, to accept a change within history. That is historicity." (p. 214)[379]

Güler diagnoses "anachronism" not only among religious *(dindarlar)* but also among other people. (p. 215) He sees anachronism at work whenever °we take over *(iktibas ediyoruz,* also: we quote) a thought irrespective of its spatial and temporal coordinates wholesale *(blok halinde olduğu gibi,* lit.: as if it was in the state of a block). Güler adduces several contemporary examples of 'anachronism' from his own country. One is a statement made "one day" by Ali Rıza Demircan[380] on television saying that any authentic Hadith would be so good—at any time—that it would easily outwit himself and his own logic. (p. 216) Güler's response to this is: "If it is authentic according to his (scil., Demircan's) criteria, it does not make any difference for him how functional, meaningful or valuable it is." (p. 216)[381]

Discussion (i): Historicity and the Transformation of Islam

(A) Enlightenment

(Cf. above, at note 373 on p. 167.) Güler's dialectical correlation of Tradition and Enlightenment is an attractive position. However, it cannot count as a solution but only as mapping a route still to be gone. These questions remain open:

a. What exactly is the Enlightenment?
b. Where does Enlightenment come from?

---

[376] In a fairly contorted manner: "But this is a feeling which I will not accept: to enter into an historical critique does not make it necessary to have at all times a third eye to see history and at the same time to observe certain things as absolute and to claim absoluteness, and there is nobody who says this, either. That is to say, an historical critique does not make such a claim." (pp. 213–4)

[377] Güler also forms an adjective of 'anakronizim': anakronik (p. 214).

[378] He is obviously thinking of ‹historicité›.

[379] Güler's 'historicity' will be revisited under *(D) Historicity*, below, p. 170.

[380] An Istanbul theologian on the Islamist side, who frequently speaks on Turkish television. His most prominent book is *İslam'a Göre Cinsel Hayat* ("Sexual life according to Islam"), Istanbul 1998.

[381] This point will be discussed under *(E) Evaluating Tradition*, below, p. 170.

c. Can every possible tradition be put through the process of Enlightenment?
d. What happens to an element of the Islamic tradition if it meets Enlightenment?

(B) Sources of Critique

(Cf. above, at note 374 on p. 167.) Güler's responses to the objections proffered against historical critique are not really tackling the problems upon which the objections touch. Especially the argument that 'historical critique is not indigenous to Islam and therefore inapplicable' cannot be parried by emphasising the urgency of Islam's modernisation. Rather, one should question the silently presupposed idea that one can only criticise a tradition with methods developed by that tradition.

(C) Sociality

(Cf. above, at note 375 on p. 167.) One wonders whether a wording "revelation is ... influenced by historicity and sociality" is not overdoing the abstraction. Is not 'being influenced by history' to be called 'historicity', and 'being influenced by society' 'sociality', so that "influenced by historicity and sociality" is simply too much? The question is not unimportant. What appears to be an oddity of expression may also be hinting at misunderstandings in terminology on either side. After all, 'historicity' is a central concept for Güler and other authors studied here. Often, 'historicity' seems to mean for them *particular historical situation* rather than 'the property of being within history'.

Secondly, it is not obvious why 'it is natural that historical criticism is influenced by the conditions the critic is in' should be *justified* by 'revelation is influenced by the conditions it is in'. The train of thought runs either this way:

a. Every utterance is influenced by its contemporary conditions; if revelation is, then all the more so, criticism. If that is what Güler is intending, he should state why revelation counts as an utterance like human utterances although it is PER DEFINITIONEM something not human.
   Or it runs this way (which would be interesting but is less likely what Güler is trying to say):
b. The proposition 'criticism is influenced by its contemporary conditions because revelation is' holds true because dealing with the historical shape of revelation critically is itself an instance of revelation.

Furthermore, the bifurcation of influences into 'history' and 'society' is anything but clear, if we are talking about a text proclaimed a long time ago. If Güler actually meant 'contemporary conditions' when he said 'society', and 'a tradition's prehistory (plus, possibly, afterlife)' when speaking of 'history', he should have clarified his terminology.

(D) Historicity

(Cf. above, at note 379 on p. 168.) Güler's concept of 'historicity', as he himself explains it, is in fact a rather superficial form of historical consciousness. On closer analysis, one discovers that it does not go beyond *temporal* consciousness. In the bluntly sequential concept of historicity which he suggests, Güler fails to include a couple of important aspects which he himself will need in the course of his paper.

1. Allocating a "before and after" (p. 214) to events does not yet say anything about their *interaction*. The concept of interaction however would have been vital for his argument because only from there can he argue (i) that the critic's present criticism is influenced by history, (ii) that the events and texts the critic wants to analyse are to be understood in their context, and (iii) that even a great temporal distance does not exclude mutual encounter between interpreter and event, between text and addressee, etc.
2. Accepting "change in history" (ibid.) does not yet express *merely punctual validity*, i.e., that the relevance of an event is limited to its surrounding conditions. Although not everybody would want to generalise this point, Güler's theory depends heavily on it. (p. 215)

(E) Evaluating Tradition

(Cf. above, at note 381 on p. 168.) Güler criticises his 'anachronists' because they decide the relevance of a tradition by its authenticity, not by its usefulness. Güler's criticism itself however is problematic. He claims more than he argued for. If Güler is suddenly asking "how functional, meaningful or valuable" a tradition is, he is no longer speaking about adapting a tradition; he is, rather, advocating ‚Sachkritik', i.e., content-criticism. Thus he is abandoning his own concept of historicity, which meant to leave—and evaluate—each event within its own context. Now he admits that this kind of (relativist!) historicity is not enough for a responsible handling of tradition today. There must be other values which allow him to judge "how functional, meaningful or valuable" a tradition is. Unfortunately,

Güler does not see that he conceals the most important point from his audience. Where does he get his values from? Surely it cannot be tradition because it is precisely tradition which he wants to sieve with them.

Güler: Uncreating the Koran

What has been summed up and discussed so far is Güler's six page survey *before* his introduction! The introduction starts with another lament about the inferior standards of Islamic thinking. "If the expression 'Islamic thinking' *('Islâm düşüncesi')* does not correspond to any historical category or body, by which criterion can we speak of a lively organic subject, identity or substance °which finds today in itself particular theoretic objects *(bugün kendine has teorik nesneleri olan),* which attempts to reflect *(teorileştirmeye,* lit.: to theorise) the practice with certain methods and entertains dialectical relations with the theoretical riggings *(donanımlar)* exterior to itself?" (p. 216) In search of the cause of that perceived backwardness, Güler has a very fundamental offer to make. The Arabian way of thinking, he says, treasured resting more than moving. It is therefore according to Güler the Arabic mentality which is responsible for the narrow and inflexible mindset typical—as he states—of medieval Islam. In this analysis, Güler relies on two books by the Moroccan philosopher M. ʿĀbid al-Ǧābirī.[382] Güler concludes that in Islamic thought, concepts like 'before' and 'after', 'developmental stage' *('merhale'),* 'sequence' and 'causality' "are fairly weak—*oldukça zayıftır*". (p. 217) In order to avoid objections, Güler qualifies: that is, "if we exclude Ibn Ḫaldūn's attempts" and (in the case of 'causality') Islamic philosophy. (p. 217)[383] Güler considers "Arabic thinking" incapable of deciding where it is necessary to remain stable and where to change. He links this incapability (causally?) to the incapability of deciding what is essential *(bizzat)* or accidental *(bilaraz)* respectively. (p. 218)

Güler's account continues thus: Arabic static thinking now materialised in a doctrine concerning the character of the Koran, viz., its uncreatedness *(Kur'ân'ın (Kelamullah'ın) 'Kadim' olduğu inancı*—lit.: the belief that the Koran, the Word of God, is beginningless). (p. 219) That doctrine, again,

---

382 Muḥammad ʿĀbid al-Ǧābirī, *Bunyat al-ʿaql al-ʿarabī. Dirāsa taḥlīlīya naqdīya li-naẓm al-maʿrifa fī t-ṯaqāfa al-ʿarabīya* ("The structure of Arab reason (‚Vernunft'). An analytical critical study of the system of knowledge in Arab culture"), Beirut 1990; IDEM, *Takwīn al-ʿaql al-ʿarabī* („The genesis of Arab reason"), Beirut 1991. Cf. Michael Gaebel, *Von der Kritik des arabischen Denkens zum panarabischen Aufbruch. Das philosophische und politische Denken Muhammad ʿAbid al-Gabiris,* Berlin 1995.

383 Güler's presentation of Arabic philosophy will be revisited under *(A) Inflexibility,* below, p. 172.

"transformed contingent history—610–632—into necessary history and thus, at the same time, became °an auxiliary cause [lit.: helper] for the stagnation of cultural time, its immobility and °lack of history *(tarihsizliğine)*, and thus petrified it" (pp. 219–20).[384]

Discussion (ii): Being Inflexible, Being Eternal, and Future

(A) Inflexibility

(Cf. above, at note 383.) Güler portrays 'Arabic thought' as
a. treasuring the static more than the dynamic, and therefore as
b. being inflexible and
c. unable to use precise concepts necessary for historical understanding.
It should already raise attention, if someone has to exclude (arguably the best) members of a group in order to be able to utter one's criticism against that group. Güler excludes Ibn Ḫaldūn and the whole of Arabic philosophy in order to be able to state (c.). On which grounds are these exclusions justified? Furthermore, it is not fair to justify a thesis as unapparent as (a.) only by dropping a name (even though it is an Arab, al-Ǧābirī, he quotes as his source for this anti-Arab ideology). Finally, how was the alleged inflexibility transported? "Through the language", (p. 217) is Güler's response. It would have been helpful if he had given some examples of linguistic transportation of inflexibility, particularly in the case of the Arabic language, which is famous for the wealth of meanings many of its words are said to have. A brief consultation of an Arabic dictionary may serve as a proof here. Polysemy is a sign of flexibility rather than inflexibility, because it means that the lexeme-meaning relation is mobile.

(B) Future in Christianity and Islam

(Cf. above, at note 384.) Güler claims that the doctrine of the Koran's uncreatedness is responsible for the transformation of a contingent history into a necessary history, and co-responsible for the stagnation of development in Islam. These questions arise:
1. Can there be necessary history?
2. Does the Koran's beginninglessness imply that the "610–632" events were not contingent?

384 This claim will be discussed below under *(B) Future in Christianity and Islam*, on p. 172.

3. Is there a causal link between the doctrine of the Koran's uncreatedness and the mental situation of Muslims today?

Conc. 1: 'History' is commonly understood to be a designation precisely of the contingent events.[385] Therefore, 'contingent history' is a pleonasm and 'necessary history' an oxymoron. But Güler may be using the words °'*mümkün tarih*' and '*zorunlu tarih*' (contingent/necessary history) tongue in cheek. After all, he is setting them in single quotation marks. (But then again, he is—like his colleagues—putting in single quotation marks half a dozen words every page, and it is not clear whether they are merely emphasising those words[386] or apologise for not having found better ones.) Another possibility is that Güler is using the word '*tarih*—history' loosely to mean 'events'.

Conc. 2: Since it is the core thesis of Güler's paper, a final discussion of this point has to be postponed. Suffice it to say here that contingence stands or falls by God's freedom. If God is conceived to be free, then there is no necessary course of events. The objection 'but if an event is foreknown, let alone planned, by an omniscient being, the event will happen necessarily' presupposes that that being is subject to temporal sequence. God however is more consistently to be conceived as not being within dilatory time. The relation between a *now* (God plans it) and a *later* (it takes place) only exists within time. It is possible—i.e., can be thought without contradiction—that God timelessly and freely causes things to happen. Consequently, they can be not-necessary, contingent and still be depending on God. The Koran does not form an exception in this respect. Only if the Koran had an origin independent of God, independent of God's will, would there be a problem.

Conc. 3: Therefore, pre-existence of the Koran can mean something quite unspectacular. If everything that will have happened at some time in the universe is eternally present in God's omniscience, then the proclamation of the Koran is there, too.[387] The point of the pre-existence doctrine however is to give to the Koran a unique authority.[388] Does this authority

---

385 Cf. Albert Veraart, "Geschichte", *Enzyklopädie Philosophie und Wissenschaftstheorie*, vol. 1, Stuttgart [1b]1995, pp. 750–2, p. 751.

386 Single quotation marks are clearly meant as emphasis, e.g., in the quote *"onun muradını bilmek için kendimizi ona yüklemek değil, onu 'dinlemek' zorundayız"*, cf. above, p. 126.

387 Güler is well aware of that. "When creatures are being created and go into the world of existence, there is no change at all in God's knowledge." (p. 222)

388 Josef van Ess, *Theologie und Gesellschaft*, vol. 4, offers two different motives for the doctrine of Scripture's pre-existence to be developed. On pp. 612–3 he considers it a logical corollary of book religions, and he puns: „Was geschrieben ist, ist auch vorgeschrieben, und zwar u.U. von Ewigkeit her—What is written is pre-written [or:

imply un-interpreted application? No such thing exists, because every act which claims to be the application of a text is already an interpretation of that text. Therefore, the question is wrong. A culture's traditionally instituted authorities need not cause that culture's petrifaction. Quite on the contrary, if 'traditionally instituted' means the continuous dialogue with a living strand of tradition, that dialogue can be a source of creative re-identification for a culture. A group which treasures certain constants may gain, through that, the self-conviction to venture into the dangerous territories of historical criticism, including self-criticism. But then the question arises whether flexibility depends only on *how* you appeal to tradition, or, rather, also *to which content* you appeal. Is there a particular content in Western tradition which opens it up to change?

One may pinpoint certain factors[389] which are likely to have played a role in the ability of Christianity (NB, rarely however of official Church Christianity!) not only to incorporate new developments but often to trigger them. Is that a fundamental difference between Christianity and Islam? If Christianity can be shown to be open to the future *as opposed to* Islam, there is a severe problem for Islam. Its doctrine could easily be held responsible for the oft-quoted backwardness of countries with a Muslim majority. And development would then be foreign and problematic to Islam. It might therefore be worthwhile asking whether any elements can be detected in the Koranic event which open its followers towards change. The Koran's great esteem for the past cannot be missed: The Islam AB ADAM idea,[390] the etiological presentation of "Islam as a return to the primitive

---

pre-scribed], possibly eternally." On p. 626, he says that 'created' means 'contingent' and the doctrine of the Koran's uncreatedness was formed to reject the Koran's contingence. But then, 'contingent' seems to be used in the sense of 'depending in its results on human action', not in the strict sense 'could not-have been'.

389 One might look for a content to which Western culture appealed in the Christian tradition. This is reasonable because no other ingredient of Western culture can claim similar formative power for that culture. These elements of Christian religion can be considered as opening Christianity to development:
(a.) The extraordinary flexibility of the Biblical people of Israel to incorporate new historical developments into their belief in God. (b.) The increasing future orientation of Israel's prophets. (These two points are elements of Christian religion because Christianity understands itself as going in the tradition of Israel.) (c.) Jesus's authoritative criticism of tradition in the light of a new decisive value, the coming Kingdom of God. (d.) The early Church's insight that in the events of Jesus's life, death and resurrection the final consumption of history has been anticipated (e.g., Eph 1:10) and therefore history after Jesus has its orientation (e.g., Eph 4:13) which comes from the goal of all events and which is therefore definite but open to be understood in new ways in each generation.

390 If the covenant passage (7:172) is to be understood thus. Cf. Richard Gramlich, "Der Urvertrag in der Koranauslegung (zu Sure 7, 172–173)", *Der Islam*, vol. 60

religion of Ibrāhīm" (2:129; 3:89),[391] the frequent honouring reference to the forbears,[392] the punishment stories,[393] and other appeals to the past[394] seem to prove that Islam is basically conservative, looking to the past, and focussed on continuity. However, these aspects should be considered:

a. The earliest message of the Koran included a warning of the Last Judgement to be at hand, the eschaton to be imminent.[395] This means, a future event is claimed to be a criterion for the value and meaning of past and presence. Living towards an all-determining future rather than living from an all-determining, all-determined past should be seen as the primeval Koranic orientation. In this light the many Koranic appeals to the past appear as AD HOMINEM arguments given for a backwards-oriented[396] culture.
b. Muhammad is characterised as the seal of the prophets *(ḫātam an-nabīyīn)* (33:40). The phrase can either mean that through him the previous prophets' messages are being endorsed, Muhammad is their certifier: *muṣaddiq*.[397] In this case, it supports what is said here under c. The phrase can however also mean that Muhammad is the last prophet.[398] This does not imply that everything ever to be said has been said. And since it was Muhammad himself who started interpreting the Koran, opening up the history of Islamic Koran exegesis, one cannot say that the umma believed everything ever to be said has been said. Quite on the contrary, now that the time of prophecy is over, the time of interpretation *has* to begin. For, from now on—Muslims can say—we must no longer look out for today's prophet to answer our questions about what is to be done today. In the post-prophetic era, reference must be

---

(1983), pp. 205–30. Cf. also the Hadith which seems to present Islam as the natural religion: "Every child is born in the natural disposition *(fiṭra);* it is their parents who make them a Jew or a Christian or a Magian". (Buḫārī, 23,80 etc., cf. Arent Jan Wensinck, *A Handbook of Early Muhammadan Tradition*, Leiden 1927, s.v. "child".) The idea seems to be building on 30:30.

391 Arent Jan Wensinck (and Jacques Jornier), "Kaʿba", *EI*², vol. 4, pp. 317–22, p. 320.

392 Salaf: 23:68 etc.

393 Cf. Josef Horovitz, *Koranische Untersuchungen*, Berlin 1926, pp. 10–32.

394 E.g., the existing value system remains in principle unchallenged (3:110; 4:19).

395 Cf., e.g., Rudi Paret, *Mohammed und der Koran*, pp. 70–3.

396 Cf., e.g., ibid., p. 21.

397 Cf., e.g., 2:101 and Josef Horovitz, *Koranische Untersuchungen*, pp. 53–4. Heinrich Speyer, *Die biblischen Erzählungen im Qoran*, Gräfenhainichen n.d., pp. 422–3 certifies Horovitz.

398 Josef van Ess, *Theologie und Gesellschaft*, vol. 4, p. 593 insinuates that the phrase might have referred to the Day of Judgement, which was expected immediately after Muhammad. van Ess remains vague about a TERMINUS A QUO for the occurrence of the second understanding, viz., that "there is no prophet after him", when he says „dann auch bald": "soon". (Ibid., vol. 1, Berlin 1991, p. 29).

made to past prophecy, this reference being a ‹relecture› oriented towards contemporary application, i.e., ethico-legal interpretation. So, declaring the process of revelation to be concluded should be seen to imply the end of direct divine direction and the opening of human finding of justice.

c. The Koran considers itself to be in line with earlier revelations. And if contradictions occur in two texts, both claiming to be revealed? The common solution to this is that then the Koran takes the lead and becomes the criterion for what can have been truly revealed in other texts. But if the doctrine of *revelatory harmony* of Bible and Koran is taken seriously, it opens the way to scholarly study of the contents of the Bible as a means of understanding the Koran. The Koranic accusation of the Jews' and Christians' changing revelation, *taḥrīf*, (2:75, 4:46, 5:13; cf. 3:78) need not refer to their having altered the revealed texts' *written wording*. It can well be heard as a criticism of their changing the (correctly transmitted) texts' *presented wording, its meaning and intention*, namely through disobedience and disrespect, and through distorting citation and interpretation, for example in controversial discussion.[399] Thus, everything that can be shown historically to be a part of Biblical teaching can, according to the Koran, be accepted by a Muslim as revealed. Therefore, quite naturally, e.g., the belief in Christ's second coming, although not mentioned in the Koran, has been held by Muslims from early on.[400] Consequently also the whole Biblical pattern of openness towards the future as sketched out above[401] can, QUA being revealed, be incorporated into Islamic theology.

d. The Koran depicts Muhammad as obtaining his prophetic authority and the content of his proclamations not from tradition and not even exclusively from a one-time experience but from God's unpredictable presence. (E.g., 75:16–9)

e. During the Koran's proclamation, a theologising openness towards contemporary historical developments can be observed. Muhammad's history is declared to contain "proofs" and "signs" of God's reality (8:7–10.42; 7:182). And the Koran takes contemporary events as occasions for teaching and even for change of previous teaching. So much so,

399 It is only in commentaries that *'taḥrīf'* comes to be interpreted unambiguously as alteration of the written wording. Hava Lazarus-Yafeh, *"taḥrīf"*, *EI²*, vol. 10, Leiden 2000, pp. 111–2, p. 111.

400 Josef van Ess, *Theologie und Gesellschaft*, vol. 1, p. 29.

401 Footnote 389.

that for some believers certain new proclamations appeared to be Muhammad's own interpretations of God's will.[402]

f. This leads on to the concept of internal abrogation, which is Koranic (2:106, cf. 16:101) and which says that it is the later passage that abrogates the one proclaimed earlier.
g. The theologies of history presented in the Koran include the view that a turn is going on from ignorance *(ǧāhilīya)* to knowledge *(ʿilm)*, moderation *(ḥilm)* and °surrender to God *(islām*; cf. also *taqwā*: fear of God) (48:26).[403]

Now, the point of this sketch of ideas for a Koranic theology of the future is completely independent of the Koran's eternity or otherwise. All these aspects hold true with a created as well as with an uncreated, eternally preexistent Koran. Islamic conservatism is, then, not up to a certain theology of revelation. The reformatory power of the Koran can be activated if it is believed to be eternal just as well as it can be overlooked if the Koran is held to be created, contingent, completely contextual. The causal link which Güler claimed to exist between the doctrine of the Koran's uncreatedness and today's Muslims' mental backwardness (cf. above p. 173, question 3) is demonstrated to be at least of no necessary nature. It would be interesting to examine whether Muslim conservatism has actually appealed to the Koran's uncreatedness to justify the prohibition of adaptation. But it is for Güler to provide the evidence, if he wants to uphold his thesis, which has to count, so far, as not proven.

Güler: Foreknowledge, Determination, and Iqbal

Güler now plunges into an historical and systematic discussion of the doctrine of the Koran's eternity. Its historical context is the Sunnite vs. Muʿtazilite controversy of the 9th century C.E. Its systematic context, he says, is the question of the nature of God's properties. He sums up the Muʿtazilite argument thus: "If one adds to God's own self other properties and if they are accepted to be eternal, together with God, then the number of the eternal entities would be multiplied." (p. 220) That seems to contradict radical monotheism. Therefore, from a purely metaphysical train of thought, the Muʿtazila concluded that the Koran has been created. Güler sides with the Muʿtazilites by declaring that 'word' *(kalām)* is always something physical ("sound"), there cannot be a completely interior *(nafsī)* word, the Koran is God's word *(kalām)*, and therefore physical and not co-

---

402 Cf., e.g., Rudi Paret, *Mohammed und der Koran*, p. 66, and above, footnote 317.
403 Cf. Ignaz Goldziher, *Muhammedanische Studien*, vol. 1, Halle 1888, pp. 219–28.

eternal with God.[404] Having his tools forged in Muʿtazilite manner, Güler can now tackle his original problem. Is everything that happens, necessary because God has eternally wanted it to happen? (In other words, have the Koran and all other decrees of God always been as they turned out to be?) No, says Güler, distinguishing implicitly between God's act of willing and the objects of God's will. Only the act, not all objects of God's will are eternal. "*Allah'ın ezelden beri murid olması, irade edeceği (yaratacağı, ortaya kayacağı) şeyleri ezelde irade etmesini gerektirmez*—the fact that God has been wanting [i.e., a being with a will] for eternity does not make it necessary that He wanted in eternity the things which He will want, will create and will bring about." (p. 223) The only eternally present objects of God's will are those referring to His own comportment *(davranışlar)*.[405]

Taking 55:29[406] "[God] is always in a new business" as his basis, Güler suggests as one meaning of 'being creator': "*yeniden irade etme yeteneğine sahip olmaktır*—having the power to will something anew". (p. 223) From that, Güler develops his idea of God's knowledge as changing. "*Dolayısıyla insanın ve Allah'ın kendinin gelecekteki – zaman olarak değil, hareket olarak – fiillerinin ezelî ilminin konusu olduğunu varsaymak, onun irade sıfatının bir defa ve bütün zamanlar (hareketler) için aktüelleştiğini savunmakla eş anlamlıdır*—To suppose, therefore, that the future acts—'future' not in the temporal sense but in the sense of motion—of human being[s] and God Himself are the object of eternal knowledge is equivalent to proposing that He actualises His will-property once and for all times, all movements." (p. 223) And that is exactly the proposition which Güler finds unthinkable. He therefore believes to have lead logically AD ABSURDUM the claim that God has always known free beings' future acts. In passing, Güler introduced a new concept of future, a future of motion rather than time.[407]

404 Some of Güler's presuppositions will be discussed under *(A) Understanding the Word*, below, p. 179.

405 Güler's theory of God's will is being discussed under *(B) Will and Time*, below, p. 179.

406 The text has: *""O her an yeni bir iştedir" (55-Rahman/2)"*. (p. 223) A phrase which could plausibly be rendered thus is not 55:2 but 55:29b: *"kulla yawmin huwa fī šaʾnin"*.

407 This new concept is discussed under *(C) Motion Future*, below, p. 180.

Discussion (iii): The Muʿtazila and Divine Foreknowledge

(A) Understanding the Word

(Cf. above, at note 404.) Güler's siding with the Muʿtazilite position of the Koran's createdness depends on his double ruling that

1. a *kalām* is always physical sound; and
2. the Koran is God's *kalām*.

Güler does not bother to establish his rulings. Perhaps because it would be difficult to. The leading dictionary of classical Arabic[408] offers two occurrences in which *'kalām'* is the direct object of 'fahima—to understand'. If it were, as Güler claims, "sound, not meaning", (p. 220) one would expect it to be the object of 'to hear' only. Since however *'kalām'* is naturally collocated in classical Arabic also with 'to understand', a verb that refers to meaning rather than to sound, *'kalām'* has clearly meant more than 'sound'. Furthermore, Güler's premise that the Koran is God's sound-*kalām* is not the common view of early Muslim thinkers. The myth that Islamic theologians have always been certain about the Koran's *verbatim* origin in God should by now be extinguished.[409]

(B) Will and Time

(Cf. above, at note 405.) Although İlhami Güler's distinction between the act of willing and the objects willed is plausible, his theory of God's will suggests a dialogue like the following.

1. 'The only objects of God's will eternally present are those referring to His own comportment'. But clearly, God's comportment is often *reactive* to human behaviour. How can I want a certain course of reaction if I do not know the action yet to which I will be reacting? Güler could respond:
   a. God may—although He does not *want* it to happen—well *know* the (human) actions to which He will be reacting.
   The consequences of that are:

---

408 Manfred Ullmann (ed.), *Wörterbuch der klassischen arabischen Sprache*, vol. 1, Wiesbaden 1970, p. 334b, s.v. *"kalām"*.

409 Josef van Ess, *Theologie und Gesellschaft*, vol. 4, pp. 622–3. Among many similar—and earlier—views, he summarises Ǧuwaynī's (d. 1085) stance as saying: „Ein Bote ist nur inhaltlich festgelegt; wie er es „herüberbringt", hängt von der Sachlage und Aufnahmefähigkeit des Adressaten ab—A messenger is bound only concerning the content; it is the circumstances and the addressee's intelligence that decide how the messenger is to get the message across." (p. 623)

i. There may be things happening which God does not want to happen. (That is a position which many would hold.)
ii. If at the same time one wants to believe that human beings are free, one has to show how human freedom goes together with God's eternal knowledge of human action. (It is not impossible to show this. The solution depends on the concept of eternity involved. (Cf. below, n. 2.) But Güler would not accept that, because he is definitive about God's knowing only what He Himself does.)

b. God does not want his comportment in a particular, specified manner. Rather, He has, eternally, general principles which He applies according to human behaviour, which is not eternally known to him.
The consequences of that are:
i. There is a limitation in God. God is not omniscient about particulars.
ii. This is not in line with the Koranic teaching (e.g., 42:12), unless one takes '*ʿalīm*' to mean only 'knowing everything which *has already* happened'.

2. 'God starts at a certain time to want something (because it has not been eternally present in His will)'. Does that not mean there is *change* in God? Does that not challenge His absolute oneness?
3. 'God has not wanted in eternity the things which He will want.' Is Güler not operating with a *temporally dilated* notion of eternity? Can the apparent incompatibility of God's omniscience and human freedom not be solved, if eternity is understood as *undivided perfection*? "Life which remains in the same because it has the whole always present—not now this, then another, but everything together." (Plotinus, *Enneades* iii.7.3) This understanding of eternity, which is not dependent on any particular religious denomination, makes it possible to think that God knows all human actions but neither before they take place nor with a changing knowledge but in His eternal presence. Within the temporal course of history, God can still be seen as acting in ever new ways.

(C) Motion Future

(Cf. above, at note 407 on p. 178.) Güler tries to replace temporal future by motion future. Which hurdle is he trying to take by that? He wants to remove temporal categories from his speaking about God. He seems to say: rather than time, which does not exist for God, there is motion only. Güler's suggestion however is a mere nominal alteration. It does not solve the problem of the compatibility of God's eternal knowledge and human freedom. As long as he cannot allow for God's knowing or willing "once for all time" he is still caught up in dilatation, no matter what he calls the parameter which separates one instant (e.g., God knows) from the other (e.g., I act). Therefore Güler is still faced with the alternative: either God knows it before it happens, or God does not know precisely what will have come about. Güler in fact opts for the second possibility when saying there is no set plan but only an indefinite possibility *("belirsiz bir imkan"*, p. 223). A real departure from dilatory categories for God has not been ventured and the explicatory power of such a different approach has been missed.

Discussion (iv): Iqbal, Newness, and History

In his conclusion that there is only an indefinite possibility of events—and God does not know what exactly will have come about—Güler depends heavily on the Indo-Muslim intellectual and poet Muhammad Iqbal (d. 1938). Iqbal pinpoints several paradoxes of theism in general and of Islam in particular, and thus also discusses the relation between temporal creation and God's knowledge of it.[410] Güler's strange concept of non-temporal future is not taken literally from Iqbal. But Iqbal starts from the same question. And he comes up with another rather unclear concept of divine time which is likely to be the origin of Güler's idea: "change without succession, i.e., an organic whole which appears atomic because of the creative movement of the ego".[411] ('The (ultimate) Ego/ego' is what Iqbal often says when speaking about God.) Perhaps Iqbal is trying to make the—important—point that since God is the origin of creation, He is not under the constraints of time. If that is what he is saying, he uses 'succession' in the sense of 'the unchangeable flow which controls everything; comprehensive necessary development'. Thus, Iqbal rejects developmental views of creation and stresses God's ever new creativity. But if God creates every single event independently, what does it then mean to say that God *knows* the events of creation? Iqbal points his finger at a fundamental problem in talk of divine knowledge.

---

410 Allama Muhammad Iqbal, *The Reconstruction of Religious Thought in Islam*, Lahore n.d. [1944], pp. 76–9. The book is the edition of a series of seven lectures delivered in 1928 at several Indian universities. (Annemarie Schimmel, "Iḳbāl, Muḥammad", *EI*^{2}, vol. 3, pp. 1057–9, p. 1057) Güler used the book's Turkish translation by A. Asrar: *İslâm'da Dinî Düşüncenin Yeniden Teşekkülü*, Istanbul 1984.

411 Iqbal, *Reconstruction*, p. 77.

Knowledge as we normally understand it is "discursive knowledge".[412] Later[413] Iqbal uses the image of the reflecting mirror for this. This cannot be God's way of knowing, says Iqbal, because it would presuppose that God is separated from the perceived objects; that would mean there are entities which exist independently of God, and God subsequently has to learn about them. But in fact, nothing is independent of God. Therefore, this cannot be God's way of knowing and there must be another type of knowledge "of an ego who knows, and at the same time forms the ground of the object known. [...] We possess no word to express the kind of knowledge which is also creative of its object."[414] This is the type of knowledge which Iqbal thinks is God's knowledge. But what about foreknowledge and eternity? If the mirror type of knowledge is attributed to God, one has only the choice to see God's knowledge as "omniscience in the sense of a single indivisible act of perception which makes God immediately aware of the entire sweep of history, regarded as an order of specific events, in an eternal 'now'".[415] For Iqbal, this is unacceptable because it "suggests a closed universe, a fixed futurity, a predetermined, unalterable order of specific events which, like a superior fate, has once for all determined the directions of God's creative activity".[416] And that is not the case, says Iqbal, because if the course of human actions were already present in God's mirror-knowledge, God would be determined; and a determined God cannot be the creator. Iqbal rejects the position 'everything is being perceived in God's eternal now' because he thinks it limits God's freedom. Iqbal sees only this alternative: "Divine knowledge must be conceived as a living creative activity to which the objects that appear to exist in their own right are organically related. [...] The future certainly pre-exists in the organic whole of Gods creative life, but it pre-exists as an open possibility, not a fixed order of events with definite outlines."[417] (This is where Güler got his "indefinite possibility".) Here, Iqbal failed to consider a series of alternatives. Therefore his conclusions are not necessary, his solutions not the only possible ones.

'If all events of history are perceived by God, then God's creative activity is determined and therefore abolished.' Firstly, Iqbal failed here[418] to

---

412 Ibid., Güler's rendering "passif" is surprising but appropriate.

413 Ibid., p. 78.

414 Ibid.

415 Ibid.

416 Ibid.

417 Ibid. pp. 78–9.

418 This is particularly strange because Iqbal uses exactly the same idea later, when proposing his own model: "No doubt, the emergence of egos endowed with the power

think of the possibility that God may have freely decreed to limit his own freedom. Secondly, then, God's knowledge—although God causes creatures to be—need not be the cause of the decisions creatures freely take; rather, their choices can be known by God in the mirror type of knowledge, because God wants them to be free. Still, that does not necessarily make creatures independent, in their existence, of God. Thirdly, even if creatures, human beings, take decisions, this does not mean that they determine eventual results, nor does it mean that they decide about everything. God can, in this model, still leave much—the result—to be decided by Himself. His own decisions are also present to Him in His eternal knowledge. Thus, what God knows in the eternal now can well be the interplay of creation and Himself. Fourthly, this does not presuppose God's temporality, nor does God's omniscience abolish creatures' freedom. There can be a lively, creative interaction between human free action (set free by God) and divine free action; and still the course and all details and its outcome can be present to God eternally, because it is only within the separating parameter of time that events take place one after the other and some are already there and others not yet. Therefore, a free God who allows creatures to be free and (mirror-)knows creatures' decisions eternally, is no contradiction to Iqbal's valuable postulate "Divine knowledge must be conceived as a living creative activity".[419]

Iqbal wants to hold at the same time that God is perfectly free and that God knows all events. But he sees this problem: God's omniscience limits his freedom. Iqbal finds only this way out of the dilemma: The future preexists in God only "as an open possibility, not as a fixed order of events with definite outlines."[420] But this way out has not taken the double challenge of freedom and omniscience. It is tantamount to saying that God does not know future particulars and that means that God's knowledge is limited. It is sacrificing omniscience to freedom. Iqbal, and subsequently Güler, should see themselves confronted with these objections: 'How does this interpretation of God's knowledge square with the Koranic passages which stress God's precise foreknowledge[421]?' If the answer is that the Ko-

---

of spontaneous and hence unforeseeable action is, in a sense, a limitation on the freedom of the all-inclusive Ego. But this limitation is not externally imposed. It is born out of His own creative freedom whereby He has chosen finite egos to be participators of His life, power, and freedom." Ibid., pp. 79–80.

419 Ibid., p. 78.

420 Ibid., p. 79.

421 *'Qaḍā''* and *'qadr'* are alternatively interpreted as God's detailed decree. Gyula Káldy Nagy, "ḳaḍā'", *EI*², vol. 4, pp. 364–5. God has assigned fixed periods to creation (30:8 par.) and to communities (7:34). Predestined particulars are specified in 6:107 parr. (unbelief of Muhammad's adversaries) and 9:51 (success in warfare). Louis

ran cannot decide about what is logically necessary, then one should ask: 'How is this ranking of logic and revelation justified?' And, leaving the Koranic questions aside, one may still wonder: 'Is the conclusion that God only knows an open possibility really logically necessary?'

The problem of God's foreknowledge, which Iqbal tries to solve, only arises if one conceives of the comprehensiveness of God's knowledge from within time. Then, God's knowledge appears to be foreknowledge and thus predestination. Iqbal was unable to remove his concept of God from the constraints of temporality.

But if we leave the question of temporality aside and take Iqbal's (inadvertently) intra-temporal point of view, then the point he is making is altogether valid. (God knowing or not knowing it:) There is creative newness every moment. Güler adopts this thought and thus prepares in terms of systematic theology the ground for a decisive category. If you remain within time and then hold that God knows all things, there is no room for change and newness. You are bound to speak of foreknowledge and predestination, there is a fixed plan, a pre-ordered course of events. But if you abandon such a divine pre-ordering and conceive of God as allowing for creatures' free actions,[422] then the decisive category you allow for is: history. Iqbal does not explicitly use the word 'history'. But he is opening the gates for an incorporation of the category of history into a theology of prayer. From that, Güler was able to incorporate the category of history, in the sense of an unforeseeable course of events, into a theology of revelation. Güler's category is 'contingent history—*mümkün tarih*', which stresses exactly this point.

Gardet, "al-ḳaḍāʾ wa 'l-ḳadr", *EI*², vol. 4, pp. 365–7, p. 365. Rotraud Wielandt, *Offenbarung und Geschichte*, p. 29.

422 And that would be possible also if God is seen as *extra-temporally* (un-dilatedly) omniscient.

Discussion (v): "Using" the Koran

Güler tries in his paper to establish or at least corroborate much of his theory through quoting the Koran. How does he use[423] the Koran? He supports his definition of 'being creator' as "wanting anew" with the Koranic proposition 55:29, in Güler's translation: "[God] is always in a new business". (p. 223) However, the middle term connecting the verse and Güler's definition of 'creator' is not in the Koran. There is no mention of 'new' in 55:29! "[God] is always in a *new* business" is a creative reading of *"kulla yawmin huwa fī šaʾnin*—He is busy every day".

In order to demonstrate the Koranicity of his view of the necessary reformation of *šarīʿa* in every generation, Güler cites 13:38fin.: *"Her dönem için ayrı bir hüküm vardır*—For each period there is a different ruling." The Arabic reads *"li-kulli aǧalin kitābun". 'Aǧal'* means 'term, appointed period', 'kitāb' can be taken to mean 'book' or 'prescription'. So, the phrase literally renders "for every term (there is) a prescription". Güler added "different" to clarify, and strengthen, his position. Güler's understanding of *'kitāb'* as "ruling" is possible in principle. The context of the verse would allow for either understanding. It is mentioning previous messengers (which would match Güler's translation) and it describes the all-

[423] Umberto Eco, *LECTOR IN FABULA*, Milano 1979, p. 59 sharply distinguishes between using and interpreting texts. The distinction appears quite unaware of Gadamer's point that there is no usage-free interpretation. (Cf. above, p. 25.) Eco has been criticised for that from a different side. Richard Rorty calls the distinction "essentialist". (Richard Rorty, "The pragmatist's progress", Umberto Eco, Richard Rorty, Jonathan Culler and Christine Brooke-Rose (ed. by Stefan Collini), *Interpretation and Overinterpretation*, Cambridge (U.K) 1992, pp. 89–108, p. 93. Rorty, being a stout pragmatist, can only see usage in human *actions* and can therefore not accept Eco's distinction of using and interpreting (i.e., not-using). Still, Rorty is suggesting a distinction which is steering towards what is being suggested below in this footnote. He calls it "methodical and inspired readings of texts", (ibid., p. 106) the difference being "between knowing what you want to get out of a person or thing or text in advance and hoping that the person or thing or text will help you want something different – that he or she or it will help you to change your purposes, and thus to change your life". (Ibid.) The problem with Rorty's "inspired" reading is that he seems to set up an almost ironical scenario of deliberate existential rapture rather than speaking about a humble readiness to be given new categories from the text in the process of reading it.) Leaving the essentialist—pragmatist controversy to one side, the distinction is valuable in giving names to two different attitudes when dealing with texts. 'Usage' is a, not necessarily derogatory, designation of the attitude of those who already know what kind of answer they want to get from the text. Text users have their questions at hand and need them answered. 'Interpretation' can serve as a designation for the attitude of those who question their own questions in the light of the text and try to listen, and to refrain as much as possible from asking. They are consciously ready to be given new questions and to be given answers in areas which seemed unquestionable to them before.

pervasiveness of God's will (which goes with the understanding of the verse presented here). But the context can only help decide between different *possible* translations. The rendering of *'aǧal'* as *'(historical)* period' however is impossible.[424] So, the case is clear. The phrase is not proposing a SEMPER REFORMANDA revelation; let alone, a SEMPER REFORMANDA understanding of revelation. This rendering, which is even closer to what Güler is saying, would additionally have to use the far-fetched interpretation of *'kitāb'* as 'applied, rather than prescribed, ruling'. The most probable meaning of the phrase is: 'The temporal duration of every being is prescribed by God'. No wonder that Güler, so strongly against predestination theology, wants to understand the verse differently.

Güler supports his thesis that the Koran is not qadīm (beginningless) but *muḥdaṯ*, (we can, if what has been said above (p. 184) is right, render this as: 'historical') by quoting verse 26:5: "°And whatever comes as a new admonition to them from the Merciful *(wa-mā ya'tīhim min ḏikrin mina r-Raḥmāni muḥdaṯin):* they turn away (from it)". (pp. 224–5) It is de-contextualising the verse if it is used as evidence of the Koran's deciding its own status as originless *(qadīm)* or created *(muḥdaṯ)*. *'Muḥdaṯ'* acquires its terminological meaning 'created' in the debates about this and other theological questions. And the debates took off in the second century after the Hijra.[425] It is a-historical to take the verse as scriptural proof of the Koran's createdness. In its original context, *'ḏikr muḥdaṯ'* reads naturally as *'another* admonition'. The proclamation of the Koran has its temporal extension. Between 610 and 632 C.E., people listening to Muhammad were able to hear many "new" words. That is to say, they were previously unheard, unheard in the previous *Koranic* proclamation. This holds true if the Koran is created just as much as if it is beginningless.

Güler adduces this verse to corroborate his stance. No matter how unhistorical it is, this usage of the verse comes in an honoured tradition. The pre-Ašʿarite theologian Ibn Kullāb (d. 855) already discussed the Muʿtazilites' and Ǧahmites' usage of 26:5 (and the similarly worded verse 21:2) as proving the Koran's origin within time.[426] In his Koranic appeal,

---

[424] Edward William Lane, *An Arabic–English Lexicon*, vol. 1, London 1863, p. 25. Cf. Heinrich Speyer, *Die biblischen Erzählungen im Qoran*, p. 3.

[425] Josef van Ess, *Theologie und Gesellschaft*, vol. 2, Berlin 1992, p. 740.

[426] Josef van Ess, *Theologie und Gesellschaft*, vol. 4, p. 184. Ibn Kullāb neither totally rejected nor accepted wholesale the position 'the Koran's origin is within time'. By not accepting the straight identification of *'ḏikr'* with the Koranic revelation, he was able to introduce the following distinction. While the reminding admonition had a temporal origin, its content has no temporal origin. (Ibid.)

Güler is in the vein of Muʿtazilite argumentation. And so is his stance in revelation theology.

Güler: Contingence and Context

Güler, approaching the conclusion of his paper, presents a triple reasoning, which should be followed here step by step. First he says: "Muhammad, the first companions, the believers, the unbelievers, the People of the Book, the polytheists and the hypocrites: all had contingent, free wills. That was the case in every divine intervention *(müdahele).*" (p. 225) Secondly, in Güler's eyes, the awareness of this fact is reflected in a passage from 5:48, which he translates "We [God] gave to each—prophet and society—a different *(ayrı)*[427] method and law *(şeriat)*". (Ibid.) Thirdly, and immediately following this, Güler demands that the Koran be understood within the milieu "which gave rise to this formulation". (p. 225) Güler's train of thought is this: *contingence* of the human actions, therefore *difference* of the many revelations, and therefore *context-dependence* of their understanding.[428]

Returning to the question of contingence and necessity, Güler says, since the Koran is referring to a contingent context, it could have turned out differently. *"Allah'ın değerlendirmeleri de (ayetler, Kur'ân, vahiy) farklı olacaktı*—God's evaluations—[individual Koranic] verses, the [whole] Koran, [all of] revelation—could have been different." (p. 225) This is, says Güler, justified by the Koran itself because it mentions when comparing itself with other revelations both its sameness (87:18–9) and its particularity (13:37).[429] The fatal dehistoricisation[430] of the Koran, which led to the doctrine of the Koran's °extrahistorical and transhistorical *(tarih dışı, tarih üstü)* character, is the lamentable product of medieval mentality and politics.

---

427 "Different" is not in the Arabic text of the Koran; it is a plausible explication of the verse, but—being an interpretative addition—not a very good *Koranic* foundation of Güler's point.

428 This train of thought will be discussed under *(A) Koranic Arguments for Interpreting the Koran*, p. 188.

429 Whether the Koran could have been different is discussed below under *(B)*, on p. 190.

430 "Dehistoricisation" is used here (but not by Güler) to designate 'making the Koran absolute', which happens if the contingent, historical character of the Koran('s form) is forgotten. This usage of 'dehistoricisation' should not cause confusion. Güler will, some lines down on p. 226, use *"tarihselleşme*—historicisation" to designate, not a scholarly attitude, not a way of seeing the Koran. Rather, for him 'historicisation' describes the entering of certain historical conditions through explicit rulings fitting to a certain contemporary setting; in other words, contextual application. But Güler does not reveal *what* exactly is being applied in this historicisation.

(p. 226) It was relative word but became absolute book. (Ibid.) Güler now operates with a pair of concepts in order to express his view of the contrast between Koran and today: *ed-Din* and *şeriat*, Religion and Sharia. He does not define either of the two but sets them in the following relation: religion has to find its adequate, contemporary, new Sharia again and again. He finds a Koranic confirmation of this contrast in 13:38: "There is a different ruling for each period".[431]

This seems to be sufficient argumentative grounding for Güler to draw his conclusion. He does it by quoting Roger Garaudy.[432] Rather than a merely literal reading of a dead document—which Garaudy calls the deductive method—one has to find, by using the inductive method, a living principle in it.

Discussion (vi): The Koran's Own Hermeneutics

(A) Koranic Arguments for Interpreting the Koran

(Cf. above, at note 428 on p. 187.) Güler justifies his plea for historical exegesis anthropologically: contingence of human acts, ergo (i.), variation of the world's religious legislations, and ergo (ii.), dependence of all understanding on the individual context of origin. Güler's syllogism does not make clear precisely how influential the human acts are on revelation. Do they only form a challenge and ambience, a mere form? Or are they responsible also for the contents of what is subsequently claimed to be revealed? Although Güler purports to have presented "the dynamic relation of God, the Universe and Human Being", (p. 225) he has not sufficiently clarified it. One important subject remains open: God's purposes. Are there any, can they be flawed, or can God bring them about through free human action, e.g., by eventually integrating even destruction into one meaningful whole? The verse which, in Güler's translation, says that God has given a different "method and law" to each society already hints at the thought that it is God who acts through human contingence. Güler does not see this hint, he rather cites Mohammed Arkoun[433] in order to justify contextual reading of revelations. But neither an authoritative author nor the appeal to human participation in the act of "divine intervention"

---

[431] Cf. what has been said above on Güler's usage of the Koran, p. 185.

[432] Roger Garaudy, *L'Islam habite notre avenir*, Paris 1981, which Güler used in its Turkish translation by C. Aydın: *İslâm ve İnsanlığın Geleceği*, Istanbul 1990.

[433] Güler used an Arabic collection of various of Arkoun's essays originally published in French: *al-Fikr al-islāmī. Qirā'a ʿilmīya*, Beirut 1986.

(p. 225) suffices to establish the necessity of historical understanding. Güler has not provided an argument against this objection: 'The distinction between context and content is human tampering with divine revelation. Abstracting a message from the original revelatory scenario always implies drawing a line between ephemeral circumstances and eternal purpose. Who guarantees for the accuracy of that line?' In order to justify application based on historical understanding over against a legalistic conservation of a past (allegedly divine) state of affairs, one has to look for hermeneutical clues within the ordering. In the present case, that would mean to find Koranic arguments for interpreting the Koran. Some such arguments will be given here:

a. If the Koran can be shown to understand itself as a message rather than the creation of an ideal state of affairs, this would be a starting point for comprehending, rather than copying, application. The first clue to that should be seen in the fact that the Koran is transmitted in a linguistic form. Thus it appeals to human beings' receiving it actively. But was it right, according to the Koran's intention, to pass it on as a language event? This can be justified by the Koran's self-designation as *hudā* ('direction (for human beings)'), *qurʾān* ('recitation', perhaps the most *textual* of all Koranic self-designations), *kitāb* (perhaps a neologism 'scription' should be introduced for this word, which is commonly rendered 'book'), *ḏikr* (and other words formed from *ḏ-k-r*: 'reminding admonition').[434] (Words pointing in another direction should however not be missed, either: if the Koran calls itself *tanzīl* (a sending down), *āya* (sign) and, most importantly, *furqān* (which may be taken to mean 'salvation'),[435] then a self-understanding of the Koran as divine action, God's effective transformation, rather than ethical information, must also be taken into account.)
b. There are many legislative passages in the Koran. (E.g., Sura 4.) Legislation is, strictly speaking, *general* and *imperative*. Being general (because it

[434] The element 'reminding' in the *ḏ-k-r* words is particularly important. It implies that the listeners (can) already know what they are being told. This is supported by the Koran's frequent incomplete temporal clauses (Nöldeke's ‚verkürzte Zeitsätze', cf. Theodor Nöldeke, "Stilistische und syntaktische Eigentümlichkeiten der Sprache des Korans", IDEM, *Neue Beiträge zur semitischen Sprachwissenschaft*, Strasbourg 1910, pp. 5–23, p. 17), which implicitly say 'already from that event, you could have known that God is God'.

[435] On *'furqān'* cf. William Montgomery Watt, *Bell's Introduction to the Qurʾān*, Edinburgh 1970, pp. 121–47, where occurrences are specified, and Horovitz, *Koranische Untersuchungen*, pp. 76–7. Concerning *'āya'*: Since a sign requires interpretation, *'āya'* could also count as re-enforcing the side which argues for the Koran's appealing to an understanding, receiving mind. Cf. also above, footnote 278 on p. 121.

refers to more than one individual case), it requires the human action of *situational application*, which again requires the human action of understanding. Questions like the following must constantly be answered: 'Does that verse, that word *refer* to this very situation?' This reference must actively be discovered. Being imperative (because it refers to intended future action rather than to accomplished facts), it requires human approval and implementation, *actualising application*. This reference must actively be accomplished. So, QUA legislation, the Koran cannot understand itself simply as God's action but requires cognitive co-operation.

c. The Koran presents God as teaching *(ʿallama,* 2:151 & PASSIM)[436], intending human reflection *(tafakkara,* 2:219 & PASSIM), hoping for °transposing application (‚Transfer') when—frequently—using the suggestive "perhaps ..." *(laʿalla-,* 2:52 & PASSIM) and *maṯal* ("example", 66:10 & PASSIM), whose consequence remains to be drawn by the recipients themselves. This demonstrates that the Koran portrays God as interacting with human beings rather than acting tyrannically; supposing, rather than imposing.[437]
d. The Koranic model of a series of identical revelations for different peoples (e.g., 35:31–2) already hints at the Koran's context-particularity as the Arabic ruling (13:36–7). Clearly, 'identical' cannot mean verbatim identity, because a sentence like "May Abū Lahab's hands wither" (111:1) does not make much sense in Moses's or Jesus's life. So, the Koranic view of the history of revelations seems to imply revelation's ‚Jeweiligkeit' (respectiveness). If that is admitted and no divine ruling after the Koran is being claimed, one should be able to draw the conclusion that a changed context requires an adaptation of the Koranic ruling, too.

(B) Accidental Foundation

(Cf. above, at note 429 on p. 187.) The Koran mentions that it is the same as the previous revelations, and that it is particular. This demonstrates, for Güler, that the Koran itself knows that it could have been different. In his stressing that the Koranic revelation could have been different, Güler fails

[436] Here, only one occurrence is stated in each case; the Arabic words are given in their dictionary form.

[437] Cf. also Josef van Ess's aside, that the Koran is constantly disputing with opponents and is therefore "not only instruction for action but also for rational thinking", IDEM, *Theologie und Gesellschaft*, vol. 4, p. 605.

to distinguish explicitly *what* could have been different: the surface contents or also its underlying orientation? When reminding the reader of the Koran's identification with former revelations, Güler may have had in mind such a distinction. The implicit claim is, then: whatever is reactive to contingent action could have been different; but in so far as the Koran and all other divine communications are identical, the views are not arbitrary, could not have been different. Güler does not draw such a conclusion. His theory is therefore open to this attack: 'Why build today's life on the Koran of all things, if it is accidental; why not rather forget about it and lay a completely new foundation?' With all his contingence, Güler has not yet tackled necessity.

Evaluation

In the essay discussed above, İlhami Güler's answers do not completely satisfy the inquiring mind.

1. If one postulates a people's—or an era's—mental inflexibility, one must justify such a view by comparing the entity in question with a *control group*.
2. His siding with the Muʿtazila is not of sufficient conceptual clarity. By bringing in Muhammad Iqbal's refutation of predestination, Güler needs a completely contingent (spontaneous) course of events. Therefore he must conceive of the Koran as an AD HOC production. That however is not what the Muʿtazila meant by the Koran's createdness *(ḫalq)*.[438] Their point was only to reject the existence of anything co-eternal with God.[439]
3. Thus Güler has proven too much. Not only does he claim more than the Muʿtazilite position; one does not have to be a Muʿtazilite. But when his theory claims that the Koran is completely contingent, and no distinction between contingent, arbitrary and meaningless is given, and no criterion is offered to discern between historical form and valid contents, then Güler can easily conclude his reflections with the plea for an historical reading of the Koran. But his conclusion hangs in the air. It does not follow from what he said before, because he has not attempted to argue why one should read the Koran in the first place!

---

438 ""Created" never meant—and not even for the Muʿtazilites—coming into existence only upon revelation at a certain point in time on the Arabian peninsula": Josef van Ess, *Theologie und Gesellschaft*, vol. 4, p. 626.

439 Ibid., p. 627.

Why not take the Orkhon inscriptions instead? Or leave all ancient texts alone?

4. In the end, his conclusion is not exactly original. If his punch line is that we have to find, inductively, a living principle in the Koran, he is back to the problems his colleagues have been struggling with for the last years.[440]
5. Güler is a systematic theologian by training and by attitude. Like many Christian systematic theologians', his usage of scripture is not exegesis, but associative illustration of his speculation, and—ironically—anachronistic.

However, Güler has presented a systematic-theological foundation for an historical reading of the Koran. Therefore his voice is unique in the otherwise philosophical and exegetical chorus that can be heard in the present study. He is in this chorus also original because he takes in other authors, viz., Iqbal, Arkoun, Garaudy and several Arabic books like al-Ǧābirī's. Güler's argument is that the concept of the Koran's eternity only got into Islamic thinking because of the Arabic medieval mentality. He, in contrast, sides with Muʿtazilite theologians and claims the Koran's contingence. Only with this theological basis, he thinks, is a contextual and therefore adapting understanding of the Koran possible. Güler's questions are vital for a renewed hermeneutics. A systematic grounding is essential.

[440] Cf., e.g., above, p. 132.

Reflecting the Conclusions: A Summary

We have studied new hermeneutical approaches to the Koran by Turkish university theologians. If studying includes critical discussion, can such a study be done by a non-Muslim? And if such a discussion is conducted within a paradigm of religious studies, how can it be critical, and how critical can it be? The thesis contended here is that religious propositions, especially theological ones, imply rational claims; these claims can be discussed by any rational being. Religious studies need not restrict itself to recording religious positions. In religious studies one can, rather, enter into a discourse with members of a religion without having to share their faith presupposition. However, such a discussion must be particularly wary of possible misunderstandings because creedal differences can involve variations in word usage. Still, one can presuppose that Turkish academic theologians and the scholar of religion studying them are in principal talking about the same things.

Why focus on Koran hermeneutics? The Koranic focus has been chosen because it is from the Koran that Islamic reform theologies have to start. It contains, as Muslims agree, a reform power which has not yet been brought to bear. And, contrary to other Islamic revisions, those starting from the Koran can be expected to meet wide Muslim acceptance. After all, they can claim to be powered by Islam's pivotal document. The hermeneutic focus has been chosen because it is only through a conscious and reflected understanding of the text that a Koranic revision of Islam can prove an upright and lasting enterprise.

The presentation of the state of research comprised a sketch on the history of hermeneutical reflection; a glance at Muslim discussions on exegetical method; and a survey of their coverage in Islamic Studies.

We observed that 'hermeneutics' can in these discussions be used on three different levels. It can, firstly, mean any way of dealing with texts, reflected or otherwise. Secondly, it can denote the historical application of normative texts. Finally, it can designate a certain tradition of Continental philosophy. This last meaning is central to the Muslim theologians under review here. Therefore, the introductory sketch on the history of hermeneutics starts from Hans-Georg Gadamer's historical view. He observed that when lawyers, classical philologists and theologians interpret texts, their intentions have always been normative. Gadamer was therefore able to see that application does not take place only after understanding and explaining. Rather, as is especially clear in the case of "interpreting" a work of the performing arts, application is a part of the process of understanding. For Romanticism, says Gadamer, understanding meant entering the other by means of a psychologically informed empathy. Gadamer himself however describes understanding as letting new views enter your own horizon. The present study accepted Gadamer's insights as elucidating. Still, four caveats had to be raised. Gadamer does not provide a method for interpreting texts, indeed, he thinks that it is impossible to devise such a method; Gadamer underestimates language's propositional character; he does not see that it is only the anticipated horizon of history in its totality which allows for a fair understanding of every element in its own right; and lastly, Gadamer's principle of understanding, which says that the question answered by a given text must be found in the text itself, misses extratextual coordinates which allow us, e.g., to see a text's appropriateness.

Then we introduced the reader to the state of Muslim research on Koran hermeneutics. Works by three European scholars guided the exploration. J. M. S. Baljon presents Urdu commentaries written between the end of the 19th and the middle of the 20th centuries. Baljon observes attempts to explain away elements of Koranic passages which the commentators considered to suggest supernatural events. He characterised their exegetical methods as demythologising, romanticising, rationalising, historicising and moralising. J. J. G. Jansen's study of 20th century Egyptian Koran commentaries diagnoses a lack of originality in many authors. The difference between classical and 20th century commentaries is often, he says, merely a difference in the type of audience addressed. Today, exegetes seem to write for secularly trained readers rather than for their theological colleagues. Jansen divides the commentaries into exegeses of three different points of view, viz., natural history, philology and everyday questions. Commentaries of the first type suffer according to Jansen from a low level of scientific information. Among the philological commentaries he points out those who deal with the Koran as literature. The most prominent question in the third type is, how Westernised may a Muslim's life be?

Rotraud Wielandt's dissertation studies modern Muslim philosophy of history. Her thesis culminates in a dilemma concerning the theology of revelation. Either one accepts that everything in the Koran is divine revelation. In that case, an historical approach to the material is illegitimate. Or one has to concede a human participation in the making of the text. In later studies, Wielandt observes however that Muslim thinkers have found ways out of the dilemma, and have gone them. In an 2002 article she proposes a sixfold typology of early modern and contemporary Muslim Koran interpretation. According to her, commentators look on the Koran in a perspective of rationalism, the natural sciences, literary criticism, history, an unhistorical immediacy, or particular themes. Thus, combining methods of literary criticism, communication theory and history, the Egyptian Naṣr Ḥāmid Abū Zayd suggests a new approach. God is the sender of the Koran, its first recipients are 7th century Arabs. In order to be understood by the first recipients, the sender had to transmit the message in the "recipients' code". Consequently, each culture has to translate the Koranic contents into its own code.

We saw that Turkish Koran exegesis has been neglected by Western research on Islam. Since the present study reviews the work of Turkish university theologians, it started the presentation with a history of academic theology in modern Turkey. Already in 1847 the Ottoman Ministry of Education decided to establish a Western style Theological Faculty at the University in Istanbul. This was one step in the movement of substituting modern education for the traditional medrese system. But it was only in 1924 under Mustafa Kemal's radical modernising programme that the medreses (working until then without State control) were closed down. Instead, state run schools for prayer leaders and preachers were opened. At the same time, the Istanbul Theological Faculty was re-established. By 1932, the new schools for prayer leaders and preachers had all disappeared. In the early days of the Turkish Republic these schools suffered from low attendance. The Theological Faculty of Istanbul was turned into an Institute for Islamic Research, subordinate to the University's Literature Faculty.

When Turkey became a multi-party democracy in 1947, a call for better training of Muslim religious staff could be voiced. In 1949, a new theological faculty was established, at the University of the modern capital, Ankara. The faculty was to be structured like Christian theological faculties in the West. Subjects like comparative religion were to be taught there, too. Since then, 23 more Theological Faculties have been founded in Turkey. Their legal status (no control by a religious authority) and founding intention (building the scientific foundation of an enlightened Islam) seem to be unique in the world of Islam. Although politicians' expectations may sometimes be felt in this system of academic theology, rethinking Islam finds promising conditions at these faculties.

Our study then lead the reader to the oldest, and in several respects leading Turkish theological faculty, Ankara Üniversitesi İlâhiyat Fakültesi. There, a group of theologians has gathered which names itself "the Ankara School". They consider themselves as "Islamic modernists". The School has a special interest in fundamental methodology. These mostly young scholars are developing philosophically and theologically sophisticated hermeneutical approaches for a rethinking of Islam.

The first theologian presented was Mehmet Paçacı. Apart from studying theology and philosophy in Ankara, he made New Testament studies in Manchester. He describes his own approach as an alternative to "orientalist" explanations and universalistic declarations. For him, the Koran is neither merely a product of monotheist tendencies on the Arabian peninsula, nor is the Koranic wording, as some Muslims claim, valid always and everywhere. We saw that Paçacı draws on Fazlur Rahman's model of Koran hermeneutics. Fazlur Rahman, born in what is today Pakistan, came forth with a three step model of interpretation. In order to understand the Koran you have to understand it in the context of its proclamation. Thus you can distil the general ethical principles from the individual norms you find in the Koran. These have to be put to action anew in every era.

In discussing Paçacı's proposals, we suggested that his sometimes quite polemical contrasting of Western and Muslim positions may be of pedagogical origin. He seems to lure a Muslim reader still sceptical towards historical methodology with this argument: while historical scholarship is dangerous for Christianity, it is fruitful, and indeed traditional, for Islam. We identified the following problems with Fazlur Rahman's three step interpretation: it presupposes, but does not justify, that the Koran is of general ethical authority; the community of Muslim believers will hardly be able to agree on formulations of the ethical principles to be abstracted from the Koran; even more difficult will it be to find a consensus on the rules of application for these principles.

According to Paçacı, the Koran's intention is ethical. All passages without direct moral appeal are subsidiary to the Koran's basic ethical aim, he says. Through the Koran, God has addressed human beings in their historical situations. Islamic jurisprudence has in Paçacı's eyes always operated thus: general principles are inferred from historically unique situations. That traditional approach had been refined by Fazlur Rahman. Now Paçacı wants to deepen it in the light of Gadamerian hermeneutics. Before one enters the three step method, one has to become aware of one's own preliminary understanding, i.e. of the historical situation from which one starts interpreting. Seeing one's own "historicality" means to seize the chance, as it offers itself today, for a responsible shaping of this world according to the Koran's ethical principles. In discussing Paçacı, we asked whether an understanding of the Koran as ethics-in-operation is not a reductionism, because it does not do justice to Koranic theology in its breadth. Furthermore, we wondered whether other insights of Gadamer's philosophy might not be fruitful for Koran hermeneutics, too, e.g., Gadamer's observation that the text transforms even the questions one asks about it.

We then looked at Paçacı's study on Sura 112. It proved to be an exegetical experiment testing the hypothesis of a "Semitic religious tradition". The Koran is according to this hypothesis one current in the Semitic monotheistic stream. Consequently, both individual Koranic words and the whole of Koranic theology can be read in the light of other religious texts in Semitic languages. We characterised Paçacı's method in the light of *Isrāʾīlīyāt*, the traditional Islamic elucidation of the Koran by mostly legendary edifying narratives on Biblical motifs. What Paçacı in fact does is to re-open the gates of *Isrāʾīlīyāt* with historical and philological instruments. For that, he uses Ancient Near Eastern, Old Testament, and Intertestamental literatures. Paçacı tries out his hypothesis on the translation of *"aṣ-ṣamad"* (112:2), a notoriously controversial point in Koranic scholarship. His explanation begins by postulating a tendency of strictly monotheist translations which began as a reaction to Christian theology. In order to distinguish itself from incarnational theology, Semitic religious tradition stopped expressing its creed in anthropomorphic terms. Concrete metaphors for God were now suppressed. Thus also the designation of God as "the rock", common in the Hebrew Bible, was already in its early translation rendered as "the tough", "the helper". According to Paçacı, *"aṣ-ṣamad"* ("the solid one"), too, is such a more abstract rendering of "the rock". In our discussion we praised Paçacı for courageously enlarging the paradigm of Koran exegesis. We recalled Claus Schedl's thesis that *"aṣ-ṣamad"* had become the standard explanation of God "the rock" in Arabic oral Bible translations during synagogue liturgies. Schedl provides a background which corroborates Paçacı's interpretation. We rejected however the term "Semitic religious tradition", because it projects a theological continuity onto a linguistic group. While in his methodological philosophical studies Paçacı claims ethics to be the Koran's primary theme, in his exegetical philological study ethical subjects are not even mentioned. We expressed the hope that thinkers of Paçacı's format will be able to combine historical, philosophical and theological questions into a Muslim fundamental theology.

The second Turkish author we presented was Adil Çiftçi. Apart from studying theology in Ankara, he was trained in sociology of religion in İzmir and London. Discussing Çiftçi proved to be at the same time deepening the discussion of Fazlur Rahman. According to Çiftçi, Fazlur Rahman's significance for theology lies in the Pakistani's redefinition of the Koran. He saw the Koran not as a law book. A law book calls for immediate application. For Fazlur Rahman, the Koran was a compendium of principles of general validity. These principles however are to be found in the Koran as exemplary applications shaped by their historical circumstances.

Therefore, the Koran's individual rulings stand for basic ethical guidelines. These need to be concretised again by every generation in order to be relevant for jurisdiction and practice. Fazlur Rahman's redefinition rests on his theology of revelation. It says that Muhammad is not God's loudspeaker, i.e., the passive transmitter of God's word. Rather, the prophet's personality has an active role in the process of revelation. Muhammad has the Divine Spirit. That is to say, according to Fazlur Rahman, that the prophet has the aptitude for taking, formulating and proclaiming decisions according to God's will. Consequently, the Muslim of today should not submit to the Koran in so far as it contains particular rulings for another time. The Muslim of today should rather submit to God's will as the Koran expresses it in concrete examples. Therefore, the interpreter of the Koran needs a method of understanding in order to make God's will explicit out of the text, in which God's will is implicit. This is Fazlur Rahman's approach to hermeneutics. He rejects Gadamer's philosophy, because for Fazlur Rahman it is a subjectivism which shakes the foundations of his Koranic ethics. Instead, he sides with the Italian historian of jurisprudence Emilio Betti, who had served as the contrasting foil for Gadamer when setting out his own position.

In the discussion, we pointed out that Fazlur Rahman weakened his own approach by rejecting Gadamer's philosophy. If Fazlur Rahman had developed a consciousness of effective history, he could have realised how traditional Muslim exegesis of the Koran shaped his own approach to the Koran, viz., his ethical reductionism. Furthermore, Fazlur Rahman has not taken seriously Gadamer's criticism of psychological historicism. If he had taken the point, he could have seen that his own approach, just like Betti's, is in fact positivist. The approach does not ask whether, from your point of view, you can see that what the text says is true. In Betti's and Fazlur Rahman's method you presuppose that the text is right. You need not and cannot justify that it is. Thirdly, Fazlur Rahman has not understood Gadamer's insight that in history nothing can be completely understood. This is not subjectivism. It means, rather, to be ready to see better and better by means of new information. Why would Fazlur Rahman want to reject that? We pointed out that Fazlur Rahman was looking for a hermeneutical foundation to ground his project "Islam and Modernity". Therefore he was grasping for something that had an appeal of solidity to him, and to the Muslims he was trying to convince. We were consequently able to evaluate Adil Çiftçi's hermeneutics along these lines: he reconstructs Fazlur Rahman's approach with instruments of Western philosophy; he is thus able to illustrate the approach; he has however not used the potential of those instruments for a critical rethinking of Fazlur Rahman.

The third voice to be heard was Ömer Özsoy. After theology and social sciences in Ankara, he studied Islamics in Heidelberg. Özsoy makes a semantic distinction between two Turkish words for 'historical'. He takes the one to mean 'has actually taken place' and 'not transhistorical', and the other to mean 'must be interpreted within its context'. Özsoy calls for a strictly historical reading of the Koran. For that, he uses the well-known formula "understanding the Koran as the first hearers understood it". For Özsoy however the formula becomes the starting point of a new approach. The first believing hearers' understanding of the Koran was an exemplary and normative interaction with the Koran's intention. Following Fazlur Rahman, Özsoy calls this believing interaction 'Sunna'. Without Sunna, the Koran would be hopelessly ambiguous. The 'tradition' of Sunna clarifies the meaning of the Koran. But Özsoy admits that the right course of action has to be translated from the Sunna situation to now. Özsoy has shown the hermeneutical relevance of action according to the Koran, and the necessity of a community of believers for understanding revelation. However, we pointed out that in his approach some questions still remain open. How can one see the first hearers' action to be normative, if not again from the text of the Koran? How can we know about the first hearers' actions, if not again through texts? Thus we are back to the problem of the ambiguity of texts. Why can later action according to the Koran not be just as normative as—or more normative than—first generation Muslims' actions? Finally, we remarked that his approach, because it refers only to correct action, again presupposes ethical reductionism.

According to Özsoy, the Koran cannot be used as a source for historical research because it does not want to say 'what God has done' but 'what God wants to do'. Does this simply mean, 'what God wants to have done'? Possibly however, this implies a new understanding of God's action. Then we could conclude that God does not act by imposing Himself but through ethical beings to whom He expresses His will. We also remarked that the Koran's historical claim should not be abandoned altogether. To say that the Koran calls for a certain course of action also implies an historical claim.

For interpretation, the Koran's message and the Koran's manner of speaking always have to be distinguished, says Özsoy. In his perception, traditional theological Koran exegesis has been obsessed in a formalistic way with the Koran's manner of speaking. Islamic lawyers on the other hand when doing exegesis have always been interested in practice. Therefore, says Özsoy, legal exegesis of the Koran has considered the first believers' practice as relevant for interpretation. Özsoy holds that the Koran was not intended as a text, that is to say, not as a systematic whole. Rather, it is speech in various particular circumstances. And that speech was subsequently written down. Therefore it is necessary for an understanding of the Koran to know the circumstances of those particular communications. The Koran is being understood as God's commentary on the first hearers' behaviour. The Koran is so context oriented that today immediate Koranic obedience would miss the point because the accidental would thus become the normative.

In discussion with Özsoy we saw that his text-speech distinction is an original contribution to Koranic hermeneutics, just as his plea for a non-textual, i.e., context-determined, understanding of the Koran. But we also pointed out the difficulties in that. Our access to the Koran is necessarily textual. The original context of the Koranic speech is not at hand. And all reconstructions of original contexts are again based primarily on texts.

Özsoy remarks that all text-based world views can fall into the fundamentalist trap. That is expecting, without historical consciousness, answers for today from the text. We saw that this is an important warning to be made, but we asked what he and his Turkish colleagues mean by 'historical'. The Turkish theologians under review take 'historical' to mean accepting the differences between two situations, between the original context and today. Thus we were able to conclude that so far only the Anglo-Saxon concept of history has been taken up in Turkish theology. Not yet taken over is the Continental European concept of history, which originates in the Biblical view of "God's deeds" as a so far open course of action which becomes an understandable whole once it is completed. We identified traces of Koranic theologies of history which see a meaning in the whole course of events. There are Koranic passages which say that all peoples are provided with revelation; that the Koran itself now offers a criterion for the unification of all peoples; that God acts through confirmatory signs.

As the last author, we introduced a systematic theologian, İlhami Güler. He studied theology and social sciences at the Universities of Ankara and Cairo. He too calls for an historical reading of the Koran, i.e., a reading which takes into account the contexts of origin and application. Güler presents Islamic thought as backward. The origin of this backwardness lies, in his eyes, in the Arab mentality, which he considers to be inflexible and conservative. In stating this, he is inspired by the Moroccan philosopher al-Ǧābirī. The Arabs like what is lasting, Güler says. That is, according to him, what gave rise to the doctrine that the Koran is uncreated, i.e., eternal without beginning. He concludes that it was this doctrine which turned a piece of contingent history, Muhammad's public ministry, into something unchangeable, viz., God's word. In the discussion with Güler, we noted the necessity of systematic theological reflection on Koran hermeneutics and praised him for taking the firsts steps on this untrodden path. However, we criticised the thesis of Arab inflexibility as weakly justified and illegitimately global. Certainly one cannot miss passages of the Koran oriented towards the past. But, we asked, does the Koran not also contain a theology that faces present and future? We pointed out that the primary contents of the earliest Suras is eschatological; that the Koran presents the source of Muhammad's prophecy to be God's present influence; and that the Koran interprets the first Muslims' military successes more and more as God's action now. On the other hand, the doctrines which say that the Koran has a beginning or none are irrelevant to the question whether Koranic theology is open towards the future.

We observed how Güler takes over the Muʿtazilite argument that positing another being without beginning besides God is tantamount to leaving monotheism. He adds the point that a word is always also sound, that is to say, something physical; therefore a word cannot be divine and eternal. Does something become eternal merely by the fact that it is willed or known by God, whose will and knowledge are eternal? No, because God need not have willed or known it from the beginning, responds Güler. He follows Muhammad Iqbal in his view of God's omniscience. God knows, according to this view, everything that could happen; God does not know however which of all possibilities are going to become reality.

Discussing Güler, we criticised his arbitrary and unhistorical manner of quoting the Koran. We questioned the suggestion that words are necessarily physical; and we raised doubts about the claim that God's knowing and willing, e.g., human free acts must be able to develop in the course of the time. Iqbal's intention is, just as Güler's, to defend the openness of history against God's foreknowledge, which, in their eyes, predestines and therefore fixes the course of events. Both authors miss the point that the concept of God's omniscience only then thwarts the openness of history if God is conceived as temporal, that is as existing within time, which separates individual events from one another. If however everything is present to God, even that which is future to us, God's omniscience does not contradict free action and the openness of the course of history.

For Güler, it is fatal that the Koran was turned from relative speech referring to particular circumstances into an absolute book. For him, the only correct way of dealing with the Koran is "inductive". That is to say, the Koran is not a dead document to be applied literally. Rather, people have to find in it a principle which can be realised in their lives.

We pointed out that an historical translation and understanding of the Koran cannot be justified only by the argument that human actions are contingent. There is better support in the Koran itself for the fact that it wants to be understood not as presenting a state of affairs to be imitated today but in comprehending, intelligent transposition. We adduced as such support the facts that the Koran is conveyed in language, thus calling for comprehension; that many of its rulings are general, thus requiring decisions about validity in each life situation; that many Koranic formulations are suggestive, thus leaving the conclusion to be drawn by the hearers; and that in the Koranic view many peoples have received the same revelation, which is still not literally identical, thus allowing for an adaptation of revelation to different situations. Finally, we remarked that Güler, by underlining the Koran's contingence, deprives it of its normative character without telling us why we should, in search of norms, bother with old documents in the first place; and why, of all documents, with the Koran?

A guiding question for our expedition into Turkish theology was: has Islamic thinking developed an historical consciousness there? We explicated the question in five criteria: [441]

(a.) awareness of the interpreter's pre-understanding,

(b.) awareness of the effects text and tradition have on the interpreter's pre-understanding,

(c.) awareness of the distance between text and interpreter,

(d.) awareness of the fact that text and interpreter are in principal confronted with the same reality and only see it from different perspectives, and

(e.) awareness of the therefore positive influence of this distance on the understanding.

We are now ready to answer the question.

All our authors are aware of the distance between the Koran and today's interpreters, (c.). They mention that distance expressly; and they talk about it indirectly by underlining the necessity of a *transposing ‹lecture›*, which they term 'hermeneutics'. Thus, the authors are consciously taking the counter-stance to an 'immediatist' Koranic reading, sometimes called 'fundamentalist'.

The fact that the Koran and its interpreters are looking at the same reality, (d.), is partly present in the approaches studied. This may apply to two different subjects. They must be treated separately. One is seen as the fundamental Koranic theme by all theologians considered here: ethics. But is the Koran's ethics good ethics? The correctness of its ethical contents is not demonstrated or debated by them. It is taken for granted. This may be understood as saying: one cannot discuss ethics, one simply has to submit to imperatives. Then, this attitude betrays no awareness of the co-

[441] Cf. above, p. 32.

situatedness of text and interpreter concerning this particular question. But their silence about the question of the correctness of Koranic ethics may also be understood as saying: one can accept the Koran's ethical message because one can see it to be good. In that case, we would have an instance of a reflected text-interpreter relation here. The other subject is monotheism. We heard Paçacı, Özsoy, and Güler stress that the Koran is a monotheistic message. But the authors added that the Koran's contribution to monotheism is not original. It rather comes in a tradition. This clearly means that they consider the Koran to be pointing at a reality human beings can see also without the Koran. So, in this point, there is an undisputable awareness of the situational similarity of text and reader. Both are confronted with the same reality.

An awareness of the positive influence the distance between Koran and interpreter has on the interpretation, (e.), is implicitely at work when the authors are happily taking in new methods and results of scholarships. This implies the belief that recently developed approaches can help us to understand the Koran even if they were unknown to the generations who had less temporal distance to its proclamation. But the productivity of that distance is not made conscious. Fazlur Rahman's approach plays an important role for these theologians. He urged Koran interpreters to move backwards to the first hearers. This has been appreciated above as an awareness of the distance between interpreter and text. But for Fazlur Rahman, this move remained the major key to what the Koran wanted to say. The same must be said of the authors studied here, too. They treasure the hermeneutic value of the first addressees' understanding (or the first practice) of the Koran. On the other hand, they strictly (and often understandably) reject "Scientific" exegesis as artificial modernisation of what the Koran could not possibly say. Along the same lines of this rejection however they come to undervalue our privileged hermeneutical position today: with the new perspectives we have gained, the Koran can be heard to say things that were previously impossible to hear. This point may be seen as overly Gadamerian. It is however not in need of labelling but of discussion.

An awareness of the interpreters' pre-understanding and its values, (a.) is explicitely there in Paçacı's reflections and implicitely in all authors, already because they are all discussiong methodology. If one thinks about how to approach a text, one is reconsidering one's own starting-point. But the possibility that the views of a reader today are already depending on the text-plus-tradition before they start asking questions, (b.), was not reflected in any of the texts studied here. How have text and tradition already shaped our approaches subconsciously? This question deserves further attention.

Concluding Reflection

Theology in Turkey has become exciting. Turkish geography (neighbouring Central Asia, Arab countries and what is called the West), Turkish history (occidentally oriented), the Turkish religious and academic scene (State-promoted Enlightenment of Islam), and also the Turkish language (precise in morphology, accustomed to neology) make for a stimulating theological climate.

In that climate, plant life is thriving. Turkish academic theology is producing high quality studies which are of great relevance for Turkey. Turkish university theologians are combining Islamic and Western strands of thought. Their work has therefore important contributions to make for the Western discourse, and for Muslim theologies elsewhere.

But once one has entered the theological jungle thriving in Turkey's stimulating climate one makes another discovery. It's a young jungle; there isn't much bio-diversity yet. The revisionists' vision is still restricted to one type of question: ethics. If they ask only, 'How can we make the Koran ethically acceptable today?', they are selling the Koran under price. Hermeneutics has then a merely mechanical function: we know what is there in the Koran, ethics; and we know what must come out, modern ethics. The only question left is, how do we get it out? Hermeneutics has become a tin-opener.

We had seen the rich gardens of Muslim tradition, and the locked gates before us. That was why we set out on our expedition. It was the quest for the lost key to the garden's fresh fruits which made us go. And now we are busy with tin-openers and baked beans. The expedition can only succeed if we remind ourselves of its initial intuition. Questions such as 'Does God exist?', 'Who are we, who are we to be?' and 'What does it all mean?' had made us uneasy enough to set out; questions which were promised answers from beyond the gate. In that light, 'The Koranic rulings were meant to bring justice' is rather disappointing a discovery. If I can't get a new insight from there into what justice is, for example, that is not much more than saying, 'The Koran can keep up', and thus the hermeneutical approach is in danger of producing nothing but apologetics.

Apologists "use" their texts. They dare not have their own questions reshaped. There is more inspiration for a modern mind to be experienced in the Koranic encounter than having one's ethical convictions confirmed. This names a problem inherent in hermeneutics. It can be so busy with translating and modernising, so focussed on the encounter between the ancient document and today, that the greater horizon gets out of perspective. The greater horizon is the whole, including the future, and therefore attempts at discovering the meaning of all of history.

But how can one study Koran hermeneutics, and then complain that what one has found is only hermeneutics? Here, one should be reminded of the ambiguity of the word 'hermeneutics'. The study investigated what Muslim theologians *do with the Koran*; and it found that they *transpose its message into their own context.* So, the question contained the neutrally descriptive usage of 'hermeneutics', whereas the answer uses it in the normative way. And hermeneutics, i.e. the art of dealing with tradition, should not be restricted to bringing a certain content from the past to the present. Studying tradition should rather be seen as the attempt to understand ourselves and everything else, including our destination, in a new light again and again.

The theologians we have met in this study are intellectuals with a vital interest in contemporary thought *and* religious tradition. They are philosophically and philologically well trained, equipped with historical methodology and systematic ambition. They are exposing themselves to the Koran (and Islamic tradition), which is ready to suggest new answers to humanity's core questions, and ready to provide new questions; indeed, one might therefore say the Koran is ready to rethink the whole world. The theological workshop we visited is promising more products. We may expect an even more theological Islam, which casts new light on our questions, visions and lives: a Muslim theology which is rethinking us. It is also in this sense that we should speak about a rethinking Islam.

Appendices

Philosophical Terms German–English–Turkish*

Andersheit	otherness	başkalık
akzident(i)ell	accidental	bilaraz
antizipierend	anticipating	öngörüsel
deduktiv	deductive	tümdengelimsel
DETERMINANTIA	determinators	belirleyicilik
essentiell	essential	bizzat
existenziell	existentiell (SIC)	varoluşsal
faktisch	factual	olgusal
Fehlschluss	fallacy	yanılsama
Geisteswissenschaften	humanities	insan bilimleri
Geschichtlichkeit	historicality (SIC)	tarihçilik, tarihselcilik
Gespräch	dialogue, talk	karşılıklı, konuşma
Hermeneutik	hermeneutics	anlabilim, hermeneutik, hermenötik, yorumsamacılık
hermeneutischer Zirkel	hermeneutic circle	hermeneutik döngü
historisch-kritisch	historical-critical	tarihsel-eleştirel
Historizität	historicity	tarihsellik
Horizontverschmelzung	fusion/ merging of horizons	ufuklar birleşimi
In-der-Welt-sein	Being-in-the-world	dünyada var olma
induktiv	inductive	tümevarımsal

* Listed are only terminological words which cannot be found in *Redhouse Türkçe–İngilizce Sözlük*, Istanbul [16]1997 (including its Supplement) in the usage encountered in the textual basis of the present study. (Karl Steuerwald, *Türkisch–Deutsches Wörterbuch*, Wiesbaden [2]1988 gives the meanings stated for *"öznelcilik"*, *"tümevarımsal"* and *"varlık".)* NB, the words are from different levels of style and linguistic tastes, and certainly there are other ways to render the terms in Turkish. The listing is according to the German, because in several cases the German term is the original, or more precise, or more widely established. The English terminology follows the suggestions of Elmar Waibl and Philip Herdina, *Wörterbuch philosophischer Fachbegriffe/Dictionary of Philosophical Terms*, vols. 1–2, Munich 2001. In Turkey philosophical dictionaries tend to be propagating somebody's private Turkish terminology. Perhaps the least idiosyncratic is A. Bâki Güçlü, Erkan Uzun, Serkan Uzun, Ümit Hüsrev Yolsal (eds.), *Felsefe Sözlüğü*, Ankara 2002. Of the words listed here they give only: *başkalık, olgusal, öznelcilik, varlık* and *varoluşsal.*

juristisch	legal	hukuksal
postmodern	postmodern	modern-sonrası
Relativist	relativist	izafetçi
Sein	being	varlık
Sprechakt	speech act	konuşma eylemi
Standort	position	durduğumuz yer
Subjektivismus	subjectivism	öznelcilik
SUI GENERIS	SUI GENERIS	nev-i şahsına munhasır
übergeschichtlich	transhistorical/ metahistorical	tarih üstü
Vorhersage	prediction	önceden görme
vormodern	premodern	modern-öncesi
Vorverständnis	pre-understanding	ön anlayış, evvelki anlaşım
Wirkungsgeschichte	effective history	etkin gelenek, etkin tarih, etki olarak tarih, etkiler tarihi
Zeitenabstand	temporal distance	zamansal mesafe

İlâhiyat Faculties in Turkey*

Akdeniz Üniversitesi İlâhiyat Fakültesi	Antalya
Ankara Üniversitesi İlâhiyat Fakültesi	Ankara
Atatürk Üniversitesi İlâhiyat Fakültesi	Erzurum
Cumhuriyet Üniversitesi İlâhiyat Fakültesi	Sivas
Çukurova Üniversitesi İlâhiyat Fakültesi	Adana
Dicle Üniversitesi İlâhiyat Fakültesi	Diyarbakır
Dokuz Eylül Üniversitesi İlâhiyat Fakültesi	İzmir
Erciyes Üniversitesi İlâhiyat Fakültesi	Kayseri
Fırat Üniversitesi İlâhiyat Fakültesi	Elazığ
Gazi Üniversitesi Çorum İlâhiyat Fakültesi	Çorum
Harran Üniversitesi İlâhiyat Fakültesi	Şanlıurfa
İnönü Üniversitesi Darende İlâhiyat Fakültesi	Malatya/Darende
İstanbul Üniversitesi İlâhiyat Fakültesi	İstanbul
Karadeniz Teknik Üniversitesi Rize İlâhiyat Fakültesi	Rize
Marmara Üniversitesi İlâhiyat Fakültesi	İstanbul
Ondokuz Mayıs Üniversitesi İlâhiyat Fakültesi	Samsun
Onsekiz Mart Üniversitesi İlâhiyat Fakültesi	Çanakkale
Osmangazi Üniversitesi İlâhiyat Fakültesi	Eskişehir
Sakarya Üniversitesi İlâhiyat Fakültesi	Sakarya
Selçuk Üniversitesi İlâhiyat Fakültesi	Konya
Süleyman Demirel Üniversitesi İlâhiyat Fakültesi	Isparta
Sütçü İmam Üniversitesi İlâhiyat Fakültesi	Kahramanmaraş
Uludağ Üniversitesi İlâhiyat Fakültesi	Bursa
Yüzüncü Yıl Üniversitesi İlâhiyat Fakültesi	Van

* This is a list of all twenty-four Turkish *İlâhiyat* Faculties. They are listed alphabetically according to university names rather than according to location, because Turkish authors tend to take for granted that the reader knows where a university is when they state only its name, or even the name's acronym. The list can, hopefully, serve as a key for indications like "D.E.Ü." (Adil Çiftçi, *Fazlur Rahman ile İslam'ı Yeniden Düşünmek*, Ankara 2000, p. 2). The list follows Yakup Çiçek and Bünyamin Açıkalın (eds.), *Türkiye İlahiyat Fakülteleri Tefsir Anabilim Dalı Öğretim Elemanları Biyografileri*, Istanbul 2000, p. 21, where however Akdeniz Üniversitesi İlâhiyat Fakültesi is not yet listed. There, teaching had not started until 2004.

Bibliography*

Açıkgenç, Alparslan, "Kur'an'da İlim Kavramı Çerçevesinde Tarisselliğe Bir Yaklaşım ve Bunun Tefsir Yönetemine Katkısı", Abay, Muhammad (ed.), *Kur'an'ı Anlamada Tarihsellik Sorunu Sempozyumu*, Istanbul 2000, pp. 183–93.

Aigrain, René, "Arabie", *Dictionnaire d'Histoire et de Géographie Ecclésiastiques*, vol. 3, Paris 1924, cols. 1158–1339.

Albertz, Rainer, *Religionsgeschichte Israels in alttestamentlicher Zeit*, vol. 1, *Von den Anfängen bis zum Ende der Königszeit*, Göttingen [2]1996.

Ambros, Arne A., "Die Analyse von Sure 112. Kritiken, Synthesen, neue Ansätze", *Der Islam*, vol. 63 (1986), pp. 219–47.

Arkoun, Mohammed (translated by Lee, Robert D.), *Rethinking Islam. Common Questions, Uncommon Answers*, Boulder (Colorado) and Oxford, 1994.

Baljon, Johannes Marinus Simon, *Modern Muslim Koran Interpretation* (1880–1960), Leiden 1968.

Baltacıoğlu, Ismayıl Hakkı, "Dine Doğru", *Ankara Üniversitesi İlâhiyat Fakültesi Dergisi*, vol. 6 (1957), pp. 44–59.

Bauer, Walter, *A Greek–English Lexicon of the New Testament and Other Early Christian Literature* (translated by Arndt, William F. and Gingrich, F. Wilbur), Cambridge (U.K.) and Chicago [4]1952.

Bayraktar, Mehmet Faruk, "Baltacıoğlu, Ismayıl Hakkı", *Türkiye Diyanet Vakfı İslâm Ansiklopedisi*, vol. 5, Istanbul 1992, pp. 36–7.

Braulik, Georg, "Das Deuteronomium und die Geburt des Monotheismus" 1985, IDEM, *Studien zur Theologie des Deuteronomiums*, Stuttgart 1988, pp. 257–300.

Buhl, Frants, *Das Leben Muhammeds* (translated by Schaeder, Hans Heinrich), Heidelberg (Danish 1903:) [3]1961.

—, "Faßte Muḥammed seine Verkündigung als eine universelle, auch für Nichtaraber bestimmte Religion auf?", *Islamica*, vol. 2 (1926), pp. 135–49.

Chadwick, Henry, *The Early Church*, Harmondsworth 1967.

Çiçek, Yakup and Açıkalın, Bünyamin (eds.), *Türkiye İlahiyat Fakülteleri Tefsir Anabilim Dalı Öğretim Elemanları Biyografileri*, Istanbul 2000.

Çiftçi, Adil, *Fazlur Rahman ile İslam'ı Yeniden Düşünmek*, Ankara 2000.

* Lest the biography be inflated, individual articles from the following encyclopaedias have been indicated only in the footnotes: *Encyclopaedia of Islam* (2nd ed.), *Enzyklopädie Philosophie und Wissenschaftstheorie*, *Historisches Wörterbuch der Philosophie*, *Lexikon für Theologie und Kirche* (3rd ed.), *Theologische Realenzyklopädie*.

Collingwood, Robin G., *The Idea of History*, Oxford 1946.

Denzinger, HENRICUS and Schönmetzer, ADOLFUS (eds.), *ENCHIRIDION SYMBOLORUM*, Freiburg [26]1976.

Ebeling, Gerhard, "Hermeneutik", *Die Religion in Geschichte und Gegenwart*, vol. 3, Tübingen [3]1959, cols. 242–62.

Eco, Umberto, *LECTOR IN FABULA*, Milano 1979.

—, Rorty, Richard, Culler, Jonathan and Brooke-Rose, Christine (ed. by Collini, Stefan), *Interpretation and Overinterpretation*, Cambridge (U.K.) 1992.

EI[2]: Encyclopaedia of Islam, vols. 1–11, Leiden (and London) [2]1954–2002.

Enzyklopädie Philosophie und Wissenschaftstheorie, vols. 1–4, Stuttgart 1980–96.

van Ess, Josef, *Zwischen Ḥadīṯ und Theologie. Studien zum Entstehen prädestinatianischer Überlieferung*, Berlin 1975.

—, *Theologie und Gesellschaft im 2. und 3. Jahrhundert Hidschra. Eine Geschichte des religiösen Denkens im frühen Islam*, vols. 1–6, Berlin 1991–7.

Fuhrmann, Manfred, Jauß, Hans Robert and Pannenberg, Wolfhart (eds.), *Text und Applikation. Theologie, Jurisprudenz und Literaturwissenschaft im hermeneutischen Gespräch*, Munich 1982.

Gadamer, Hans-Georg, *Hermeneutik*, vol. 1, *Wahrheit und Methode. Grundzüge einer philosophischen Hermeneutik*, Tübingen ([1]1960:) [6]1990; vol. 2, *Wahrheit und Methode. Ergänzungen, Register*, Tübingen 1993.

—, "Rhetorik, Hermeneutik und Ideologiekritik. Metakritische Erörterungen zu 'Wahrheit und Methode'" (1967), IDEM, *Hermeneutik*, vol. 2, *Wahrheit und Methode. Ergänzungen*, pp. 232–50.

—, "Klassische und philosophische Hermeneutik" (1977), IDEM, *Hermeneutik*, vol. 2, *Wahrheit und Methode. Ergänzungen*, pp. 92–117.

— (translated and revised by Weinsheimer, Joel and Marshall, Donald), *Truth and Method*, New York 1989.

Gaebel, Michael, *Von der Kritik des arabischen Denkens zum panarabischen Aufbruch. Das philosophische und politische Denken Muhammad ʿAbid al-Gabiris*, Berlin 1995.

Goldziher, Ignaz, *Muhammedanische Studien*, vol. 1, Halle 1888.

—, *Die Richtungen der islamischen Koranauslegung*, Leiden 1920.

Görgün, Tahsin, "İnşa–Haber (Performative–Constative) ve Kur'an'ın Anlaşılması. Sözeylem Teorisinin Tarihi Üzerine", Kara, Ömer (ed.), *Yüzüncü Yıl Üniversitesi İlahiyat Fakültesi 17–18 Mayıs 2001 Kur'an ve Dil – Dilbilim ve Hermenötik – Sempozyumu*, Erzurum 2001, pp. 443–60.

Grondin, Jean, *Introduction to Philosophical Hermeneutics*, New Haven (German 1991:) 1994.

Güler, İlhami, *Allah'ın Ahlakîliği*, Ankara 1998.

—,"Muhtar Bir İrade (Allah'ın İradesi) ve Mümkün Bir Tarihin (610–632) 'Kelam-ı Kadim'e ve 'Zorunlu Tarih'e Dönüşmesi", Kayaer, Osman (ed.), *III. Kur'an Haftası. Kur'an Sempozyumu. 13.–19. Ocak 1997*, Ankara 1998, pp. 211–27.

—, *Sabit Din–Dinamik Şeriat*, Ankara 1999.

Habermas, Jürgen, *Zur Logik der Sozialwissenschaften*, Tübingen 1967.

von Harnack, Adolf, *Lehrbuch der Dogmengeschichte*, vol. 1, Tübingen ([1]1886:) [5]1931.

Henrich, Dieter, "Rahmenbedingungen der Rationalität. Überlegungen zum Verhältnis von Kulturform und Kunstform" (1982), IDEM, *Fixpunkte. Abhandlungen und Essays zur Theorie der Kunst*, Frankfurt am Main 2003, pp. 221–32.

Hermann, Rainer, "Den Koran lesen. Ein türkischer Gelehrter will den Islam gegen die Last von Tradition und Dogmatik erneuern", *Frankfurter Allgemeine Zeitung*, April 4, 2002, p. 12.

Hirschfeld, Hartwig, *New Researches into the Composition and Exegesis of the Qoran*, London 1902.

Historisches Wörterbuch der Philosophie, vols. 1–, Basel 1971–.

Horovitz, Josef, *Koranische Untersuchungen*, Berlin 1926.

Iqbal, Allama Muhammad, *The Reconstruction of Religious Thought in Islam*, Lahore n.d. [1944].

b. Isḥāq, Muḥammad (translated by Guillaume, Alfred), *The Life of Muhammad*, Oxford 1955.

İslâmî Araştırmalar, vols. 1– (1986–).

İslâmiyât. Üç aylık araştırma dergisi, vols. 1– (1998–).

Jansen, Johannes J. G., *The Interpretation of the Koran in Modern Egypt*, Leiden 1974.

Jäschke, Gotthard, "Der Islam in der neuen Türkei. Eine rechtsgeschichtliche Untersuchung", *Die Welt des Islams*, N.S. vol. 1 (1951), pp. 1–174; corrections and additions: ibid., vol. 2 (1953 (SIC)), pp. 278–87.

Jeffery, Arthur, *The Foreign Vocabulary of the Qur'ān*, Baroda 1938.

Kaiser, Otto (ed.), *Texte aus der Umwelt des Alten Testaments*, vols. 1–3, Gütersloh 1981–95, Supplement (*Ergänzungslieferung*), Gütersloh 2001.

Kermani, Navid, *Gott ist schön. Das ästhetische Erleben des Koran*, Munich 1999.

Kluge, Friedrich, *Etymologisches Wörterbuch der deutschen Sprache* (ed. by Seebold, Elmar), Berlin [23]1999.

Köbert, Raimund, "Das Gottesepitheton aṣ-ṣamad in Sure 112,2", *Orientalia*, N.S. vol. 30 (1961), pp. 204–5.

Der Koran (translated by Paret, Rudi), Stuttgart [7]1996.

Körner, Felix, *Muḥammad Šaḥrūrs Koranhermeneutik in al-Kitāb wa-l-qurʾān*, Bamberg 2000 (unpublished M.A. thesis).

Koştaş, Münir, "Ankara Üniversitesi İlâhiyat Fakültesi (Dünü Bugünü)", *Ankara Üniverisitesi İlâhiyat Fakültesi Dergisi*, vol. 40 (1998), pp. 141–84.

Krawietz, Birgit, *Hierarchie der Rechtsquellen im tradierten sunnitischen Islam*, Berlin 2002.

Kreiser, Klaus and Wielandt, Rotraud (eds.), *Lexikon der islamischen Welt*, Stuttgart [2]1992.

Lane, Edward William, *An Arabic—English Lexicon*, vols. 1–8, London 1863–93.

Laut, Jens Peter, *Das Türkische als Ursprache? Sprachwissenschaftliche Theorien in der Zeit des erwachenden türkischen Nationalismus*, Wiesbaden 2000.

—, "Zur Sicht des Islam in der Türkischen Republik bis zum Tode Atatürks", Schluchter, Wolfgang (ed.), *Kolloquien des Max Weber Kollegs VI–XIV (1999/2000)*, Erfurt 2000, pp. 59–75.

Lazarus-Yafeh, Hava "Some Neglected Aspects of Medieval Muslim Polemics Against Christianity", *Harvard Theological Review*, vol. 89 (1996), pp. 61–84.

Lewis, Bernard, *The Emergence of Modern Turkey*, Oxford [2]1968.

Lewis, Geoffrey, *The Turkish Language Reform. A Catastrophic Success*, Oxford 1999.

Lexikon für Theologie und Kirche, vols. 1–11, Freiburg [3]1993–2001.

Madigan, Daniel A., *The Qurʾân's Self Image. Writing and Authority in Islam's Scripture*, Princeton 2001.

—, "Book", McAuliffe, Jane D. (ed.), *Encyclopaedia of the Qurʾān*, vol. 1, Leiden 2001, pp. 242–52.

Marshall, David, *God, Muhammad and the Unbelievers. A Qurʾanic Study*, Richmond (U.K.) 1999.

Meier, John P., *A Marginal Jew. Rethinking the Historical Jesus*, vol. 1, *The Roots of the Problem and the Person*, New York 1991; vol. 2, *Mentor, Message, and Miracles*, New York 1994; vol. 3, *Companions and Competitors*, New York 2001.

Motzki, Harald, *The Origins of Islamic Jurisprudence. Meccan Fiqh before the Classical Schools*, Leiden 2002.

Neuwirth, Angelika, "Koran", Gätje, Helmut (ed.), *Grundriß der Arabischen Philologie*, vol. 2, *Literaturwissenschaft*, Wiesbaden 1987, pp. 96–135.

—, "Vom Rezitationstext über die Liturgie zum Kanon: Zu Entstehung und Wiederauflösung der Surenkomposition im Verlauf der Entwicklung eines islamischen Kultus", Wild, Stefan (ed.), *The Qur'an as Text*, Leiden 1993, pp. 69–105.

Nöldeke, Theodor, "Stilistische und syntaktische Eigentümlichkeiten der Sprache des Korans", IDEM, *Neue Beiträge zur semitischen Sprachwissenschaft*, Strasbourg 1910, pp. 5–23.

— and Schwally, Friedrich, *Geschichte des Qorāns*, vol. 1, *Über den Ursprung des Qorāns*, Leipzig 1909; vol. 2, *Die Sammlung des Qorāns*, Leipzig 1919.

Özsoy, Ömer, *Sünnetullah. Bir Kur'an İfadesinin Kavramlaşması*, Ankara 1994.

—, "Kur'an Hitabının Tarihselliği ve Tarihsel Hitabın Nesnel Anlamı Üzerine", *İslâmî Araştırmalar* vol. 9 (1996), pp. 135–43.

"Ömer Özsoy ile "Tarihsellik" Üzerine", *İktibas*, September 1997, pp. 24–33.

Paçacı, Mehmet, "Kur'an-ı Kerim Işığında Vahiy Geleneğine—Kitabı-ı Mukaddes Bağlamında—Bir Bakış" (1991), IDEM, *Kur'an ve Ben Ne Kadar Tarihseliz?*, Ankara 2000, pp. 81–127.

—, ""Allah'ın Krallığı" Sendromu ve Günümüz Müslümanları" (1994), IDEM, *Kur'an ve Ben Ne Kadar Tarihseliz?*, Ankara 2000, pp. 9–29.

—, "Anlama (fıkh) Usulüne Dair" (1995), IDEM, *Kur'an ve Ben Ne Kadar Tarihseliz?*, Ankara 2000, pp. 31–52.

—, "Kur'an ve Ben Ne Kadar Tarihseliz?" (1996), IDEM, *Kur'an ve Ben Ne Kadar Tarihseliz?*, Ankara 2000, pp. 53–79.

—, "The Role of the Subject (mujtahid) in al-Shafi'i's Methodology: A Hermeneutic Approach", *The American Journal of Islamic Social Sciences*, vol. 14 (1997), pp. 3–15.

—, ""De Ki: Allah Bir(אחד/أحد)'dir." Sami Dini Geleneği Perspektifinden İhlas Sûresi'nin Bir Tefsiri Denemesi" (1998), IDEM, *Kur'an ve Ben Ne Kadar Tarihseliz?*, Ankara 2000, pp. 155–84.

— and Aktay, Yasin, "75 Years of Higher Religious Education in Modern Turkey", *The Muslim World*, vol. 89 (1999), pp. 398–413.

Pannenberg, Wolfhart, "Die Aufnahme des philosophischen Gottesbegriffs als dogmatisches Problem der frühchristlichen Theologie" (1959), IDEM, *Grundfragen systematischer Theologie*, vol. 1, Göttingen 1967, pp. 296–346.

—, "Heilsgeschehen und Geschichte" (1959), IDEM, *Grundfragen systematischer Theologie*, vol. 1, Göttingen 1967, pp. 22–78.

—, "Dogmatische Thesen zur Lehre von der Offenbarung", IDEM (ed.), *Offenbarung als Geschichte*, Göttingen 1961, pp. 91–114.

—, "Hermeneutik und Universalgeschichte" (1963), IDEM, *Grundfragen systematischer Theologie*, vol. 1, Göttingen 1967, pp. 91–122.

—, *Grundzüge der Christologie*, Gütersloh ^{2}1966.

—, *Wissenschaftstheorie und Theologie*, Frankfurt am Main 1973.

—, *Anthropologie in theologischer Perspektive*, Göttingen 1983.
—, *Systematische Theologie*, vols. 1–3, Göttingen 1988–93.
Paret, Rudi, "Der Koran als Geschichtsquelle", *Der Islam*, vol. 37 (1961), pp. 24–42.
—, *Der Koran. Kommentar und Konkordanz*, Stuttgart [3]1986.
—, *Mohammed und der Koran. Geschichte und Verkündigung des arabischen Propheten*, Stuttgart [7]1991.
Pretzl, Otto, "Aufgaben und Ziele der Koranforschung", Paret, Rudi, (ed.), *Der Koran*, Darmstadt 1975, pp. 411–2.
Pritchard, James B., *Ancient Near Eastern Texts Relating to the Old Testament*, Princeton [3]1974.
Fazlur Rahman, *Islamic Methodology in History*, Karachi 1965.
—, *Islam*, Chicago [2]1979.
—, *Islam & Modernity. Transformation of an Intellectual Tradition*, Chicago 1982.
—, *Major Themes of the Qur'an*, Minneapolis [2]1989.
—, "An Autobiographical Note—Kısa Otobiyografi" (translated by Demirkol, Bekir), *İslâmî Araştırmalar* vol. 4 (1990), pp. 227–31, p. 228.
Rahner, Karl, "Grundlinien einer systematischen Christologie", IDEM and Thüsing, Wilhelm, *Christologie – systematisch und exegetisch. Arbeitsgrundlagen für eine interdisziplinäre Vorlesung*, Freiburg 1972, pp. 15–87.
Redhouse Türkçe—İngilizce Sözlük, Istanbul [16]1998.
Ricœur, Paul, *Hermeneutik und Strukturalismus*, Munich 1973.
Rippin, Andrew, (ed.), *Approaches to the History of the Interpretation of the Qur'ān*, Oxford 1988.
Rosenthal, Franz, "History and the Qur'ān", McAuliffe, Jane D. (ed.), *Encyclopaedia of the Qur'ān*, vol. 2, Leiden 2002, pp. 428–42.
Rumpf, Christian, "Das Präsidium für Religionsangelegenheiten", *Zeitschrift für Türkeistudien*, vol. 2 (1989), pp. 21–33.
Schaeffler, Richard, "Sprache als Bedingung und Folge der Erfahrung. Das religiöse Wort als Beispiel für die Geschichtlichkeit des Verhältnisses von "Sprache" und "Rede"", Beinert, Wolfgang (ed.), *Sprache und Erfahrung als Problem der Theologie*, Paderborn 1978, pp. 11–36.
Schedl, Claus, "Probleme der Koranexegese. Nochmals ṣamad in Sure 112,2", *Der Islam*, vol. 58 (1981), pp. 1–14.
Schöler, Gregor, *Charakter und Authentie der muslimischen Überlieferung über das Leben Mohammeds*, Berlin 1996.
Speyer, Heinrich, *Die biblischen Erzählungen im Qoran*, Gräfenhainichen n.d.
Trimingham, J. Spencer, *Christianity Among the Arabs in Pre-Islamic Times*, London 1979.

Spuler-Stegemann, Ursula, "Der Islam", Grothusen, Klaus-Detlev (ed.), *Südosteuropa-Handbuch*, vol. 4, *Türkei*, Göttingen 1985, pp. 591–612.

Steuerwald, Karl, *Türkisch–Deutsches Wörterbuch*, Wiesbaden [2]1988.

Stolz, Fritz, *Einführung in den biblischen Monotheismus*, Darmstadt 1996.

Sülün, Murat and Çelik, Ömer (eds.), *Türkiye Kur'an Makaleleri Bibliyografyası*, Istanbul 1999.

Taeschner, Franz, "Ilâhiyat [SIC] Fakültesi Dergisi", *Die Welt des Islams*, N.S. vol. 2 (1953), pp. 305–6.

Theologische Realenzyklopädie, vol. 1–, Berlin 1977–.

Thiselton, Anthony C., *New Horizons in Hermeneutics*, London 1992.

Troll, Christian W., *Sayyid Ahmad Khan: A Reinterpretation of Muslim Theology*, New Delhi 1978.

—, "Islamische Stimmen zum gesellschaftlichen Pluralismus", IDEM (ed.), *Der europäische Islam. Eine reale Perspektive?*, Berlin 2001, pp. 55–94.

Ullmann, Manfred, *Wörterbuch der klassischen arabischen Sprache*, vol. 1, Wiesbaden 1970.

Usta, Mustafa, *Türkiye'de Yüksek Din Eğitimin Korumlaşma ve Ekolleşme Sorunları*, Istanbul 2001.

Wach, Joachim, *Religionswissenschaft. Prolegomena zu ihrer wissenschaftstheoretischen Grundlegung*, Leipzig 1924.

Waibl, Elmar and Herdina, Philip, *Wörterbuch philosophischer Fachbegriffe/Dictionary of Philosophical Terms*, vols. 1–2, Munich 2001.

Waldman, Marilyn R., "New Approaches to "Biblical" Materials in the Qur'ān", *The Muslim World*, vol. 75 (1985), pp. 1–13.

Watt, William M., *Free Will and Predestination in Early Islam*, London 1948.

—, *Bell's Introduction to the Qur'ān*, Edinburgh 1970.

Webster's New Collegiate Dictionary, Springfield (Massachusetts) 1979.

Wensinck, Arent J., *A Handbook of Early Muhammadan Tradition*, Leiden 1927.

Wiegand, A., "Der Gottesname צור und seine Deutung in dem Sinne Bildner oder Schöpfer in der alten jüdischen Litteratur", *Zeitschrift für die alttestamentliche Wissenschaft*, vol. 10 (1890), pp. 85–96.

Wielandt, Rotraud, *Offenbarung und Geschichte im Denken moderner Muslime*, Wiesbaden 1971.

—, "Wurzeln der Schwierigkeiten innerislamischen Gesprächs über neue hermeneutische Zugänge zum Korantext", Wild, Stefan (ed.), *The Qur'an as Text*, Leiden 1996, pp. 257–82.

—, "Exegesis of the Qur'ān: Early Modern and Contemporary", McAuliffe, Jane D. (ed.), *Encyclopaedia of the Qur'ān*, vol. 2, pp. 124–42, Leiden 2002.

Wilckens, Ulrich, *Das Evangelium nach Johannes*, Göttingen 1998.

Zusammenfassung

Die vorliegende Arbeit untersucht koranhermeneutische Neuansätze in der gegenwärtigen türkischen Hochschultheologie. Diese Ansätze werden nicht nur archivierend vorgestellt, sondern kritisch dargestellt. Daher muss eine vorgeschaltete wissenschaftstheoretische Überlegung das Paradigma einer Religionswissenschaft begründen, die sich mit theologischen Aussagen (propositions) auseinandersetzt, ohne selbst einen bestimmten religiösen Standpunkt beziehen zu müssen. Ein solches Vorgehen ist religionswissenschaftlich möglich, ja sinnvoll, da es den Wahrheitsanspruch religiöser Aussagen als allgemeinen ernst nimmt und Theologie auf gleicher Ebene, nämlich argumentativ aufgreift. Bei der Auseinandersetzung mit theologischen Positionen muss sich der Religionswissenschaftler jedoch der Gefahr bewusst sein, mit falsch verstandenen Begriffen zu hantieren, weil er deren Erfahrungshintergrund nicht teilt.

Die Arbeit untersucht Koranhermeneutik wegen deren Schlüsselstellung für islamische Reformtheologien. Der *Koran* muss in einer solchen Theologie den Ausgangspunkt bilden, da er, wie auch Muslime sehen, ein ungehobenes Erneuerungspotential birgt, das anders als jede sonstige Reformgrundlage mit einer breiten muslimischen Akzeptanz rechnen kann. Schließlich entstammt es dem islamischen Zentraldokument. Die *hermeneutische* Frage muss hierbei gestellt werden, da nur ein bewusster und reflektierter Rückgriff auf den Text denkerisch rechtfertigbare Auslegungen ermöglicht. Und nur sie können sich auf Dauer vor einer kritischen und aufrichtigen Befragung bewähren.

Die Darstellung des Forschungsstandes muss einen philosophiegeschichtlichen Rückblick auf die Behandlung der texthermeneutischen Frage, einen Einblick in die innerislamische auslegungsmethodische Diskussion sowie einen Überblick über deren islamkundliche Erforschung umfassen.

Das Wort ‚Hermeneutik' kann hierbei auf drei Ebenen verwendet werden; als Benennung jeglicher Umgangsformen mit Texten (und zwar als implizite, d.h. praktizierte sowie als explizite, d.h. reflektierte Methodik), als Beschreibung des geschichtlichen Transfers normativer Textgehalte sowie als Kennzeichnung einer bestimmten kontinental-philosophischen Tradition. Da diese letztgenannte Ebene bei den untersuchten muslimischen Autoren einen Angelpunkt der Reflexion darstellt, nimmt der einführende hermeneutisch-philosophische Rückblick ebenfalls HANS-GEORG GADAMERs Sichtweise zum Ausgangspunkt. Sein Blick auf die Geschichte des Verstehens zeigt, dass juristische, klassisch-philologische und theologische Textinterpretationen seit je normatives Interesse hatten und, wie insbesondere bei der „Interpretation“ von Aufführungswerken in der Kunst abzulesen ist, die Anwendung des Verstandenen kein dem Verstehen und Erklären nachklappender Vorgang ist, sondern Teil des Verstehensprozesses. Statt einer psychologischen Einfühlung in das andere, wie die Romantik vorschlug, beschreibt GADAMER alles Verstehen als Einlassen neuer Gesichtspunkte in den eigenen Gesichtskreis. Die erhellenden Einsichten GADAMERs werden unter viererlei Rücksicht kommentiert. GADAMER bietet keine Textinterpretationsmethode, ja er hält eine solche für nicht entwerfbar; GADAMER unterschätzt den Aussagecharakter von Sprache; er sieht nicht, dass erst der antizipierte Horizont der Gesamtgeschichte vereinnahmungsloses Verstehen ermöglicht; und sein Prinzip, dass die verständniserschließende Frage, die der Text beantwortet, aus dem Text selbst gefunden werden muss, übersieht außertextliche Maßstäbe, die auch ein Urteil wie ‚Thema verfehlt’ ermöglichen.

In den innerislamischen koranhermeneutischen Forschungsstand wird anhand der Arbeiten dreier europäischer Islamwissenschaftler eingeführt. J. M. S. BALJON (1968) stellt urdu-sprachige Korankommentare vom Ende des 19. bis zur Mitte des 20. Jahrhunderts vor, die neue methodische Wege gehen. Er beobachtet Versuche, mit philologischen, moderne naturwissenschaftliche Erkenntnisse voraussetzenden oder psychologischen Methoden Elemente aus Koranstellen wegzuerklären, die von den Autoren als übernatürlich beurteilt wurden. Er charakterisiert die Vorgehensweise der von ihm untersuchten Kommentatoren als Entmythologisierung, Romantisierung, Rationalisierung, Historisierung und Moralisierung.

Die breit angelegte Untersuchung ägyptischer Korankommentare des 20. Jahrhunderts durch J. J. G. JANSEN (1974) diagnostiziert mangelnde Originalität bei vielen Autoren. Oft bestehe der Unterschied zu klassischen Kommentarwerken lediglich in der angesprochenen Leserschaft (‚der interessierte Laie’). JANSEN teilt die von ihm gefundenen Kommentare in drei Kategorien ein: naturgeschichtliche, philologische und alltagsbezogene. Den ersteren attestiert er einen geringen naturwissenschaftlichen Informationsstand. Unter philologischen Kommentaren nennt er Versuche, den Koran als Literatur, das heißt auch als literaturwissenschaftlich erschließbar, zu lesen. Nach JANSENs Beobachtung gehen schließlich die alltagsbezogenen Kommentare vor allem von der Frage aus, inwieweit das Leben der Muslime verwestlicht werden darf.

ROTRAUD WIELANDTs Dissertation (1971) erforscht moderne islamische Geschichtsphilosophie. Ihre geistesgeschichtliche Vorgehensweise eröffnet auch koranexegetische und offenbarungstheologische Einblicke. Die Studie spitzt sich auf ein theologisches Dilemma zu. Entweder man akzeptiere die vollkommene Göttlichkeit alles im Koran Offenbarten; dann sei eine historische Herangehensweise unzulässig. Oder man gebe eine menschliche Beteiligung beim Zustandekommen des Textes zu. In späteren Forschungen beobachtet WIELANDT jedoch, dass muslimische Denker hier Auswege gefunden und beschritten haben. In ihrem 2002 erschienenen Enzyklopädie-Artikel entwickelt sie eine sechsfache Typologie frühmoderner und zeitgenössischer muslimischer Koraninterpretation. Sie teilt die Gesamtszene ein in rationalistische, naturwissenschaftliche, literaturwissenschaftliche, historische, ahistorisch-unmittelbare sowie thematische Exegese. Ein literaturwissenschaftlich und historisch forschender Muslim kann nun beispielsweise vorschlagen, der Koran sei, um Menschen auf der Arabischen Halbinsel im 7. nachchristlichen Jahrhundert – den ersten Koranempfängern – verständlich zu sein, von Gott – dem Sender – im Empfängercode übermittelt worden. Jede Kultur müsse in der Folge einen Transfer des Koran in ihren eigenen Code leisten.

Türkischsprachige Koranexegese wurde von der islamkundlichen Forschung bisher wenig berücksichtigt. Da die vorliegende Arbeit Quellen aus der Hand türkischer Hochschultheologen untersucht, stellt sie die akademisch-theologische Szene der Türkei vor. Die Geschichte einer neuen islamischen Theologie in der Türkei kann im Jahre 1847 ansetzen, nämlich bei dem Beschluss des osmanischen Erziehungsministeriums, an der Universität in Istanbul eine theologische Fakultät westlichen Zuschnitts einzurichten. Dieser Schritt muss als Teil der Gesamtbemühung gesehen werden, das traditionelle Medresen-System durch moderne Bildungsanstalten zu ersetzen. Doch erst 1924 wurden unter dem radikalen Modernisierungsprogramm Mustafa Kemals die bislang ohne staatlichen Zugriff operierenden Medresen geschlossen und statt ihrer staatliche Ausbildungsstätten für Vorbeter und Prediger eingerichtet. Zugleich wurde wieder eine theologische Fakultät an der Istanbuler Universität – sie war 1917 von einer Fachhochschule an der Süleymaniye-Moschee abgelöst worden – eingerichtet. Die Vorbeter-und-Prediger-Schulen fanden in der Frühzeit der türkischen Republik wenig Zulauf und waren 1932 allesamt eingegangen. Die Istanbuler theologische Fakultät wurde in ein Institut für Islamforschung umgewandelt und der Literaturwissenschaftlichen Fakultät eingegliedert. Mit der Einführung des Mehrparteiensystems 1947 konnte in der Türkei auch öffentlich eine bessere Ausbildung des Religionspersonals gefordert werden. Private Seminarien wurden erlaubt, setzten aber eine säkulare staatliche Sekundarbildung voraus. Schon nach einem Jahr jedoch wurde die Wiedereinrichtung staatlicher Vorbeter-und-Prediger-Schulen gefordert. 1949 wurden, nun unter Aufsicht des Erziehungsministeriums, die ersten Vorbeterschulungen eingerichtet. Mit der Begründung, reaktionär-islamischen Bewegungen zu wehren, wurde ebenfalls 1949 eine theologische Fakultät an der Universität Ankara eingerichtet, die wie westliche theologische Fakultäten aufgebaut sein und auch Fächer wie vergleichende Religionswissenschaft unterrichten sollte. Bis zum Jahr 2004 wurden in der Türkei 23 weitere theologische Fakultäten gegründet. Ihr rechtlicher Status – sie unterstehen keiner religionsbehördlichen Aufsicht – und ihre Gründungsintention – einen aufgeklärten Islam wissenschaftlich zu fundieren – sind in der islamischen Welt wohl einzigartig und für die Entwicklung theologischer Neuansätze außerordentlich vielversprechend.

Die Arbeit führt nun an die älteste der türkischen islamisch-theologischen Fakultäten, an die Ankaraner, die in der Türkei eine Führungsrolle innehat. Hier hat sich eine Gruppe von Theologen gebildet, die sich selbst „Ankaraner Schule" nennt, ihre Ausrichtung als „islamischen Modernismus" bezeichnet, insbesondere methodische Grundsatzfragen behandelt und auf hohem philosophischem und theologischem Niveau hermeneutische Ansätze für ein neues Islamverständnis vorträgt.

Der erste vorgestellte Theologe ist der 1959 geborene MEHMET PAÇACI, der in Ankara Theologie und Philosophie sowie in Manchester Neues Testament studiert hat. Er stellt seinen eigenen Ansatz als Alternative einerseits zu „orientalistischen" Erklärungsversuchen des Koran als Produkt monotheistischer Tendenzen auf der Arabischen Halbinsel und andererseits zu islamischen Allgemeingültigkeitserklärungen des koranischen Wortlautes vor. PAÇACI schließt sich dem koranhermeneutischen Modell des aus dem heutigen Pakistan stammenden islamischen Theologen FAZLUR RAHMAN (st. 1988) an. Dieser schlägt ein dreischrittiges Auslegen vor. Um den Koran zu verstehen, muss man ihn im Kontext der Zeit seiner Verkündigung verstehen. Aus dem so Verstandenen sind die den Einzelregelungen zugrundeliegenden allgemeingültigen ethischen Prinzipien zu destillieren. Diese schließlich sind in jeder Zeit neu zu verwirklichen. – In Auseinandersetzung mit PAÇACI bemerkt die Arbeit, dass die teilweise recht polemisch vorgetragene Gegenüberstellung westlicher und islamischer Positionen wohl didaktische Ursprünge hat. Ein historischen Methoden gegenüber noch skeptisches muslimisches Publikum soll offenbar durch das Argument überzeugt werden, dass Geschichtsforschung zwar für das Christentum gefährlich, für den Islam aber fruchtbar, ja traditionell sei. Als Probleme des vorgetragenen Dreischritts sind aufzuführen: Er setzt bereits voraus, dass der Koran ethisch Allgemeingültiges zu sagen hat, ohne dies zu begründen; die Glaubensgemeinschaft wird sich schwerlich einigen können auf Formulierungen für die aus dem Koran zu abstrahierenden ethischen Prinzipien; und auch neuformulierte ethische Prinzipien brauchen wieder Anwendungsregeln, für die man um so schwerer einen Konsens findet, als ja schon die Neuformulierung umstritten sein wird.

PAÇACI zufolge ist der Skopus des Koran ethisch. Alle nicht sollensförmigen Passagen des Koran seien seinem moralschaffenden Grundanliegen untergeordnet. Durch den Koran habe Gott Menschen in ihrer historischen Situation angesprochen. Rechtsfindung laufe in der islamischen Tradition seit jeher über die Gewinnung allgemeiner Prinzipien aus dem geschichtlich Einmaligen. Jedoch sei dieser traditionelle und von FAZLUR RAHMAN verfeinerte Ansatz nun anhand der GADAMERschen Hermeneutik zu erweitern. Vor Eintritt in den Dreischritt muss das Vorverständnis, die geschichtliche Ausgangslage der jeweils Interpretierenden, zu Bewusstsein kommen. Für PAÇACI bedeutet dieses Wahrnehmen der eigenen Geschichtlichkeit vor allem, die sich jeweils heute bietende Gelegenheit der verantwortlichen Weltgestaltung nach koranisch-ethischen Prinzipien zu nutzen. – Die Arbeit fragt an, ob es sich beim Verständnis des Koran als konkretisierter Ethik nicht um einen Reduktionismus handelt, der der Breite koranischer Theologie nicht gerecht wird; und ob die Rezeption hermeneutischer Philosophie nicht noch weiter gehen kann, indem z.B. der von GADAMER beobachtete Vorgang, dass der Einfluss des Textes auch die Fragestellung des Auslegers verwandelt, koranhermeneutisch genutzt würde.

Eine Untersuchung zu PAÇACIs Studie über Sure 112 zeigt, dass es sich dabei um eine experimentelle Exegese handelt, die die Hypothese einer „semitischen Religionstradition“ überprüft. Der Koran wird als ein Niederschlag der gemeinsemitischen monotheistischen Strömung verstanden. Daher könnten sowohl einzelne koranische Vokabeln als auch die koranische Theologie insgesamt im Lichte anderer semitischsprachiger religiöser Texte gelesen werden. Die traditionelle islamische Beleuchtung des Koran durch Anführung meist legendärer, erbaulicher Geschichten biblischer Thematik – der so genannten Isrāʾīlīyāt – wird von PAÇACI mit historisch-philologischer Methodik erneut unternommen, indem er altorientalische sowie alt- und zwischentestamentliche Literatur koranexegetisch nutzt. Das Hapaxlegomenon „aṣ-ṣamad“ in Vers 112,2, dessen Bedeutung in der Forschung umstritten ist, erklärt er aus einer streng-monotheistischen Übersetzungstendenz, die nach dem Auftreten christlicher Theologie einsetzt. Um sich von inkarnationstheologischen Vorstellungen abzusetzen, habe die semitische Religionstradition ihren Glauben nun nicht mehr anthropomorph ausgedrückt, sondern konkrete Gottesmetaphern durch abstraktere ersetzt oder aufgelöst. So wurde auch die Gottesbezeichnung „der Fels“, die in der Hebräischen Bibel häufig ist, schon in ihren frühen Übersetzungen als „der Harte“, „der Starke“, „der Helfer“ wiedergegeben. Auch das koranische „aṣ-ṣamad“ („der Feste“) ist nach PAÇACI nun eine solche abstraktere Wiedergabe von „der Fels“. – Die Auswertung würdigt zuerst, dass PAÇACI hier das koranexegetische Paradigma mutig erweitert hat. Die Einzelerklärungen jedoch sind zum Teil übereilt und beruhen auf unbegründeten Zwischenannahmen. Es wird an die These CLAUS SCHEDLs erinnert, dass „aṣ-ṣamad" das eingebürgerte Ersatzwort für die Gottesmetapher „der Fels" in der mündlichen arabischsprachigen synagogalen Bibelübersetzung war, was PAÇACIs Auslegung formal ergänzt und inhaltlich erhärtet. Der Terminus „semitische Religionstradition" wird jedoch abgelehnt, da er eine tatsächlich nicht gegebene Kontinuität suggeriert. Hatte PAÇACI in seinen methodisch-philosophischen Studien Ethik zur Hauptaussage des Koran erklärt, so finden sich in seiner exegetisch-philologischen Arbeit zum Koran zwar Themen der Gotteslehre und Offenbarungstheologie behandelt, aber kein Wort über Ethisches. Es ist jedoch zu erwarten, dass Denker vom Kaliber PAÇACIs die zeitgenössisch-philosophischen und historisch-theologischen Denkstränge in einer islamischen Fundamentaltheologie zusammenbringen.

Als zweiter türkischer Denker wird der 1963 geborene ADİL ÇİFTÇİ vorgestellt, der außer Theologie an der Ankaraner Fakultät auch Religionssoziologie in Izmir und London studiert hat. Die Auseinandersetzung mit ihm erweist sich zugleich als Vertiefung der Auseinandersetzung mit FAZLUR RAHMAN. Für ÇİFTÇİ liegt die Bedeutung der Theologie FAZLUR RAHMANs vor allem in dessen Neueinschätzung des Koran. Der Koran ist ihm zufolge kein Gesetzbuch, also unmittelbar anzuwenden, sondern ein Kompendium allgemeingültiger Prinzipien, die jedoch in Form von exemplarisch-zeitgebundenen Anwendungen vorliegen. D.h. die koranischen Einzelregelungen stehen für ethische Grundlinien, die erneut konkretisiert werden müssen, um justiziabel und entscheidungsleitend zu werden. Dieses Verständnis beruht auf FAZLUR RAHMANs Offenbarungstheologie, die Muhammad nicht als Lautsprecher Gottes sieht, also als passiven Übermittler des Gotteswortes, sondern die Persönlichkeit des Propheten am Offenbarungsvorgang beteiligt. Muhammad ist vom göttlichen Geist erfüllt. Dies bedeutet für FAZLUR RAHMAN, der Prophet besitzt die Einstellung, die es ihm ermöglicht, die Gottes Willen entsprechenden Entscheidungen zu treffen, zu formulieren und zu verkünden. Daher hat sich auch der heutige Muslim nicht dem Koran zu unterwerfen, insofern er früher geltende Einzelregelungen enthält, sondern dem Gotteswillen, wie er im Koran anhand von Beispielen formuliert ist. Folglich braucht der Koraninterpret jedoch eine Verstehensmethode, die es ihm ermöglicht, den ja nicht ausdrücklich benannten Willen Gottes aus dem Korantext zu erheben. So gelangt FAZLUR RAHMAN in die hermeneutische Diskussion. Er lehnt GADAMERs Philosophie als einen Subjektivismus ab, der die Grundlage seiner koranischen Ethik erschüttere. Statt dessen schließt er sich der Methode des Rechtshistorikers EMILIO BETTI an, der GADAMER als Kontrastfolie für die eigene Position gedient hatte. – Die Auseinandersetzung weist darauf hin, dass FAZLUR RAHMANs Ablehnung der GADAMERschen Philosophie der Haltbarkeit seines eigenen Ansatz schwer schadet. Hätte er ein wirkungsgeschichtliches Bewusstsein entwickelt, so hätte er bemerken können, wie die bisherige muslimische Koranexegese sein eigenes, ethisches, Befragen des Koran bewirkt hat. Hätte FAZLUR RAHMAN GADAMERs Kritik an psychologisch-historistischen Interpretationen ernstgenommen, wäre ihm klar geworden, dass sein eigener, wie BETTIs, Ansatz positivistisch ist: Er fragt nicht, ob man den in einem Text benannten Inhalt vom eigenen Standpunkt aus als wahr erkennen kann; dass der Text recht hat, behauptet ein so vorgehender Koranethiker oder Jurist, ohne es begründen zu müssen oder zu können. Hätte FAZLUR RAHMAN GADAMERs Einsicht verstanden, dass man in der Geschichte nichts vollständig verstehen kann, hätte er dies nicht als subjektivistisch ablehnen müssen, sondern als um Sachlichkeit bemühte Bereitschaft annehmen können, durch stets neue Informationen besser zu erkennen. Jedoch muss auch gesehen werden, dass FAZLUR RAHMAN nach einer Hermeneutik greift, die seinem Projekt „Islam und Moderne“ eine feste, und Muslimen als fest vermittelbare, Verankerung bietet. – ADİL ÇİFTÇİs Auseinandersetzung mit FAZLUR RAHMANs Ansatz wird als eine Rekonstruktion eingeschätzt, die unter Zuhilfenahme einiger Anregungen westlicher Philosophie den Ansatz illustriert, das Potential dieser Philosophie aber nicht für eine kritische Neubeleuchtung FAZLUR RAHMANs nutzt.

Als dritte Stimme lässt die Arbeit den 1963 geborenen Theologen ÖMER ÖZSOY zu Wort kommen, der außer Theologie und Sozialwissenschaft in Ankara, Islamwissenschaft in Heidelberg studiert hat. ÖZSOY nimmt eine semantische Unterscheidung zweier türkischer Wörter für „geschichtlich“ vor. Dem einen legt er die Bedeutungen „tatsächlich“ und „nicht übergeschichtlich“ bei, dem anderen „muss kontextbezogen ausgelegt werden“. Diese Unterscheidung entspricht nicht der im Deutschen geläufigen zwischen „geschichtlich“ und „historisch“. ÖZSOY fordert eine streng historische Lektüre des Koran. Er verwendet dafür die bekannte Formel, „den Koran so verstehen, wie ihn die ersten Hörer verstanden“, eröffnet unter diesem Motto jedoch eine neue Zugangsweise. Er beschreibt das Verständnis der gläubigen Ersthörer als exemplarisch-normativen Umgang mit dem im Koran Gemeinten und nennt diesen Umgang im Anschluss an FAZLUR RAHMAN „Sunna“. Der andernfalls hoffnungslos vieldeutige Koran wird durch diese „Tradition“ vereindeutigt, wenn auch eine Übertragung richtigen Handelns aus den damaligen Lebensumständen in jeweils heutige notwendig bleibt. – ÖZSOYs Erschließung des hermeneutischen Wertes von korangemäßem Handeln ist eine weiterführende Erkenntnis, da sie die Uneindeutigkeit textlicher Regeln offenlegt und die Notwendigkeit einer

Glaubensgemeinschaft für das Offenbarungsverständnis aufzeigt. Ungeklärt bleibt bei ÖZSOYs Gedanke jedoch, wie das Handeln der Ersthörer als normativ erkannt werden kann, wenn nicht aus dem Koran; wie das korangemäße Handeln der gläubigen Ersthörer heute anders als über Texte – und damit ebenso uneindeutig – zugänglich sein soll; und wieso nicht späteres korangemäßes Handeln ebenso oder mindestens so normativ sein kann wie das der Muslime der ersten Generation. Außerdem setzt der Ansatz, da er Koraninterpretation nur auf rechtes Handeln bezieht, wiederum einen ethischen Reduktionismus voraus.

ÖZSOY zufolge ist der Koran nicht als Geschichtsquelle nutzbar, da er keine Aussagen vom Typ ‚was Gott getan hat' machen will, sondern nur vom Typ ‚was Gott tun will'. Falls dies nicht eine sprachliche Unsauberkeit für ‚was Gott getan haben will' ist, handelt es sich hier um ein neues Verständnis von Handeln Gottes. Gott handelt demnach nicht mittels Durchsetzung, sondern durch ethikfähige Wesen, denen gegenüber Er Seinen Willen ausdrückt. Allerdings sollte der historische Anspruch koranischer Aussagen nicht, wie ÖZSOY es tut, vollständig aufgegeben werden, da auch die Behauptung, der Koran fordere ein bestimmtes Handeln, einen historischen Anspruch beinhaltet.

ÖZSOY fordert die Beachtung der Unterscheidung zwischen koranischer Botschaft und koranischer Sprechweise bei der Auslegung. Traditionelle theologische Koranauslegung schildert ÖZSOY als formalistisch auf die Sprechweise fixiert, während juristische Auslegung stets praxisinteressiert gewesen sei und daher auch die frühste Koranbefolgung für interpretationsrelevant gehalten habe. ÖZSOY zufolge war der Koran nicht als Text, d.h. nicht als systematisches Ganzes, intendiert. Er ist verschriftlichte Rede in diversen Einzelzusammenhängen. Kenntnis der Mitteilungsumstände ist daher für sein Verständnis notwendig. Der Koran wird als Gottes Kommentar zum Verhalten der ersten Hörer verstanden. Der Koran ist dermaßen kontextgebunden, dass es nicht um eine direkte Koranbefolgung gehen kann. Sonst würde das Zufällige normativ. – In der Auseinandersetzung werden ÖZSOYs Unterscheidung von Text und Rede und sein Plädoyer für ein „nicht-textliches" (d.h. kontextdeterminiertes) Koranverständnis als originelle Beiträge gewürdigt, aber auch deren Schwierigkeiten benannt. Unser Zugriff auf den Koran ist nun einmal nur textlich möglich, weil wir heute den ursprünglichen Sprechkontext nicht mehr erleben können; und alle Kontext-Rekonstruktionen müssen sich wiederum auf Texte berufen.

ÖZSOY bemerkt, dass alle auf Texten basierenden Weltanschauungen in die fundamentalistische Falle gehen können, den Text ungeschichtlich auf Antworten für heute zu befragen. – Die Auseinandersetzung stimmt dieser Einsicht zu, fragt aber, ob die untersuchten Autoren mit „geschichtlich" dasselbe meinen, was in kontinental-europäischer Geschichtsphilosophie damit benannt wird. Die türkischen Theologen verstehen unter ‚geschichtlich' das Anerkennen der Unterschiede und der Übersetzungsnotwendigkeit zwischen zwei Situationen, nämlich dem Originalkontext und dem Heute. Nur der angelsächsische Historiebegriff, nicht jedoch der kontinentale Geschichtsbegriff, der aus der biblischen Sicht der „Taten Gottes" als offene, aber als Gesamt verstehbare Handlung entstand, ist bisher rezipiert. Es wird aufgezeigt, dass der Koran durchaus geschichtstheologische Linien bietet, die eine Bedeutung des Gesamtgeschehens sehen. Der Koran sagt zum einen, dass alle Völker gleichermaßen mit Offenbarung versorgt wurden, zweitens, dass er selbst nun einen Maßstab für die Völkervereinigung bietet, und schließlich, dass Gott durch Bestätigungszeichen handelt.

Die Arbeit stellt als letzten Autor den 1959 geborenen Systematischen Theologen İLHAMİ GÜLER vor, der in Ankara und an der Universität Kairo Theologie und Sozialwissenschaft studiert hat. Auch er fordert eine historische, d.h. eine den Entstehungs- und Anwendungskontext berücksichtigende Koranlektüre. Das islamische Denken ist GÜLER zufolge zurückgeblieben. Die Ursache hierfür sieht er in der seiner Ansicht nach unflexiblen, konservativen arabischen Mentalität. Aus der angeblichen arabischen Sympathie für das Dauerhafte begründet er nun auch die Entstehung der Lehre von der Ungeschaffenheit, also anfangslosen Ewigkeit, des Koran. Durch diese Lehre sei aus einer kontingenten Geschichte, dem öffentlichen Wirken Muhammads, etwas Unveränderbares geworden, das Gotteswort. – In der Auseinandersetzung mit GÜLER kritisiert die Arbeit die schlecht begründete und pauschale These der arabischen Unbeweglichkeit und fragt dann, ob es im Koran neben den tatsächlich unübersehbaren rückwärtsgerichteten Aussagen auch eine gegenwarts- und zukunftsorientierte Theologie gibt. Hingewiesen wird darauf, dass die frühesten Suren primär eschatologischen Inhalts sind, dass in der koranischen Darstellung die Quelle für Muhammads Prophetie der gegenwärtige Einfluss Gottes ist und dass die kriegerischen Erfolge der ersten Muslime zunehmend als Handeln Gottes gedeutet werden. Ob der Koran anfangslos ist oder nicht, trägt dagegen für die Frage nach der Zukunftsoffenheit koranischer Theologie nichts aus.

GÜLER übernimmt das mu'tazilitische Argument, dass die Annahme eines weiteren anfangslosen Seienden neben Gott den Monotheismus verlasse. Er ergänzt, dass ein Wort immer auch Schall, also etwas Physisches sei und folglich nichts Göttlich-Ewiges sein könne. Und allein dadurch dass Gott, der ewig Wollende und Wissende, ein bestimmtes Seiendes will oder weiß, werde dies nicht ewig, weil Gott es ja nicht von Anfang an gewollt oder gewusst haben müsse. In Anlehnung an den indo-muslimischen Reformdenker MUHAMMAD IQBAL (st. 1938) vertritt GÜLER diese Deutung der Allwissendheit Gottes: Gott kennt die unendlich vielen möglicherweise eintretenden Geschehen alle. – Die Auseinandersetzung moniert GÜLERs oft recht leichtfertige, unhistorische Verwendung von Koranzitaten; sie zweifelt an, dass ein Wort immer etwas Physisches sein muss und dass Gottes Wissen und Willen, z.B. bezüglich menschlich-freier Handlungen, sich im Laufe der Zeit erweitern können muss. IQBAL und GÜLER wollen die Offenheit der Geschichte gegen das ihrer Meinung nach alles Geschehen festlegende, prädestinierende Vorherwissen Gottes verteidigen. Bei der denkerischen Verwirklichung dieser Absicht übersehen sie jedoch, dass Gottes Allwissendheit nur dann eine offene Geschichte verunmöglicht, wenn Gott als innerhalb einer Einzelgeschehen voneinander trennenden Zeit gedacht wird. Wenn Gott jedoch alles, auch das uns Zukünftige, gegenwärtig ist, wie dies schon PLOTIN dachte, sind freies Handeln und ein offener Geschichtsgang mit Gottes Allwissendheit vereinbar.

Für GÜLER handelt es sich bei dem Vorgang, der aus dem Koran als auf bestimmte Umstände bezogenes, also relatives Wort ein absolutes Buch machte, um einen Unglücksfall. Der einzig richtige Umgang mit dem Koran sei der „induktive", der nicht ein totes Dokument wörtlich anwendet, sondern darin ein lebbares Prinzip findet. – In der Auseinandersetzung wird darauf hingewiesen, dass eine historisch-vermittelnde Koranlektüre nicht nur mit der Kontingenz menschlicher Handlungen begründet werden kann, aber auch nicht muss, da es im Koran selbst Hinweise darauf gibt, dass er nicht als nachzuahmender Zustand, sondern zustimmend, mitdenkend, übertragend verstanden sein will. Solche Hinweise sind: die Sprachlichkeit des Koran, die ja Verstehen erfordert; die Allgemeinheit vieler seiner Regelungen, nach deren situativer Gültigkeit also stets gefragt werden muss; die suggestive Redeweise vieler seiner Formulierungen, die es den Hörern überlässt, die Schlussfolgerung zu ziehen; und seine Sichtweise, nach der viele Völker dieselbe, aber eben doch nicht wortgleiche, also eine jeweils angepasste, Offenbarung erhalten haben. Außerdem entzieht GÜLERs Betonung der Kontingenz des Koran diesem die Normativität, und er liefert keine neue Begründung dafür, warum man sich überhaupt mit normativer Absicht um ein altes Dokument und warum ausgerechnet um den Koran kümmern sollte.

In einer Schlussbetrachtung wird die gegenwärtige türkisch-theologische Szene als produktiv charakterisiert. Es wird scharfsinnig und mutig gedacht. Allerdings scheint die gesamte koranhermeneutische Fragestellung bisher auf einen einzigen Bereich fixiert: das Ethisch-Juristische. Da jedoch die vorgestellten türkischen Theologen sich als in hohem Maße kritik- und selbstkritikfähig erwiesen haben, ist zu erwarten, dass sie bald auch mit anderen theologischen Fragen an den Koran und die islamische Tradition herangehen.

MISK. MITTEILUNGEN ZUR SOZIAL- UND KULTURGESCHICHTE DER ISLAMISCHEN WELT

herausgegeben von

Rahul Peter Das – Werner Ende – Erika Glassen – Angelika Hartmann
Jens Peter Laut – Stefan Leder – Ulrich Rebstock – Rotraud Wielandt

Band 9
Loimeier, Roman (Hrsg.)
Die islamische Welt als Netzwerk
Möglichkeiten und Grenzen des Netzwerkansatzes im islamischen Kontext
2000. 515 S. – 155 x 225 mm.
Kartoniert
€ 37,00
ISBN 3-933563-80-1

Band 10
Steinberg, Guido
Religion und Staat in Saudi-Arabien
Die wahhabitischen Gelehrten 1902-1953
2002. 690 S. – 155 x 225 mm.
Kartoniert
€ 86,00
ISBN 3-89913-266-1

Band 11
Damir-Geilsdorf, Sabine
Herrschaft und Gesellschaft
Der islamistische Wegbereiter Sayyid Quṭb und seine Rezeption
2003. 426 S. – 155 x 225 mm.
Kartoniert
€ 39,00
ISBN 3-89913-319-6

Band 12
Lier, Thomas
Haushalte und Haushaltspolitik in Bagdad 1704-1831
2004. XVI/234 S. – 155 x 225 mm.
Kartoniert
€ 36,00
ISBN 3-89913-318-8

Band 13
Riexinger, Martin
Ṣanāʾullāh Amritsarī (1868-1948) und die Ahl-i Ḥadīṣ im Punjab unter britischer Herrschaft
(in Vorbereitung)
ISBN 3-89913-374-9

Band 14
Eschment, Beate – Harder, Hans (eds)
Looking at the Coloniser
Cross-Cultural Perceptions in Central Asia and the Caucasus, Bengal, and Related Areas
2004. 384 S. – zahlr. z.T. farb. Abb.
155 x 225 mm. Kartoniert
€ 42,00
ISBN 3-89913-359-5

Band 15
Körner, Felix
Revisionist Koran Hermeneutics in Contemporary Turkish Theology
Rethinking Islam
2004. 230 S. – 155 x 225 mm.
Kartoniert
€ 29,00
ISBN 3-89913-373-0

Band 16
Stolleis, Friederike
Öffentliches Leben in privaten Räumen
Muslimische Frauen in Damaskus
2004. 199 S. – 7 Krtn.
155 x 225 mm. Kartoniert
€ 29,00
ISBN 3-89913-375-7

ERGON VERLAG · WÜRZBURG

MISK. MITTEILUNGEN ZUR SOZIAL- UND KULTURGESCHICHTE DER ISLAMISCHEN WELT

herausgegeben von

Rahul Peter Das – Werner Ende – Erika Glassen – Angelika Hartmann
Jens Peter Laut – Stefan Leder – Ulrich Rebstock – Rotraud Wielandt

Band 17
Glaß, Dagmar
Der *Muqtaṭaf* und seine Öffentlichkeit
Aufklärung, Räsonnement und Meinungsstreit in der frühen arabischen Zeitschriftenkommunikation
Erster Band: Analyse medialer und sozialer Strukturen
Zweiter Band: Streitgesprächsprotokolle
2004. zus. XVI/749 S. – zahlr. Abb.
155 x 225 mm. Kartoniert
nur zus. € 94,00
ISBN 3-89913-379-X

Band 18
Oberauer, Norbert
Religiöse Verpflichtung im Islam
Ein ethischer Grundbegriff und seine theologische, rechtliche und sozialgeschichtliche Dimension
(In Vorbereitung)
ISBN 3-89913-382-X

ERGON VERLAG · WÜRZBURG